W9-AQW-676

Praise for *Urban Magick*

"I've been waiting a long time for a book like *Urban Magick* to arrive. Not only does Diana include a complete guide to harnessing power and integrating the city into your magical practice, she also includes often left-out history and design patterns for why cities develop into what they are. Start navigating your city pathworking with *Urban Magick* today."

—Jaymi Elford, author of *Tarot Inspired Life*

"For too long, the Pagan and New Age movements have fixated on the magic of wilderness while ignoring the urban environments in which they live. Rajchel's *Urban Magick* is a necessary and revolutionary step forward in that desperately overlooked arena."

—Jeffrey Groves, author of *The Mark of the Wolf*

"Diana Rajchel shows that a city is a magical environment that has its own rules and laws that impact how you work with it. In this book, you'll learn what those rules and laws are and how to create a relationship with your city that changes your magical practice. This is cutting-edge magic that you'll want to take advantage of to help you transform your spiritual practice."

—Taylor Ellwood, author of *The Magic of Art*

"*Urban Magick* is an exciting exploration of deep city sorcery. Diana Rajchel takes us on a beautiful journey through spaces that are unassuming yet brimming with spiritual life. This work shows that for those with eyes to see, we urban creatures can thrive in our own enchanted worlds."

—David Salisbury, author of *Witchcraft Activism*

"Reading this book has forever changed the way I view my relationship—my love affair—with the city I live in. I'm left brimming with new ideas that I'm eager to explore and new practices I'm looking forward to trying out."

—Robin Scott, creator of Urban Tarot

URBAN MAGICK

© Nathan McCann

About the Author

Diana Rajchel (San Francisco, CA) is the author of *Mabon* and *Samhain* in the Llewellyn Sabbat Essentials series and is a long-time contributor to Llewellyn annuals. She is in a lifelong, passionate love affair with magick itself and runs the Emperor Norton Magickal People social. Rajchel has gone through many transmutations: from Wiccan to witch, from Pagan to animist, from magician to alchemist. She serves as a city priestess to the spirit of San Francisco and offers tarot life coaching and spell technique consulting to the public.

A GUIDE FOR THE CITY WITCH

URBAN MAGICK

DIANA RAJCHEL

Llewellyn Publications
Woodbury, Minnesota

Urban Magick: A Guide for the City Witch © 2020 by Diana Rajchel. All rights reserved. No part of this book may be used or reproduced in any manner whatsoever, including internet usage, without written permission from Llewellyn Publications, except in the case of brief quotations embodied in critical articles and reviews.

FIRST EDITION
First Printing, 2020

Book design: Samantha Penn
Cover design: Shira Atakpu
Editing: Laura Kurtz

Llewellyn Publications is a registered trademark of Llewellyn Worldwide Ltd.

Library of Congress Cataloging-in-Publication Data (Pending)
ISBN: 978-0-7387-5274-7

Llewellyn Worldwide Ltd. does not participate in, endorse, or have any authority or responsibility concerning private business transactions between our authors and the public.

All mail addressed to the author is forwarded but the publisher cannot, unless specifically instructed by the author, give out an address or phone number.

Any internet references contained in this work are current at publication time, but the publisher cannot guarantee that a specific location will continue to be maintained. Please refer to the publisher's website for links to authors' websites and other sources.

Llewellyn Publications
A Division of Llewellyn Worldwide Ltd.
2143 Wooddale Drive
Woodbury, MN 55125-2989
www.llewellyn.com

Printed in the United States of America

I dedicate this book to the many spirits and beings that helped me make this book happen. There are many crossroads in this work, and I have stood in them all.

CONTENTS

INTRODUCTION

When I began working with city spirits, I did not see myself as a priest. I saw myself as a person with a passionate interest in magick who wanted to get really good at it. Cities and their magickal potential certainly called to me, but so did many things. The occult is a bursting closet with behemothic layers of interesting. When you begin the study, you become that prize contestant standing in a wind tunnel, trying to grasp the dollar bill equivalents of different topics. Even now, twenty years later, putting together a coherent narrative for other urban magickal people feels like flailing in that tunnel. I had too many interests within the topic to settle for one. Becoming something specific—especially something city-related—snuck up on me.

I wasn't looking to engage the city spirit when I moved to Minneapolis. After a divorce, I had to move to the nearest big city because the city had the jobs. With what was going on in my life at the time—mainly being broke in my late twenties—I invested most of my study into figuring out why some of my spells worked and others didn't. I could feel the city spirit of Minneapolis watching but paid little mind. I was too busy working magick like the rent was due tomorrow, because usually it was.

About the time of my move, Llewellyn published *Urban Primitive*. This was the first time I saw any acknowledgement of the intelligence I felt hovering over me. It read to me like a palliative for nature workers living in cities; the premise hinged on someone "stuck" in the city and negotiating the necessity of a job while feeling that call to a pristine, idealized nature. I winced a little at that idea without fully knowing why but kept reading. I already knew that I rarely aligned fully with other people's magickal perspectives. I found it valuable, even if I disagreed with some of it on a subterranean level.

For me, city life was medicine for too many years in places of controlling isolation. Knowing this about myself, I took much of what Kaldera and Schwartzstein presented into my personal practice and reframed it for someone who *needed* life in a large city.

Not long after moving into my new urban apartment, an old college friend came to visit. During this visit she introduced me to a hipster obsessed with the architecture and urban design of Minneapolis. By the end of our first date, so to speak, I recognized him: the priest to the city of Minneapolis. As an atheist with a degree of contempt for "woo" folk like me, he probably still has no idea. For about two years, he and I went on weekly outings always centered on exploring some aspect of the city. Once we walked the labyrinthine skyways. Another time we watched clouds obscure the city skyline. Yet another time we explored a lock station on the Mississippi River.

Every adventure tapped me into some part of the city that he already instinctively knew. While he would never admit it, he seemed pulled along by some intuitive call to bring me to these oft-obscure places. I became aware of the magick of Minneapolis and Saint Paul and felt its untapped potential on a visceral level. The place had more magick to work with than I could possibly conceive, even now.

City spirits have their own hierarchies, and those of us that it chooses for priests usually know nothing about the specifics of that hierarchy. Most of the time we don't even know who the other priests are. I suspect Minneapolis already knew when I arrived that some other city had already claimed me, and so it supplied me a teacher for the work I would do later in life. I became expert at finding hidden opportunities, free things to do, and mysterious skyway corners visited by maybe fifty people a day. It didn't have many needs of me—it got those met by someone else. It just wanted to show me things that other people might not notice, and it often asked me to think about different ways to tap into the magick of what it showed me. Without knowing, I trained as a city priest, and at the same time my development as a witch continued unabated.

This (usually) gentle guidance from the city spirit of Minneapolis had the long-term effect of unbinding me from religious dogma, even Pagan religious dogma. As I became progressively untethered from the religious trappings of the type of witchcraft I trained in, the recognition of me as a priest by spirits and spiritual people lingered and strengthened. I am here to help. I am here to deliver messages that need hearing. I am here to listen. The other particulars, like picking a religion or some god to worship, aren't important in city work.

It's proven a difficult task to organize and align what I learned with what my intuition told me others needed to know into something as coherent and systemic as a book. While this work has broken me out of a great deal of calcified thinking—such as nature only existing outside of human-made spheres—I have had to overcome several internalized bugaboos. I believe the Spirit/Source (or whatever it is) that drives these things needed me to see for myself that without cities, many things we enjoy and most things we rely on would not exist. Along the way, I was given the privilege of guidance from a city spirit that wants very much to be seen.

The Mystery of Civilization—what prompted humanity to create written language, to develop engineering, and to build communities with an intent beyond that of mere survival—is also the mystery of the city. None of these things could happen until humans built the first city. Only then, with that small relief from the burden of survival, could they feel the urge to create beyond that of procreation and sustenance. By attempting to point out the ways in which cities were born and the ways in which they are crafted now, I am hoping to show other magickal people new spiritual discoveries hidden in between the lines of city streets and parkways. There are cycles—death and rebirth, devastation and miraculous healing—all contained in the microcosm that we call "city."

ONE
WHAT IS URBAN MAGICK?

Urban magick has three aspects: working with the spirit of a given city, tapping the energy generated by a city for your own use, and using energy you generate to benefit the city spirit and your neighbors. Aside from believing in the metaphysical, urban magick has no religious framework, and its practice at this point is mostly through practitioners that work magick alone or with one partner.

In some ways, it is a forgotten ancient practice, and in others, a version of magick for modern pioneers. If you happen to be Wiccan or Christian or Druid (for example), you can work with city magick while still honoring your tradition. If you happen to see yourself as aligned with nature, that doesn't preclude you from city magick; nature lives in the city just as much as it does outside of it.

Each city has its own energy and spirits. I have traveled enough to know that they differ greatly from one another, but they also exist and come about in similar ways. I would love to travel the world and write a grimoire based on every major city and be able to offer you a comprehensive book with a chapter for each city. However, at the time of this writing, such a thing is cost prohibitive. Also, I am not sure my own lifespan would be long enough to gather all that data.

My own style of magickal working is deeply relational; I spend time with a city and work on that connection over years and decades. While living in a city helps, it is possible to forge friendships with cities you visit. Most city spirits will work with anyone sincere. Those who prefer formalized ritual have as much of a place with urban magick as those who perform magick from a place of spontaneous intuition.

However, city priesthood is solely a calling that happens at the discretion of the specific city spirit. You can live in a city for twenty years and never sense a thing… and visit another city for a day and hear it say, "I want you." Suddenly you may find yourself moving to the city that called when you had no plans for relocation. These callings move on tides far larger than human perception.

When possible, I give examples from a broad range of cities, but my own experiences are limited to Europe and North America. Minneapolis trained me for the work I do in San Francisco, and San Francisco sought me out. Because of that, most of my examples come from these two cities. Until then, I will leave it to you, intrepid experimental magicians and city lovers, to use what I have here as a launching point for you to develop your own grimoires and guides.

To guide you along the way, let's start with a broader introduction to the concepts behind urban magick.

What's a City?

Legally, a city is an incorporated geographic area where one governing body manages sanitation, power, roads, and education. Towns do not have legal incorporation, and citizens must determine for themselves how to manage their power, water, and road maintenance. Towns often incorporate into cities after a drastic increase in population.

The magickal definition of a city includes the legal definition. In addition, for urban magick the following conditions must exist:

- an identity shared by the city's residents (Londoner, Parisian, New Yorker, Minneapolite)
- a steady, multichoice mass transit system
- at least one area where buildings exceed ten floors

There is no doubt in my mind that by defining it someone will find at least ten exceptions—and this is good. These are just guidelines shaped from one personal practice. The only definition that has thus far proved a hard-and-fast rule is the first one: the area must have some shared identity, whether localized to the city, like New York, or regional, like Chicago, to harbor a true city spirit.

Does that mean someone living in a suburb or a rural area can't practice urban magick? No, but for those in rural areas, you will need to visit a city if you want to work with a city spirit. You don't need to live there, but you do need to be around city energy often enough to develop a relationship. Some city spirits are friendlier to tourist energy than others, and it's often a matter of having a sincere, respectful approach.

What Do I Need to Know About Cities?

It helps to have an appreciation for urban design and architecture. Both affect human behavior and can solve or cause social problems while escaping our conscious awareness. Different urban designs can manipulate our moods, our thoughts, and even where we walk. Buildings can act as containers, roads as energy paths, gardens as power sources, and so on. If you understand the behavior and emotions these spaces are designed to stir, you can better calibrate your own magickal work.

Do Suburbs Have City Spirits?

It depends. Sometimes a suburb may contain collective self-identification sufficient to form and feed a city spirit. Sometimes its dependence on the city as an energy inlet makes it part of a regional spirit. Even if a suburb has a shared identity, it may have less power than it would in an area that has a higher population density and a fully formed city spirit. While you can't work with a city spirit where one doesn't exist, smaller spirits and entities are everywhere.

In rare cases, suburbs become cities as their population grows enough to become independent from the original city spirit. A particularly ambitious suburban magician might create a city spirit. While this would take enormous personal energy and feeding, it would make for a fascinating experiment in how far a created spirit's impact can spread over a specific geographic area.

What Do I Need to Know About Magick?

City magick can include all spiritual paths, but at its root it is a form of folk magick. In folk magick, you use what's around you. While people who practice specific traditions may try to emulate the tools of their ancestors, city magick embraces the new and the old equally. Even if the substance—plastic, for example—didn't exist in the past, if it's available now, you can engage it for your magickal workings.

Urban magick does not require formal training, initiations or elevations. You practice the magick by experiencing it and, when possible, by sharing your experiences with open minds. A city magician may well weave in material from other trainings and traditions. In the course of a month, a city magician may incorporate Qabala, traditional witchcraft, and chaos sigils—and that would be a slow month. The practice is strange, uncharted, and fluid—much like a day wandering your city can be. I suspect that city priests in Lagos, Cairo, New Delhi, or Beijing have an entirely different approach than mine, with very different toolkits. I truly hope to hear from some of them someday.

What Is a City Spirit?

Since working with city spirit and urban energies is the focus of this book, it helps to know what one is and what one is not. A city spirit is *not* a *genius loci*. The genius loci is the intelligence inherent in the land of an area, including the land a city stands on. The city spirit manifests by forming an intelligence from the collective intelligence and energy generated from the people living in a city. Major cities have both a genius loci (land spirit) and a city spirit, in addition to the several smaller spirits that can populate a landscape.

What Are the Goals of Urban Magick?

Because urban magick does not follow a specific religious or ethical path, the goal of urban magick depends on the goals of the magick worker. Currently, the four most common are:

- the Civic Path
- the Chaotic Path
- the Hearth/Home Path
- the Priesthood Path

What urban magick path a person chooses may or may not align with any chosen or called religious path. For example, a person that venerates Pan in his pre-civilization aspect may experience some energetic conflict when working with the most visible measures of civilization.

The **Civic Path** of urban magick engages city energy for social change. People who work this path petition the city spirit to solve social problems that happen in cities. They may use their magickal skills and relationships to reduce crime in their neighborhoods, to find the homeless housing, or to sway political bodies to give money to certain communal needs. People who practice Druidry, Reclaiming Tradition Witchcraft, or that subscribe to Humanism may feel especially inclined to work the Civic Path of urban magick.

The **Chaotic Path** is for those inclined to experiment with the unknown and even invent new deities and servitors just to see what happens. While chaos magicians often still perform workings for personal goals, they thrive off the wilder energies of the universe—and certain cities generate mayhem. The Chaotic Path is the path of the mad scientist, and it is often chaos magicians who discover or invent new ways of working with urban magick.

Chaos magicians have their own approach well in hand, so this text focuses on other paths.

The **Hearth and Home Path**, in other areas of magickal practice, might also be called the path of the hearth fire. This path consists of people who prioritize keeping their homes and families safe and provided for. They work within the city in much the same way they might anywhere else. While these magicians might venture to influence their neighborhood for some greater good—quieter summer nights so a baby can sleep or amicability with all neighbors—they have little interest in any far-reaching results of their work. They prefer instead to benefit from the safety and peace they can build into their domestic routine.

The **Priesthood Path** has the fewest travelers and is by far the most difficult to explain. Some, but not all, city spirits select one person or a few people to act as priests, assigning to certain magick workers the spiritual care of itself. These priests may or may not know of one another. They may work in cooperation with each other or seemingly at random as the city spirit guides them. This avocation is often strange, even in the world of magick workers.

Some city spirits require death and resurrection ceremonies; others want their workers to heal wounds in the fabric of the city psyche when deep violence has happened. Sometimes the city spirit wants help playing mostly harmless pranks on its inhabitants. Since the last publicly identified city priests disappeared when the Catholic Church overtook Rome, the city Priesthood Path has little in the way of a map for the people on it—if the city spirits they serve have even bothered to inform them they've got the job.

All causes and beings, whether their magickal path is left, right, or center, have a place within a healthy city. Because city spirits function as living organisms, they require the same balance of light and shadow as human beings. Destruction, creation, and chaos keep organisms alive.

All This Talk of Spirits is Fine, but What If I Can't See/Hear/Feel Energies?

You do not need strong psychic talent to work magick. There are city priests who have no idea they even do. If you happen to be one of those people who believes something is out there and that magick works, but must take it on faith, you're far from alone. If you feel love for things ineffable, you still have a place at the table in the magickal community. You may need to use some alternate methods to confirm that something is happening. For example, you can ask for specific signs when performing a working or meditation—feathers in your path, for instance, or even a literal billboard with a message for you. Over time, you'll get a conversation going with your city spirit over the channels you can perceive, and the lack of psychic sensitivity won't matter as much.

Where Does Your City Magick Come From?

The techniques laid out in this book are my personal practices, developed while working with the city spirits of Minneapolis and San Francisco, unless otherwise credited. The modern practice of magickal urbanism is new enough that I can freely admit I am making things up. I try things out, see what works, and discard what doesn't. What I share here is what has worked *for me*. Techniques I discarded may work for you. City spirits have unique personalities and so none of this can possibly work as "one size fits all."

If you're already working city magick, you are already making things up as you go along, too. What works in London might just piss off New York. All we can do is make a note of what happens, and when possible, report our efforts to each other.

Is Urban Magick Anti-Nature?

Urban magick is not a practice where you look at nature as something pristine, virginal, and far away. Cities came to exist because nature can kill you. To a city spirit, Mother Nature and genius loci are always right there, watching everything you do. Beings that live in nature—including humans—find ways to adapt to and survive in these conditions. It's an aspect of evolution. While most animals evolved body parts to help them survive, humans adapted to conditions using tools around them.

City dwellers remain vulnerable to natural disasters, climate conditions, and weather. While architects and urban planners design buildings and streets intended to mitigate these concerns, Mother Nature has a mind of her own and more resources than any city. Cities are, to nature itself, just another ecosystem. Understanding that ecosystem is a key part of urban magick.

What Cities Are You Talking About?

This book has a strong bias towards the United States, especially the Midwest, because this is where I learned my own urban magick. Because I can't account for experiences unknown to me, I encourage international readers to adjust these techniques and to share results via social media and blogging. For instance, the history and architecture of Sao Paulo, Brazil, differs from that of Washington, DC, and what you might do with a skyscraper during drought season may differ quite a bit from how you anchor your energy to a monolith on the DC mall during a blizzard. Also, I realize not everyone can do some of what I recommend in the book physically or legally. It is always okay and good to develop your own workarounds and I encourage you to share them.

Ethics and Philosophy

Ethics is considered by most a method used for determining right from wrong. From my perspective, it is more an area of thought to consider whom our actions affect and how. While I am not introducing a magickal tradition so much as a magickal mindset, I do feel obligated to acknowledge some ethical considerations. Chief among the concerns raised are those of environmental care, colonization, and civil disobedience. That any of these concerns can mix, match, and conflict—and that they all appear aplenty in urban settings—is not a coincidence.

City magick by its nature crosses many boundaries that magicians in the late twentieth century were often encouraged to avoid, especially in the areas of politics, chaos, and mass manipulation. More people than ever before feel called to use all their abilities to shape their lives and their countries into places they want to live. Using magick in response to politics isn't new; since time immemorial, it has been the way humanity takes power in the face of its own powerlessness. The reason that most people are advised to avoid attempting to influence political outcomes with magick is that their targets are too big: trying to influence the outcome of a US presidential election is roughly on par with using magick to win the lottery. It might work, but there's a lot of competing energy for the same thing.

City magick can show you how political energies move. The smallest political systems are those most easily influenced—and that consists of neighborhood and city government. When casting something as simple as a "good neighbor spell," you can see with immediacy how a seemingly benign intent, such as "improving the neighborhood," can lead to unintended consequences, such as evictions and foreclosures.

If civic urban magick is your path, it's important to be aware of consequences and accept the risks. Many see "monkey's paw"–type consequences as the reason to refrain from moving around energies. My philosophy deems inaction worse than action, even in the face of failure. Every action, even something as trivial as, say, putting on a pair of socks, has consequences somewhere.

Because magicians do not universally subscribe to one ethical practice and don't all come from a singular religious background, I won't advocate the correctness of any specific philosophy. The needs of Flint, Michigan, are distinctly different from the needs of Moscow. Whatever ethical model works for you, please found it on introspection and thorough questioning. Before working any magick, pause and think carefully about everyone it might affect and in what way they might be affected. The more you shape a concrete result as a sign of success, the more you can manage the ethical fallout. In urban magick, even small workings have potential to affect large populations, no matter how well you lay the boundaries. Divination, meditation, and opening a conversation with city spirit all can form the foundations of this type of ethical work.

Urban Magick and the Environment

People who place high spiritual value on healing and protecting the environment may have concerns about the overall safety and cleanliness of city magic. Some may worry about engaging with energy that is in some cases literally machine-and-fossil-fueled because it might contribute further to the poisoning of natural resources. As much as I'd like to give a blanket answer that it doesn't, the reality is much more complex. A lot of what's considered common knowledge on these topics no longer applies. First, we must shift our perspective on cities from resource consumers to resource conservers. After that, you also have to take the first law of thermodynamics into account—energy can be neither created nor destroyed. Environmental cleanup is important, *and* the stuff we're cleaning up doesn't just go away. Even after we resolve the damage it does to the land, we have to figure out what to do with the substances that caused that damage.

To inadequately break it down within the popular environmental slogan, much city magick involves reducing and reusing (or repurposing), and yes, just a bit of recycling. But to act on that particular green triad, the bad stuff has to be present to be repurposed. The urban magick I recommend in this book should for the most part not add to the damage; I encourage you to work with what's already around you rather than adding non-organic material to the land.

As in all things concerning environmental health, every action taken to benefit one aspect of the environment trades off with a negative effect somewhere else. While the industrial world has a long way to go, more municipalities recognize economic and public health benefits to green design. While very much a slow work in progress, many cities are slowly becoming places with smaller overall carbon footprints and less strain on local soil.

All environmentalism comes back to preserving the longevity of humans and animals on Earth. We started by understanding not to poison ourselves. We have extended that care to animals. Now we are looking at how our technology impacts the environment before we unleash it on the world. While the progress is frustrating and slow, when it comes to urban planning and technological innovation, there have been significant strides in reducing negative environmental impact. Urban magick may follow a similar path.

How Magick Affects the Earth

When it comes to doing environmental harm while working magick, much of the concerns remain the same as they do in any other situation. In the minds of many magick workers deciding whether to cast or call spirits, the question of "What are the possible consequences?" includes the impact on surrounding nature. Urban magicians must account for the supplies they use, where those supplies came from, and how to dispose of them. A petroleum-based paraffin candle pollutes just as much in a city as it does on a farm, although the smoke runoff has the potential to irritate more people in a city. Burying old spell materials that don't biodegrade might affect the groundwater and so on.

The more ways workers find to use and repurpose byproducts, the more they nurture the city itself. The accumulated effort reduces environmental strain. An extreme example is *freegans*, people who dumpster dive for food and other reusable items. Artists—often also magickal people—may appropriate pieces of waste for their works. Drivers that build cars to run on renewable fuel take grease that restaurant owners might otherwise have to pay to have disposed of. In a society prosperous enough to generate so much waste, the waste itself provides opportunities. The waste still exists in places where people spread out more, but the cost-benefit of finding that waste and using it dwindles in a rural environment as opposed to an urban one.

Choosing to embrace the city on a magickal level means a few things: first, that you recognize that there are nonbiodegradable synthetic things that are part of our lives, and they are here to stay. Finding new and creative ways to work with them—adapting them to art, magick, and justice—is really the only thing to be done with them until the day someone grows just the right bacteria to eat the nonbiodegradable things without turning into termites for all. Second, that virtue lies in change over abstinence. While you can certainly refuse to engage with city life (and many do have good, mental health-related reasons for doing so), embracing city magick on a personal and ethical level means getting involved. Third, you open yourself to experiment—manufactured substances are not automatically without magickal potential. Only pewter and lead fail completely to hold magickal charges.

One of the areas of greatest technological advancement at this time is in correcting environmental damage. These changes will definitely affect the way we work city magick. Until then, do your best and know that living in the city does not mean you are doing more harm to the earth.

The Dark Side of Urban Magick

Most magickal people, especially Pagans, talk about shadow work as a metaphor for recognizing our weaknesses and blind spots. For some reason this discussion usually happens separately from exploration of ethics even though our shadow sides are why we need those guidelines. In city magick, our shadow selves become visible quickly. The way we cordon off city neighborhoods by money and race shows us our prejudices, and that is energy that must be recognized and honored before we have any hope of redirecting it.

Magick is disquieting at its most advanced. The most disturbing and unsettling discoveries will be about yourself. You have to make peace with your own ugly to work urban magick, because your innate responses will come out.

Large cities have unpleasant things. Homelessness, drug addiction, casual emotional and physical violence, and mental illness all come into naked view. While these problems themselves may seem like the city's dark underbelly, the real darkness lives in how you respond when you see these unpleasant realities. You may find, over time, that your virtuous responses to these realities are the source of perpetuated evil.

City spirits sometimes use panhandlers, those suffering perceptual illnesses, and even uncomfortable/weird interactions with neurotypical people to communicate. This often means that you must work to break through your own projections and prejudices to read the real situation. Sometimes the panhandler is just another grifter making your parking lot experience a little more difficult; sometimes it's a manifestation of spirit. Sometimes someone genuinely needs help. You won't be able to tell the difference until you move from a place of reacting to a place of responding to what presents itself.

The most visible disquiet appears on mass transit. Taking transit gives you a chance to practice checking your filters. For instance, if you encounter someone with visible mental illness on the bus, observe yourself first. What are your gut reactions? What do you hear yourself think? Do you feel judgment, disgust, fear?

What about pity? What does pity make you feel about yourself? Root out the "why" of every response. Look deep into your reactions. Some of these people are ill, some of the clean-cut ones are criminals, and some of the strange ones are non-human sentient spirits that have integrated into city life.

Looking first at your own reactions reveals underlying attitudes that can block your spiritual perceptions. The dirt also covers you. The shadow of the city lies within our reactions just as much as it does in those who experience misfortune as a byproduct of city life.

On Colonization, Appropriation, and Your Safety

Some reading this book have concerns for misappropriation. I can't promise the book is totally de-colonized and appropriation free. I am 50 percent colonizer descendant and 50 percent descendant of a non-colonizer who lucked into cultural normalization eventually. Even when I strive, there are simply things I cannot see because of my privilege. The rituals included come from my own private development. Anything borrowed that I don't specifically acknowledge is because it is so commonplace that it hasn't occurred to me to question its origin.

There are several places in this book where I suggest activities that while not illegal (for the most part) might still put certain individuals at risk of violence for no other reason than because of how they look or speak. I wish I could do more to protect you. If something isn't safe for you to do because of this, please speak up about it—city magick is forever a work in progress, and that particular part of the progress is important work you will be doing for yourself.

Civil Disobedience

Later chapters include rituals you may wish to perform in public. If you live in an area where the law has an arbitrary attitude about your right to freedom of assembly, you may end up breaking the law. In some cases, you may perform public rituals as acts of protest. Not all acts of civil disobedience are camera grabbers. Sit-ins and marches grab cameras, but people painting crosswalk lines themselves rather than waiting for the city to do it also make a difference in the lives of others. Some of the most iconic public art came about as acts of civil disobedience; in a pinch, you can always claim what you're doing is performance art. Authorities never know what to do with performance artists.

I do feel obligated to point out that you can also work city magick without breaking the law. But if you are coming to magickal urbanism with that intent, your city spirit is probably going to have some interesting jobs for you. I only ask that if you decide to fight cultural entrenchment, you approach it with thought, strategy, and a plan for bail. Neither I nor my publisher can accept liability for your actions.

If you have a love for cities and a love for magick, you are fully qualified to practice magickal urbanism. You need only love the city in your own way. Some of you may love the glamour of night life and the creative spirit rising from arts and culture, or from the underground of raucous weirdos ever city harbors somewhere. Some of you may want to use your skills to effect powerful social changes. Some of you may prefer a quiet approach, working with spirit from home. Some of you may still not see yourselves in this text and are off doing your own thing with your city spirit; that thing that is also urban magick. You'll let us see you when you feel ready. Welcome to the city, magickal people. There is room for you.

TWO
LAWS OF URBAN MAGICK

M agickal urbanism demands a degree of invention. However, invention can bring about what artists know as the intimidation of the blank page: you know you need to create something, but without an idea or two to nudge you, you may suffer brain freeze. While magick is not science and hasn't been since alchemy and chemistry split up, the non-science of magickal laws and their theoretical application can really help when you need to engage in some creative problem solving.

Magick theories and laws come from anthropological observation, practice at gathering results, and wild guesses very loosely based on physics. These theories range from how energy works to a classification of magickal types. Law and theory are often used interchangeably in the occult because we are dealing with phenomena that can neither be quantified nor reproduced under laboratory conditions. The words really just give us a verbal grip so we can talk about phenomena we think we see repeating often.

A mix of magickal laws distilled from exploration of magickal theories and philosophies from diverse origins apply the most to urban magick. While you need not cite these laws to practice city magick, a basic understanding can help you form new ideas for how to work with your city energy. This can also help you determine why an attempted working failed. The more you internalize these laws, the less time you will spend checking lists of magickal correspondences or looking for someone else who did the thing you want to try.

The First Law of Urban Magick: Heinrich Cornelius Agrippa's Five-Element Theory

All elements converge from their respective dimensions to form the material plane.

Heinrich Cornelius Agrippa was a German philosopher and scholar who studied natural magick at the eve of the Renaissance. He developed several theories still used today about the relationship between humanity and the spirit world, published in his *Three Books of Occult Philosophy.*[1] His first law, based on experiments that extrapolated at-the-time untested rationalistic elemental theories of Aristotle and the philosophy of Empedocles, is still a foundation framework of the natural world for Western occultists. Agrippa, after performing alchemical experiments, theorized that the elements of earth, air, fire, and water exist on their own planes. The convergence of those planes forms the material world. He agreed

---

1. Vittoria Perrone Compagni, "Heinrich Cornelius Agrippa von Netteschem," *The Stanford Encyclopedia of Philosophy,* edited by Edward N. Zalta, 2017. https://plato.stanford.edu/archives/spr2017/entries/agrippa-nettesheim/.

with Empedocles[2] that spirit/aether acts as the binding mediator on the material plane we call the physical world. Based on this theory, every object we perceive as present in our world has at least some small amount of every element—earth, air, fire, water, and spirit. Following this idea, you could call fire from out of a table or air from the shirt you're wearing, even though that might not be the dominant element present in the material.

For example, if you have a leaky faucet and can't call a plumber right away, try calling out the element of water from within the faucet itself and ask it to draw off the flow in a way that doesn't leak. When struggling with the heating bill in your apartment, draw out the element of fire in your walls and ceiling to encourage the ambient temperature to rise so you need not turn your thermostat so high.

This law/theory only applies to the Western five-element model. Different traditions of magick use different elements: you may want to compare how those differing elements and structures compare when you do call on those energies. For example, traditional Chinese medicine uses fire, metal, wood, water, and earth. While the structure mainly addresses a complex system for treating elements based on organ disturbance, it could also apply to non-organic material. The Celtic three-element system of land, sea, and sky might apply less to inorganic material but could apply to speeding or slowing certain transportation systems in a city.

---

2. Tracy Marks, "Elemental: the Four Elements from Ancient Greek Science and Philosophy to Poetry," (originally published 1998), www.webwinds.com /thalassa/elemental.htm.

The Second Law of Urban Magick: Microcosm/Macrocosm

The universe is a house. The world we see is the
dollhouse version of it. If we move the couch in the
dollhouse, it moves the couch in the giant house, too.

The law of the macrocosm and microcosm is stated as the occult maxim "As above, so below." Different spiritual disciplines have identified this theory in different ways. The concept appears in the works of Agrippa, in Buddhist and Hindu philosophy, and in the Qabala. While some may perceive this visually, with the human as the miniature of the greater universe, others sense the microcosm/microcosm as higher/faster and lower/slower vibration. Because we are part of the universe, when we take an action on ourselves—the *microcosm* of the universe—the action also impacts the universe itself.

This microcosm/macrocosm law also means that even small actions can cause change. Placing a bright flower in a dreary place can open an avenue for positive energy. Giving a small donation to a homeless shelter can bring one family off the street for a night, shifting the general balance and pressure on a neighborhood. Small, intentional actions taken daily can build paths of opportunity for yourself or others.

In urban magick, small changes to one aspect of the city will impact the whole city. These changes, which happen in closer proximity than might be experienced by those living in suburbs or rural areas, contribute to the constant sense of motion—and to some degree to the discomfort of sensitive people.

The Third Law of Urban Magick: Law of Sympathy

Like produces like.

Much of modern magick has roots in this law and its history. Nineteenth-century anthropologist Sir James Frazer studied indigenous traditions throughout the world and collected them into his work *The Golden Bough*. From observing magickal rituals around the world, he developed a theory of how magick operates. While much of the research held the biases of its time, his observations and theories around magick, divine sacrifice, and the universality of sorcery have influenced European Pagan practices since the 1940s.

As far as anyone can tell, Frazer was right: most spells bank on some aspect of sympathetic activation. The Law of Sympathy dictates that "like produces like." In this structure, a person might create a likeness of another person, such as a poppet or drawing. Acts upon that created object were believed to also alter the person that the object was like. Much as the macrocosm/microcosm theory states that the miniature affects the greater, in the law of sympathy, the imitation affects the original.

The first corollary of this law, the Law of Similarity, posits that "the effect resembles the cause." A practitioner wishing to cause an effect acts it out upon an object representing the thing they desire to change. For example, if someone wanted to work magick to fertilize a community garden, they might ritually act out rain, engage in sexual rites, or dance in imitation of cornstalks waving in the breeze to encourage the crops to grow.

The second corollary, the Law of Contagion, posits that positive or negative energy spreads through contact. People who practice folk magick traditions know this well, as some rely on people smelling oils or touching powders for their spells to take effect. People who live in cities know all about the law of contagion in the physical world: touch the wrong bus seat during flu season and the disease finds you.

Much of what happens in any magick comes back to Frazer's Laws of Sympathy. In urban magick, often the law of contagion has more applications than the law of similarity. One of the chief aspects/energies of urban magick is using population density. While we hear more about the negative infections in the world, this doesn't negate that positive infections are possible with intentional magick. Flu season, for instance, could benefit from someone placing a healing or immunity powder on the buses with the intention of that energy spreading through the population.

The Fourth Law of Urban Magick: Authentic Thaumaturgy As It Applies to Urban Magick
The only thing that really matters is that it works
Isaac Bonewits, a Neopagan scholar who evolved many ideas about how magick works, initially presented his rules in the book *Real Magic*.[3] While they were intended as guidelines for tabletop roleplaying games, the theories he presented came from research on magick in real life. For the sake of brevity, only his laws that apply the most to city magick appear here. The fourth Law of Magick draws directly from this because it is, at this point in development, pass/fail magick. A practitioner tries something, and if it appears to work, tries it again. This action can be as simple as pouring a libation to settle an area disturbance to performing a complex ritual with candles, incense, and chanting to increase the chances of finding affordable housing. The mechanics and symbolism only matter if they work; if the magickal actions end with a successful result, then it counts as a true result of the work.

---

3. Isaac Bonewits, *Real Magic* (San Francisco: Weiser Books, 1989), 1–12.

The Law of Names

Knowing the true name of an object grants control over it.

The law that knowing an entity's true name can break a spell or grant control over an entity—think Rumpelstiltskin—has a long folklore tradition. While most often used in Goetia or fairy magick, it can also apply to urban magick: If you want to perform a long-distance cleansing on a house, knowing the street address helps. If you want to work with the neighborhood spirit, knowing the name that the locals call an area rather than what the Chamber of Commerce does can help you find that specific energy channel. Naming a city or settlement in itself has a spiritual element. To name a place gives it alignment and intention. To give it intention activates energy. A city spirit, once named, has the potential to manifest.

The Law of Personification

If you act like it's alive, treat it like it's alive.

Acting as if the city is alive, sentient, and personified is the key to engaging with an active city spirit. Even if the city is too new for active personification, choosing to act in this manner can set the process of sentience in motion. Talk to your city spirit like it can hear you, and the city will eventually form the energy needed to talk back.

To understand this on a microcosmic level, look at how some drivers name their cars. Along with the name, they may confer a gender and personality. These people often report that their cars manifest personality traits. At times, the energy behind making those attributions may allow the car to operate despite needing repairs. The power of personification may also appear in certain mechanical quirks or in a general mood hovering in the the car interior. In a similar fashion, if someone wants to create a city spirit in a place with a population below a hundred thousand, taking the attitude of conscious personification opens a pathway for that spirit to form the intelligence necessary to manifest.

The Law of Pragmatism
If it works, it's true.
This may be the only law of magick that truly matters. Given the experimental nature of most city workings, reality is best determined by results. This has the caveat that failure needs acknowledgement, and to recognize failure, you must establish measurable results. If you think a particular working might help, whether burning a sigil so the homeless find shelter in the cold or muttering a prayer to help you find a parking spot, the result counts towards the legitimacy of the initial effort.

The Fifth Law of Urban Magick:
The Collective Unconscious
Collective shared cultures and belief form their own bodies of energy.
In urban magick, the city exists in some way within each of its residents. Because cities form complex ecosystems unto themselves, most of the microcosmic/macrocosmic changes happen through the channel of attention. What the most people notice gets the most energy. This is why seeing graffiti art, or a well-kept garden, can create a continuous impact on a city spirit and collective identity. For example, Central Park is both a landmark and a touchstone to the shared identify of New Yorkers. Most people living in the city can create a psychic anchor in the park. Those repeated memory markers—whether it's a sculpture or simply "sold" scrawled on an overpass—build mile markers in the collective unconscious that become part of the shared mental map of that city.

Each person who lives in a city builds an internal map that begins on their very first visit and continues as long as that person spends time in a city. The more time spent, the stronger the internal map. In this way, a second, personalized, incomplete city lives inside every citizen.

If you extracted a visual of the city map in your head, it likely has large chunks missing: neighborhoods you've never visited, street names you don't know, possibly even a landmark or two missing. For example, a sports fan may have clear internal markers for all the stadiums in a city, but another person may have all the markers for public parks instead.

Even with those aspects missing, each person likely has many of the same areas marked on their internal maps—a highway exit, a welcome sign, or even a famous building that all drivers see lit up at night. For example, North Mankato, Minnesota, has the last Happy Chef statue in the US. Most people who live in North Mankato or visit the city more than once can picture that statue, assess how tall it is, and possibly name the businesses next door to it. If someone wanted to perform an astral working and move through the city out of body, that statue can serve as an anchor for that travel. If person A, who knows the stadium system, and person B, who knows the parks, want to meet and work in the astral, they could agree to meet at the Happy Chef statue because it's already on both of their internal maps. They can then combine their internal maps and thus expand the energy access to certain areas for both parties.

After a person is away for several years, the internal map becomes less accurate and thus also becomes a time travel tool. This time travel can be used to locate origins of energy or for drawing on something inherent in a city spirit that no longer exists in the present-day spirit.

For example, if a person wants to check the origin of an energy (usually used when tracing the source of negative energy), bringing up the memory of a city landmark that no longer exists but did in a specific year, and using that image travel in the astral through the marks of the now overwritten map, can help discern when and how a negative event happened. It can also allow a magick worker to create a solution for a present-day energy imbalance by addressing the issue when it happened, even if it happened long before the magician's time.

Diana Rajchel's Law of Magick
Magick does not multitask.

This is my own law, determined after years of trial and error. Kitchen sink spells—where you throw all the power you can muster at several targets—can work *but* are far less effective than concentrated efforts. Loading too many intentions into a spell only allows a few charged atoms for each purpose. One intention per spell works best. If you would like a better night's sleep and more money in your pocket, perform separate spells for each intention. If you're working with city energy, you may need to raise a lot of power. Don't dilute your efforts.

Magick is ultimately a discipline. Coming back and doing a little bit of work each day is part of the practice. Magickal urbanism at this point extends beyond discipline—it is part theory, part lifestyle, and part *avant garde* experiment. Until we really evolve our ideas beyond "yes, this building has a spirit," and "yes, these shared perceptions come from something in concrete reality," we have to borrow from the theories of magicians that went before us. Those theories and how they apply to this work are a helpful launching place, especially when you're constructing spells and rituals for needs no one could possibly anticipate.

THREE
FOUNDATION SKILLS FOR URBAN MAGICK

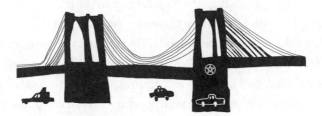

Urban magick requires much the same foundation skills as any other type of magick. Those basics—grounding, centering, checking ambient energy, channeling energy, trance, and relationship building—are how you train for the marathon of city energy work.

Once you have firmly anchored your practice of energy practice basics discussed in the beginning of this chapter, you can prepare for the deeper skills of city spirit work. In order to expand into city energy, you need to develop two complementary yet contradictory skill sets in addition to those that allow you self-care and recovery: the skills of *acclimation* and the skills of *disconnection*. Flowing between acclimation and disconnection prevents burnout, which in turn allows you to practice and sustain magick and/or interact with much larger energy bodies for longer periods of time. Acclimation lets you find flow states—

in this case, the flow of city energy—enabling you to feel the collective "mood" of a region and, over time, to influence that mood and direction. Disconnection is the skill set that allows you to shield from energy, stand in it unaffected, or to completely remove yourself from a pattern.

To learn city energy, you must acclimate to it. To acclimate to it, you must expose yourself to its rhythms. Expose yourself to your city by walking (if able), taking mass transit, breathing the air (if it's safe), touching the water (swimming pools count), and learning its daily and seasonal rhythms to the point that you can feel it on your skin. Simple information, like when rush hour starts or what blocks serve as common parade routes, can and should affect how you time your workings. It may not seem significant to someone working in a city they were born in, but for someone from the outside, for the first few months to the first few years, you are a foreign cell introducing yourself into a complex organism. The sooner you make yourself part of the city's internalized body, the sooner you become part of that natural flow. This alignment eases everything in city life, from finding parking to dating to finding affordable groceries.

Observing

City spirits like attention, and that's good because inattention in dense populations can endanger you. So, if you go out into the city, plan on total engagement. Put phones away and leave the headphones at home. Try wearing something with pockets. Overalls and utility jackets come in especially handy for urban magick because they make carrying supplies easy and let you worry less about forgetting or losing something valuable. Fewer distractions and burdens improve your ability to read the energy around you and add to your personal safety because you can focus on your surroundings.

Practical self-protection emphatically constitutes a skill for urban magick. You need to know what happens around you for your safety and those you encounter. Some people may balk at disconnecting with phones or setting aside headphones. Phones can help people manage social anxiety; headphones are a common way to signal disinterest in interaction. At the same time, people with headphones on or who pay too much attention to their phones are often marks for robbery and other violence. You can pay attention and prevent one unpleasantness but then remain exposed to another kind.

If you find yourself vulnerable to catcalling, fat-calling, or similar harassment, then perhaps compromise by leaving your headphones on but the sound off when doing city work. While this can expose some unpleasantness, it retains some remnants of a social filter. You know your cities and your safeties. Use careful judgement for when and how to have your music filters on or off.

Once you establish these safeties, observation comes down to going out and seeing what happens. Pick a city street, sit on a bench, and make a note of who walks past you. Look around when taking the bus—listen to what people talk about, and look out the window for construction projects, business changes, even shifts in traffic patterns. Take one day and count the different types of plants you see growing along sidewalks or through cracks and keep an eye out for different flora and fauna—what you see when you pay attention may surprise you.

Walking

If you can walk, go for one twice a week. Knowing the streets and sidewalks intimately builds the city map in your mind. This inner map helps you acclimate to the territory and can feed your inner vision when you need to work in the astral rather than the physical. If you can't walk, try sitting outside, or if it is at all reasonable to do so, take public transportation lines from beginning to end to discover lesser-known details of your city. While physical limitations come up for everyone eventually, it shouldn't shut you out of city magick altogether. There is always another way to connect to your city spirit. This walking process builds that inner map, yes, but it also allows the city spirit a chance to recognize you and to show you its own map, such as what streets have ley lines or similar energy pools running beneath.

The Body and the City

There is a strong relationship between bodily awareness and magick. Improving your understanding of what goes on in your body when working magick or when you have strong emotions can help a great deal when exposed to high population density. One useful method for figuring out what is going on with you on a spiritual and personal level is to run through a series of questions by chakra. It can let you know if you need help in a certain area, if you are experiencing an energy from outside yourself, or if you need to disconnect.

While none of the following exercises can ever replace care from a well-qualified therapist, the simple acts of recognition, release, and expression can help make progress both in self-healing work and in magickal energy management. The following self-inventory is only a beginning tool, questions to ask yourself before you begin any magickal working—especially magickal workings with possible community effect. Many energy communications happen solely through bodily sensation, so this inventory begins the work of distinguishing what sensation and what communication. Each question is aligned loosely along the seven major chakras (energy centers) in the body. Working through these is intended to help you identify your own emotional states, so that you know where you store certain emotions in your physical body. These questions also help you distinguish between metaphysical events and physical ones.

The Root Chakra Questions

- Am I hungry?
- Am I tired?
- Am I sick?
- Do I feel threatened?

The Sacral Chakra Questions

- Is sexual attraction a factor in my behavior and judgments right now?
- Is sexual repulsion a factor in my behavior and judgments right now?
- Am I feeling a normal amount of pleasure given the situation?
- (For all genders) Where am I on my hormone cycle?

The Solar Plexus Chakra and Belly Chakra Questions

- Do I feel a need to control this situation?
- Did I just eat something weird?
- Have I swallowed any anger?

The Heart Chakra Questions

- Am I sad?

- Am I worried?

- What is happening in my relationship with others in this moment?

- Does my chest feel tight or compressed?

- (For people who wear bras) Is my bra size correct? (This can add feelings of tightness/discomfort.)

The Throat Chakra Questions

- Does my throat feel tight? Does something feel caught in it?

- Where else does that stuck feeling repeat in my body?

- Am I experiencing a "bite my tongue" feeling? Why?

- (If you literally just bit your tongue) Where was my attention focused in that moment?

The Third Eye/Forehead Chakra Questions

- Am I experiencing anxiety?

- At what speed are my thoughts coming?

- How much information am I processing right now?

- Does it help or hurt to close my eyes?

The Crown Chakra Questions

- If I stand in a patch of light, am I feeling only my own energy?

- If I sense energy that isn't mine, what is the shape of that energy?

- Where in my chakras am I feeling a response to the energy that isn't mine?
- What is my emotional response to these other energies?

City magick, even for the most diligent, is dirty work. People who work magick in urban spaces are exposed daily to the energies, emotions, histories, and degraded practices of workers long gone. Even for relatively insensitive people, it can be hard to tolerate. The better we understand where we respond to our emotions (internal energies) and that of others (external energies), the better we'll be able to cultivate the right boundaries between ourselves and our metaphysical/physical worlds.

Curiosity

Curiosity, especially after several decades of adulthood, can take some rekindling. It isn't just an emotional condition—it's a skill. It takes skill and discipline to have new questions about things, and to want to know what things and people are. It's also the single best way to form a relationship, whether with a person or a spirit. Show some curiosity about who that person is, about what hidden things the city contains, and about the stories and history languishing underneath the cement. Because city magick is simultaneously ancient and forgotten and modern and experimental, it demands curiosity. Ask the people around you why they live in your city and how they came there. This will expand your understanding of whom the city calls and help you know what you bring to it yourself. Look at everything around you. Why do trees line one street while another stands bare to the sky? Why did the city install that park there? Why is everyone afraid of that house? Why do so many

people plan their lives around that church's events? A good magician never passively accepts conditions. All aspects of life receive at
least one pass through rigorous thought.

Some reading this may argue that curiosity is more personality trait than skill. In early childhood, this may be true, and
it seems that most kids begin as curious and then run into the
allowed and not-allowed questions. Adults, having had decades
of that same conditioning, tend to either not ask questions or
ask questions only from a mysteriously vetted unknown script.
They assume their questions have been answered or they've been
trained to no longer ask them. Cultivating curiosity—wanting
to know why things are the way they are—helps you understand
what needs to change and what needs to stay the same. Curiosity cultivation differs from the path of internet debate, where
questions are meant only to find flaws in thinking. Curiosity as a
magician's skill comes from a place of genuinely wanting to learn.
Ask questions until your assumptions break, and you need to
form new ones. Continuous questions elevate your connection to
city spirit like no other method.

Acting in Accord and Measurable Results

In Scott Cunningham's *Living Wicca*, he raises the principle of
acting in accord. This concept has faded from view in recent
years, and it's a shame, as it is about making sure magick gets
results. Cunningham used the example of someone casting a
spell to get a new job—and how the job still wouldn't come unless
the caster sent out résumés. Hearth and Home witches especially
need this principle—to make their lives stable, they must also
perform practical tasks to open the paths of delivery.

In contrast, other types of city working may not need this
because the action often is the accord. If you want to do a neigh-

borhood peace working, sending the energy is your act of peace. That energy may manifest through unexpected conversation with a neighbor, a lit candle, or even another person's random act of kindness.

Urban magick calls for you to reach a specific and, when possible, measurable goal. When you work that spell for neighborhood peace, are you looking to reduce noise complaints, lower the crime rate, or have friendlier neighbors? Determine your desired result before you begin. Also, at that time decide what tools measure success. Assess the progress of your goals by checking police blotters or other reporting agencies weekly to spot shifts or trends in your area.

Once you build up a practice of walking and observing, and excavate your body language to yourself, you can move on to a relationship with nature seen and unseen. In cities, nature can seem hidden in certain spots. Learning how to find the nature in everything around you can help you overcome that cut-off feeling, by remembering that all things natural and not are merely a convergence of planar forces to establish what we perceive as the material. The following exercises, rooted in elements and practical concepts, also apply to the emotional bodies: your anger may indeed bear some of the plane of fire, or the plane of earth. Understanding these on the physical plane can assist you in understanding your own emotional makeup, and thus understand the emotional makeup of your city spirit.

Disconnection

When the ancient Greeks said "know thyself," they meant that self-awareness mattered far more than the most esoteric information, and it still holds true. Magick workers must make every effort to understand themselves because, after energy and magick work becomes practiced, it can also become subconscious. Many magickal errors come from someone unaware that they did anything. The more awareness you build of your own energy—who touches it, who uses it, and who you are connected to and disconnected from—the more effective your magick (and the less accident-prone you become). Boundaries, both personal and geographic, are significant to city magick. Part of this containment is knowing where your energy begins and the city's ends. This sense of self matters in city magick because you can more easily recognize when a city problem is also somehow your problem, and when the city and its energy might bleed on you until you blur. Feeling connected is good but slipping into altered consciousness as soon as you step outside your door is too much for normal day-to-day function.

Certain spaces in your city may trigger subtle reactions, so subtle you may not question them. You may avoid places, citing "convenience" rather than the actual discomfort you feel. You might sense curiosity about places and wander to areas that fall far out of what is easy for you to get to. Until you fully understand how your opinions, inclinations, traumas, and background affect your behavior, you may overlook how your energy impacts your environment or fail to recognize that you feed certain entities. This feeding comes from your emotional body, arguably the most ignored—and most important—auric body in all Western esotericism. Good mental health is just as contagious as poor mental health, and a well-kept magician can spread either because magick pulls from the strongest energy sources it can find. Emotions make up a massive amount of that energy.

Shielding and Filtering

Shielding disconnects you from your environment by placing a barrier between yourself and what surrounds you. While meant to protect the shielded, it also reduces that person's impact on those who encounter that person. Most beginners learn to visualize a bubble of blue or white light around their bodies. As they advance, their style of shielding changes. Some practitioners eventually stop using them in favor of overall environmental awareness.

I prefer the multilayer, multipurpose approach to shielding. Remember, magick doesn't multitask, and that applies to shielding as well. Add layers of light, each with a different singular purpose, until you have enough layers to block out the surrounding environment as best serves you. For example, you might begin with a three-layer method: The first layer fends off psychic intrusions—mind reading, manipulation, overt attack, or generic astral parasites. The next layer can filter without totally blocking strong emotions from people around you, so that you recognize them without feeling their influence. The third can act as a ventilator, inhaling fresh prana for you to fuel your shields while releasing any negative buildup that comes from inside yourself. These beginner shields act like one-way mirrors; you can see and sense what goes on, but what you shield against can only get a vague sense of you.

The following exercises, from basic light to designer edition, will help you develop your own method of shielding. If you find the practice beneficial, you can gradually make these methods your own by adding textures, light effects, an interesting tool borrowed from science fiction, and so on. You might even want to add your own version of two-factor authentication. For example, if you have clairaudience but don't trust all spirit communications, you might establish a numeric code that spirits must provide in order to send their message. Once you master the basics, get really creative!

Exercise 1: White or Blue Light Shielding

Scores of guided meditation recordings begin: "Imagine yourself surrounded by a white light," a visualization that creates a basic shield. The next most popular version guides practitioners to picture blue light. Sometimes the guide explains the color choice but often not. Color shielding is a popular go-to because most people can imagine colors with ease. The two most common colors, white and blue, have Western cultural associations with purity, heavenliness, and cleanliness. These qualities do make for useful shielding wavelengths. White light automatically "cleans out" most run-of-the-mill spiritual negativity while drawing positive energy into the caster.

Blue light adds a subtle layer of invisibility—not full invisibility, but rather a "notice me less" aspect to the shield. The frequency of blue promotes calm to the point of detachment. It also requires less energy and concentration than white light shielding. White calls on the presence of all colors; blue only calls to the wavelength of blue. We may not notice the mental strain, but it can affect the effectiveness and stamina we have for shielding. When someone shields constantly using only their own energy, they also end up feeling tired most of the time. To see what works most easily for you, practice holding a color in your mind while running a stopwatch. White takes the most effort; black the least. If prone to depression, you may want to stick with white or explore rose-colored shielding, something that evokes a light, sweet response in observers. You will need to turn this method on and off depending on where you go in your city. Start with something easy to maintain—the pressure of cacophonous energies is stress enough, without the stress of trying to block them out completely.

Exercise 2: Two-Direction Shielding

Casting a circle before ritual is an example of two-directional shielding. It contains and protects those within it, and any energy brought into that circle stays there until released rather than influencing what lies beyond it. It prevents outside energies from wandering in and protects those outside energies from unintended/nonconsensual influence. Such styles of shielding are important if, for example, you conjure something in a space where your neighbors' four-year-old might see that energy form pushing through his wall more plainly than the adults in the household. Adding layers of outer shielding to keep your own energy from spilling onto others, as well as the shields you use to limit what spills onto you, can drastically enhance safety and comfort for you and for any unwitting yet sensitive neighbors.

Other Shields

Color shielding doesn't work for everyone and that's okay—there are other methods. Once you understand how a shield can feel you can create your own using what symbols speak to you. This next level shield, a more advanced method, may offer the alternative you need.

However, if you are a more tactile or emotive person—or simply have a vivid imagination that needs room to play—the only limits are what works and what doesn't. What works for you may not work for others and vice versa. Here are some elements you can experiment with for your shield.

Textures

- Silk—smoothness, gliding on by
- Black Cloth—blending in, invisibility
- Corduroy—abrasion
- Wool—abrasion and insulation

Animals

- Lizards and snakes—become ambient to the environment
- Predatory animals—"do not approach" feeling
- Large animals (elephants, rhinoceros, horses)—animals that take up space without apology
- Spiky animals (porcupines)—fend off intrusive energy

Plants

- Roses—seemingly innocuous; hidden thorns
- Nettles—sticky, encourages avoidance
- Onions—hidden layers

Shield Filters

Shield filters act like specific spells planted within and over top of your shields. Often, they form a layer of offensive protection, although some workers prefer filters that encourage subtle mood shifts in their immediate environment. Most people who use light and color shielding imagine them as porous. This allows them to sense when someone with bad intentions is in their sphere or when a mood shifts in a room. You can add a layer that projects "I'm not interesting" or "I'm the wrong person to pick on." You may add a slightly more aggressive response planted in your shields if someone tries to push past even those limits, or you may opt for a glamour that filters out the wrong people but invites the right ones to come flirt with you.

Filters can really help when walking through "minefield" city blocks. In downtown Minneapolis, people stopped me so often to ask for money or make (usually unwelcome) comments that I often missed my train home. Along with learning what non-verbal signals were causing me to stop and training myself to not respond to them, I also spent a few minutes at the end of my workday rehearsing my resting witch face and projecting platypus darts extending outside of my shields. It took a bit of practice, but after about a week I could get from the office to my commuter train with little disruption.

The Chakra Clamp

From time to time, certain energies we encounter may push through all our shields, no matter how thick and tricky. In those situations, clamping down on your chakras can prevent energy from attaching, especially energy or entities out to drain energy or cause fear. Closing and opening energy centers takes practice, even for those with innate awareness of their own energy. Practice at home before you go out.

To learn to do this, lie down and scan your body. You may want to find a guided body scan meditation to help this. First, look for aches and pains and compare them to areas of your body that feel fine. This is an inside-out scan. Next, mentally scan your skin from the outside in and notice spots that move a little faster or feel a little "stickier" than the rest of you on average. Breathe into those sticky/fast spots to regulate the energy. Often these areas indicate some type of energy intake that disagrees with you—most people have a few patches on their body. Once you master this awareness, center your attention to the chakra points along your spine. For those unfamiliar, the seven most common chakra points fall along the base of your spine, your genitals/belly, your solar plexus, your heart, your throat, the center of your forehead and the crown of your head. You can use the body scan exercise to find these points and check in on their motion—each center should have some sense of motion and be pain-free. If these spots feel sluggish or you sense pain, you may need healing.

Those seven spots are the areas to close when something breaks through shields. For most, the instinct is to tense muscles to close these areas. Resist this! You do not want to train yourself to tense up the minute something crosses a boundary. It restricts energy flow and you risk pinching a nerve later. Instead, focus on one trouble spot at a time, feel the shape of the energy, and ask, "What's going on?" Imagine pulling those spots inward while keeping your muscles relaxed. As you close the chakra, inhale slowly, imagining the sound of a lock clicking. Once the danger has passed, make sure to re-open your chakras and give them a good spin/shake out. You may want to do this as part of exercise, just to get all your organ and energy systems flowing well again.

———

As mentioned, some workers prefer not to shield. The next section covers alternate methods of self and neighbor protection. They may have no innate psychic ability and work magick from a different place of perception, making shields unnecessary, or they may prefer to remain alert to all information sans filters. Not shielding works better for people with high levels of extroversion and a strong immune system, who feel energized after crowd exposure. For empaths, introverts, and the allergic, stick with shielding.

Open Defenses

Open defenses come in handy when a magick worker really needs to know everything going on, to the point where shields leave out vital information. These methods can include invisibility, glamours, and offensive defenses. Most people prefer personal boundaries to these types of magick, but things happen in cities, especially with so many egos sharing close physical and psychic space. When "things happen" we need some extra tools. We live in a day and age where more people can learn about magick and learn how to throw it at one another—and where we have much less emotional maturity when it comes to how and when to use these tools. This can force people to change their defense methods, since in some situations ignoring a person's obnoxiousness is exactly the thing, but other times you need something that pushes back for you while you go about the business of minding your own business. Invisibility and glamour reduce the necessity of pushing back, while offensive defense methods automate pushbacks so you need not waste your conscious energy and time on someone else's ego burst.

Invisibility

Occult lore is filled with spells of invisibility, ranging from the sublime to the ridiculous—and a few of the methods detailed in old grimoires could lead to hospitalization or jail. In modern work-ings, people have several methods for escaping notice or simply staying engaged in a subliminal way. In his series *The Hitchhiker's Guide to the Galaxy,* science fiction author Douglas Adams wrote about a ship with a cloaking device called the "somebody else's problem field." The ship sat in the middle of a cricket field, and the players played right over it as if it weren't there because it regis-tered as "somebody else's problem." This is exactly how invisibility magick works. Technically you remain part of the scenery, but eyes never quite focus on you or the target you wish to escape notice. This works on items as small as a ring or as large as a building. For magickal people in a city, you may wish to use invisibility selec-tively. Project a "not your problem" field to get past canvassers and street preachers or when you must walk past someone aggressive.

Some people take naturally to invisibility work while others struggle. For those who can do so easily, performing your normal grounding and centering and then matching your energy as com-pletely as possible to your immediate atmosphere should work fine. You become the scenery to anyone not especially looking for you. This also usually requires some degree of stillness. The especially talented can calibrate automatically, retaining invisibil-ity as they move through different environments—for example, the energy of the ambient energy of the street differs from the ambient energy of the library. Someone in the library will likely notice something with street energy because it does mismatch the environment. For most people, you need to pause and recali-brate energy when you walk through any doorway.

For those where from-the-body energy work does not hap-pen so easily, you have a host of herbs and folklore to pull from. A common invisibility herbal formula includes bay leaves and almost any kind of black seed, such as poppy or black mustard.

You may need to mix and activate them by asking them out loud to do what you want them to do. Often you can get more energy from these plants by grinding them with a mortar and pestle, or you can get the most by growing them from seed. Carry these herbs in your pockets or a muslin bag pinned to the inside of your clothing. If you prefer a more ritualized way to make yourself invisible, the Key of Solomon has a spell for doing so. Often praying or making offerings to the angels named is enough to help you gain invisibility for short periods of time. Remember to keep your invisibility time to the bare minimum you need: you may not want the person likely to follow you home to notice you, but you definitely want the driver peeling through the intersection to recognize your presence.

Ambience, the "Not Quite" of Invisibility

Rather than cloaking yourself from notice, you may instead become ambient. This differs from invisibility in that instead of escaping notice, you simply seem like you Belong There, wherever there may be. This happens naturally to some people—do you know someone who always gets approached by other shoppers in the store because they think that person works there? Does this happen even when the person wears clothing that in no way resembles the employee uniform? That is a form of natural ambience. It's much less irritating when deliberate.

To achieve ambience, calibrate yourself to the energy of an area, and then tap into the oldest object in an area and give the impression your presence has been in place for almost that long. This is especially useful if going into a place where you might project a "fish out of water" vibe. Imagine a chameleon that changes color to match its environment.

To achieve this calibration requires strong grounding and centering skills. Ground and center as you would normally. Then notice the energy around you; compare your energy to it. Is it moving faster, hotter, louder? Adjust your own energy to match that energy. Now, look around for some background object, possibly one a bit dusty, and sense any impressions you get from that. Picture taking a tiny slice of that energy into your own and spreading it over your outermost layer. You may have a hard time holding this for long periods at first. You may want to experiment with this in a nightclub or any other place where a lot of socialization happens—turning the ambience off and on to see who notices you or who loses interest. You can use this exercise on mass transit, in a shop, or anywhere you visit. Compare how people react to you when you choose to make yourself different from the energy around you. What effects and results can you produce?

Glamours

Glamours, for the purposes of city magick, are making sure people see you the way you want them to see you. You can use this to give off an air of respectability, to make yourself seem like the most charismatic person in the room, or to seem a tiny bit sillier than you really are. To some this may seem like shallow magick, but altering perceptions—that's powerful stuff.

In the most basic form of glamour, you build a 360-degree projection of how you want others to see you. Picture a flattering outfit, good hair, good skin—and then add a layer of how you want those in perceptual range to feel. Usually if you're going with a glamour, you want a positive emotional response. You may want to do this before you speak to a group, so that they respond to your air of authority. You may want this when going out for fun so that people see you as fun and thus want to join you.

You can also use the most common tools of altering appearance to boost magickal glamour. Using makeup, hair styling, and clothing with intent can help these projections last longer and also assist you in building your confidence in real ways. Colors in makeup and clothing especially come in handy—using colors to symbolize energies you wish to put outwards. You may have to pick and choose where you use makeup depending on who you are, but it's worth reminding people that eye liner looks good on almost everyone.

Offensive Defenses

For those who subscribe to "harm none," this type of protection needs some clarification. This style of protection attacks no one; however, just as someone might put an ink bomb in a safe that they don't want opened, you can similarly add traps to your auric body. The most famous of such methods is a hoodoo/conjure work called Fiery Wall of Protection. Rather than a shield, the spell creates a fire wall around your energy and your home; if someone tries to have a go at you, they get burned. City workers may do something similar, but portable, since crowds can make random attacks more likely. Carrying a charm that casts a curse on any energy intrusion, or carrying stones like aegirine and tourmaline that trap energy and spirits that might otherwise cause trouble, can reduce the impact of people going out just looking to cause a little unwarranted chaos.

People who need open defenses usually already draw a lot of attention to themselves for different reasons, or they wind up in the crosshairs of magicians that want a little too much control over everyone else. It happens, and it happens more these days than it has in the past. Try to live a life where you don't need to carry defensive curses for more than a few months at a time. It won't protect you totally—there's always someone out there looking to make trouble just for you—but it can keep these inevitable interactions to a manageable minimum.

Over time, you will develop the defenses and self-checks that best work for you. You may find that you do need to upgrade your protections every so often—more people work with magick than you might think, and many people tap into spiritual energies without realizing that they do so. The exposure to this can cause some uncomfortable surprises among spiritually sensitive neighbors. The tools covered in this chapter give a reasonable start for practice for the new, and perhaps some new tools to the more experienced worker.

The skills of urban magick can apply to magick in other areas but are usually not nearly as needed in areas of lower population density. This is because magick basics remain the same no matter what branch or tradition you practice. It is in the repetition of those basics that you learn the minutiae, such as what specific habits apply to city work or at the very least apply to your city spirit. All magicians must learn by walking the earth. City magicians learn by walking and riding the city, and by learning the bounds of that city and by extension their own boundaries. The tools given here should give you a very good start to working with your city spirit and the city's energy in a safe, strong way.

FOUR
THE BIRTH OF CITIES

ities appeared at the end of a long evolutionary process and as a direct byproduct of agricultural development. This period, called the Neolithic Revolution, started in the Fertile Crescent around 8500–8000 BCE, with the Americas seeing their own revolution between 7500–7000 BCE and Europe's and Africa's almost coinciding, appearing at roughly 6500–5000 BCE.[4] At this time, human cultures moved away from hunter-gathering as they discovered ways to cultivate crops, domesticate animals, improve food storage, and form permanent settlements.[5] The relative stillness borne of this new permanence gave humans more free time. With less burden to just survive, humans began crafting

---

4. Cait Caffrey, "Neolithic Revolution" *Salem Press Encyclopedia*, (Ipswich, MA: Salem Press, 2018), via EBSCO.

5. Paul Kriwaczek, *Babylon: Mesopotamia and the Birth of Civilization* (New York: St. Martin's Press, 2010), 20.

and building, and soon skilled labor and art emerged. People also started building walled enclosures for their communities. Gathering community behind a fortified wall eased issues with predators and flooding.[6] It also caused settlers to form a sense of shared identity.

Around 3500 BCE, the Urban Revolution began.[7] People began forming dense settlements, sometimes incorporating groups of nearby villages into a population dense enough for a city. While scholars debate the exact requirements for what made an ancient city different from a large farming village, archaeologist Vere Goden Childe proposed ten qualifiers: government, taxes, religion, a social hierarchy, foreign trade (foreign meaning with other nearby cities), scientific exploration, skilled artisans, writing, architecture, and art. Ancient cities, from Childe's perspective, were the birthplace of complex cultures.

Even though each city developed its own languages and customs, certain patterns of development recurred across disparate zones. The earliest cities—especially those in the Fertile Crescent—dedicated their settlements to a specific deity. Usually if a community built a temple at the point it shifted from village to city.[8] Along with places of worship, temples served as hospitals, trading centers, government centers, and food distribution sites. Artisans often built and maintained the temple, artists lived and worked in them making amulets and statues, barbers cut hair for

6. Annalee Newitz, "Why Do We Build Walls Around Our Cities?" *Gizmodo* (blog), September 3, 2014: https://io9.gizmodo.com/why-do-we-build-walls-around-our-cities-1630142347.

7. Ruth Michael, "Urban Revolution" *Salem Press Encyclopedia*, (Ipswich, MA: Salem Press, 2017), via EBSCO.

8. Richard Miles, *Carthage Must Be Destroyed: The Rise and Fall of an Ancient Civilization* (New York: Viking, 2011), 31.

those wishing to give it as offering to the gods, sex workers served as healers, and teachers transmitted writing and other knowledge that stabilized society.

As human society evolved, another common theme emerged: some degree of separation of church and state. This usually happened as the result of some political schism. As social hierarchy evolved, governance moved outside of the temples. Tribal leaders began building palaces, sometimes strategically in the center of their cities, to pull power away from the temples. Soon enough, these palaces were in competition with the temples for wealth and power.[9] In some cities, the palace inhabitants declared themselves gods. Early urban citizens usually built their temples at a city's outskirts and as part of a grid. Palaces were built in the center of the city, forcing traffic to revolve around them.

City-States

The invention of the boat led to the rise of the city state. As humans found this way to travel faster, they also found new territories for trade. City-states began appearing around islands and coastlines, as access to the water made these ideal trading locations. These cities amassed wealth that also made protection of the wealth necessary, as pirates and raiders began targeting resources beyond food.

The city-state became the first government structure to include both military and agricultural interests. Prior to the Urban Revolution, different tribal groups would attack one another for resources, but war as an ideological rather than practical concept evolved as a byproduct of trading among city-states.

---

9. P. D. Smith, *City: A Guidebook for the Urban Age* (New York: Bloomsbury, 2012), 50.

These cultures then protected themselves or gained resources by conquering neighboring cities.

Every ancient city, even those forgotten, brought something important to the development of civilization. These cities also venerated their land spirit/genius loci to godhood, and gods were born out of their shared collective belief. In many cases, over time, a god of the city emerged that was not the genius loci. Those gods and spirits evolved from the power of collective human attention and belief.

Early City Planning

One of the pieces of wisdom that priests of early cities held close: engineering and ways to make cities more defensible through conscious design. Most cities aligned themselves with the geographic features of their region—thus trade cities built up around seaways and rivers, mountainous areas might have pathways along rocks and ravines, and agriculture-centered cities formed grids. Beyond geography, the earliest cities manifested with little conscious planning.

Cities fell often from war, famine, and disease. After enough wars, civilizations began to take note of this large-scale cycle of life and death, and invented ways to reduce the death cycle by creating longer-lasting buildings and roads. Archaeologists found maps of planned cities from the time of Alexander the Great in the eighth century BCE; these maps showed an understanding of the land and its resources, as well as real intention behind the distribution of dwellings. For example, the city of Krane in Greece had an even layout and a partial wall, showing military planning and execution of Greek mathematical ideals. Despite the advantages that planned cities enjoyed, the practice of urban design and city planning did not become a standard engineering practice until the twentieth century. In some ways, this absence of deliberate planning shows us a map of the earliest collective consciousness.

Mortality in Ancient Cities

Keeping a population alive was one of early civilization's great challenges. Ancient cities had much smaller populations than modern cities, often barely capping the population required to be recognized as a small town in the modern Americas. At its most populous, Sumerian city Eridu had 10,000 people; by modern standards, this would constitute a village.[10] Its sister city, Uruk, grew to an estimated 80,000 people, while the population of Memphis ran 30,000. Carthage, including its transient population, had around 150,000 citizens at its peak.

In addition to the larger problems of famine, disease, high infant mortality, and low life expectancy, these cities also suffered from problems of population density unresolved to this day. Poor street lighting at night made travelers vulnerable to robberies.[11] Unsanitary waste disposal spread disease, as did superstitions about hand-washing and other now common hygiene practices.[12] Fires in dense housing often led to many deaths and sometimes the destruction of entire cities.

Environmental pollution as we know it did not exist in ancient times. That said, pollutions of close proximity and climate changes

---

10. Smith, *City*, 30.

11. David Matz, *Daily Life of the Ancient Romans* (Westport, CT: Greenwood Press, 2002), 50.

12. Paul Kriwaczek, *Babylon: Mesopotamia and the Birth of Civilization* (New York: St. Martin's Press, 2010), 33.

did exact a price on some ancient cities. Permanent weather shifts in Mesopotamia combined with poor livestock farming practices brought a once fertile area to famine. Dense populations often led to widespread plagues, creating a cycle where all the settlers of a city died out. Usually about twenty years after one population died out, a new population came and built on top of the original cities—until disease or war wiped them out as well, a continuous layer-on-layer cycle that confounds archaeologists.

Ancient Attitudes Toward Cities

Ancient city life was famed for smells, disease, discomfort, and animal waste. During the times of ancient Rome, a saying one often heard was "the greater the stench, the greater the city." The invention of poverty only made this stench worse.

The appearance of coins to exchange for goods led to uneven distribution of resources. City walls, created to preserve the safety and collective identity of a settlement, also made a dividing line between those wealthy enough to live in cities and those so poor they had to remain on the outskirts near the temples.

The psychological effect of city walls may also have factored into why people remained in cities despite the unclean and unsafe conditions.[13] The walls created a sense of safety through separation from the outside world. Only strangers came from outside the gates, and those outsiders were treated with suspicion. The poor building their houses just outside of city walls became the roots of the modern suburb.

Even though strangers did not always receive a warm welcome, larger settlements began to serve many of the same people that modern cities do: They housed the queer, the creative, and

---

13. Smith, *City*, 37.

the disenfranchised. Many of these wandering folks came to temples for their support and became the artisans, inventors, and scholars that moved their cities to the next level of cultural development. Hospitality became a complex value—the community needed protection, but welcoming the right strangers brought healing, change, and prosperity.

Founding City Myths

The earliest cities always had deities at their foundation, and so cities did not merely have history, they had mythology.[14] City myth cycles usually consisted of a climate disaster, followed by a hero conquering the elements of nature. In these stories some monster or ancient chaos deity represented the forces that early humans overcame.

Just as cities fell and built on top of one another, city cosmologies and their patron deities also layered and blended. These pantheons and their stories inform the concept of modern city spirits. For example, in one account, the patron god of Ur is Marduk, a Herculean figure sometimes deemed interchangeable with the genius loci;[15] in another, the moon god Sin takes ascendance.[16] This usually happened after a population shift, such as an immigration influx, if not from one of the city's cycles of death and rebuilding. Often proponents of the earlier pantheon continued their worship even as newer versions of the same gods rose to primacy. Ancient Egypt handled these cultural shifts by accepting

14. Matz, *Daily Life,* 127.

15. Nicole Brisch, "Marduk" in *Ancient Mesopotamian Gods and Goddesses,* http://oracc.museum.upenn.edu/amgg/listofdeities/marduk/.

16. Mogens Trolle Larsen, *Ancient Kanesh: A Merchant Colony in Bronze Age Anatolia* (New York: Cambridge University Press, 2015), 88.

parallel deities and giving them equal honor—no one version was the "right" version, though different cities claimed different aspects of these parallel deities.[17] Egypt began this pluralism; Rome perfected it,[18] going so far as to propitiate the gods of their enemies and bring them into Roman worship after those cultures were conquered.[19]

The Myth of Eridu and Uruk

The first known city myth is that of the Eridu, sister city to Uruk. In the myth, the god Enki served as protector and provider to humanity, similar to Prometheus. According to myth, Enki created humanity from clay and taught humans how to build canals, plan temples, and produce abundant food. In some stories, he also "divided the speech of people" as an explanation of why humans spoke multiple languages. As the patron spirit of the city of Eridu, he kept the *Me* (sometimes written *Meh*). The *Me* contained all the secrets of civilization, and Enki himself knew the power of incantations, exorcism, and divination, which he kept in his temple, *Apsu*. This story reflects not only the secrets of civilization, but the pride of a city in the creation of wisdom. The people of Eridu invested their city with their own belief in its

17. Marsha E. Ackerman, Michael J. Schroeder, et al., eds., "Egypt Culture and Religion" in *Ancient World History: The Ancient World Prehistoric Eras to 600 C.E.*, volume 1, (New York: Facts on File, 2017), xxxv.

18. Jörg Rüpke, "Religious Pluralism and the Roman Empire," *From Jupiter to Christ: On the History of Religion in the Roman Imperial Period* (Oxford, UK: Oxford University Press, 2014), accessed DOI: 10.1093/acprof:oso/9780198703723.003.0011.

19. Stephen L. Dyson, *Rome: A Living Portrait of an Ancient City* (Baltimore, MD: Johns Hopkins University Press, 2010), 23.

creativity and mystery. It also ritualized knowledge, organization, and planning—all necessary aspects of maintaining a city.

The mystery aspect of Eridu's story also hints at how shared culture spread between cities in one region. Enki certainly gave of his wisdom to his own city and used the *Meh* to keep records of it, but he did not share his wisdom with people of other settlements, even when those gods were his own children. He exemplified a pristine patriarchy—and his sister city eventually conned him into sharing his wisdom. It is the quintessential story of tribalism and how one culture relented in order to transmit knowledge to another.

Uruk's patron deity was a goddess of love and war—and also a daughter of Enki. A temple was built for Inanna, and the city named her as its patron.[20] In the translated accounts, Inanna visited her father Enki and, over beer, persuaded him to share all his secrets of magic and power. The story resonates with the Egyptian myth of Isis gleaning the powers of magic from Ra. By the time Enki sobered up, Inanna had loaded her boat with all her father gave her. She shared this knowledge with her own city so that her people could enjoy better health and greater prosperity. There are other tales of Inanna that focus on the mysteries of life and death, but this seemingly human one speaks to the ways knowledge can be used as capital.

City deities expressed what a people considered most important. Harsher climate and political conditions meant harsher gods. Gentler living led to nurturing gods. Marduk, for example, conquered Tiamat, the ancient goddess of primal chaos. Zeus, in ancient Greece, was a mountain god because mountains formed

20. "The Electronic Text Corpus of Sumerian Literature," http://etcsl.orinst .ox.ac.uk/cgi-bin/etcsl.cgi?text=t.1.3.1&charenc=j#.

their landscapes. Ancient Rome adopted Jove because of its outlook towards consolidating power. Athens had concerns centered in military, agriculture, and trade, so Athena became its patron deity.

City Deities

You can invoke the energy of ancient cities and draw on their wisdom. To do so, it helps to understand as much as you can about the city. The following chart may help you research for creating your own approaches. These cities each chose their deities as an indicator of what they valued most: in the case of Babylon, overcoming the forces of chaos; in the case of Uruk, the female body and life cycles because the infant and mother mortality rate was so high.

Experimenting with connecting to these ancient spirits can offer insight into your own city by recognizing how some of the same things affecting the ancients still affect you.

City	Patron Deity
Babylon	Marduk
Uruk	An and Inanna
Rome	Jove
Athens	Athena
Sparta	Athena Poliachos
Thespiae	Eros
Thebes (Greece)	Dionysus
Corinth	Poseidon
Argos	Hera

City	Patron Deity
Carthage	Tanit and later Juno
Delphi	Apollo
Olympia	Zeus
Memphis	Ptah
Alexandria	Serapis
Heliopolis	Ra
Bubastis	Bast
Cnidus	Aphrodite
Eridu	Enki
Nippur	Enlil
Argos	Hera
Cynopolis	Anubis

Ritual 1: Connecting to Ancient City Deities

Exploring the energy of this ancient practice of revering a city spirit as a god can help you recognize where and how collective spirit manifests. It will also help you recognize the difference between a city spirit and a god. While it's simple enough to tell you gods can get up and visit other cities, while city spirits stay put, performing this ritual makes that knowledge visceral.

This ritual working plays with the concept of time travel. It is complex, and your results may feel strange. Anything you learn from these rituals can serve you in your own magic and personal symbolism but will not be admissible in any academic arena.

Since we can't, for example, book a tour package to ancient Babylon, we must rely on other psychic methods to experience it. You have two options: astral travel and remote viewing.

For those unclear on the difference, astral journeying is when the soul/essence/consciousness leaves the physical body and travels to different points in space. Some people take to this naturally; others need practice. Remote viewing allows you to remain in the body while observing different places in time and space. For those who have a harder time leaving the body or just feel safer staying connected, remote viewing offers a viable alternative that lets you circumvent any limits to magical perception.

Once you decide how you want to get to the city on a psychic level, you can prepare for the ritual itself. Choose an ancient city you want to experience and at what point in time. Spend at least two weeks researching that city. Gather what images and stories you can to represent that city in your working. You might print out line drawings and maps from antique books, collect prayers written for the city gods, and prepare offerings and libations originating from the culture of your chosen city. (This may have practical limits. Most urban dwellers do not have an apartment setup that allows for sheep slaughter, and public park commissions can be iffy about such practices.) Look for any material you can on etiquette and the magick of that culture, especially protective symbols or workings. If you are in the astral and you hit the time/place you aim for, there will be people from that time that can see you. Understanding both the etiquette and the dress code of the time will do much to ensure a positive experience. Language rarely becomes a problem. When you have your understanding of costume, language, and manner, build a mental projection of how you wish to look while traveling within the city.

Next, set up a room with restful space around you. You may need to spend some time cleaning up an area, and during that time burn cleansing incense, add protective wards (this can be as simple as a pentacle drawn in the air in front of each wall as well as the floor and ceiling), and include tools that ground you, awaken you to normal consciousness, and repair psychic injuries. If you live in a small space, I recommend any area you commonly inhabit that is not your normal sleeping space. Set up blankets and mats or prepare a comfortable chair. Comfort and safety are the most important parts of this.

After you've established your safe zone, set up the tools you have gathered in the course of your city research. Create an altar of the symbols of the city on a table or small serving tray. Put any protective symbols from that culture on your person, whether you draw them on yourself, wear jewelry with those symbols, or simply keep something you made yourself in your pockets. Light any candles or incense and bring yourself into a controllable altered state, using slowed breathing. If it's available to you, I also recommend using binaural files for astral travel or remote viewing as you enter this working. Do this work only while sober.

Imagine the time and place you want to visit with as much detail as you can muster. See or feel yourself standing in front of the city gates and petition the deity of that city for entrance. Name your purpose for entering, and if you know it, make the appropriate offering to that being.

Walk through the gates (or extend your awareness through them) and take in whatever impressions come to you.

Visit at least three points in the city: the temple, any palace it might have, and where people collect water. If you're feeling brave, visit just outside the city walls. When you feel ready to go (sometimes the city spirit itself might just kick you back to your own time—it happens), thank the city for its hospitality and move your body, wiggling fingers and toes, to bring yourself back to normal consciousness. Take time as soon as possible after this working to gather your impressions. Use a voice recorder to report them on your phone or write them down. Then spend extra time grounding, healing, and returning to full consciousness. Drink water, and if it feels right, eat something so that you can rebalance your physical and astral body.

You may only want to try this ritual once, or you may do it for different cities to better understand the feeling of ancient urban energies and pantheons. Visiting the same city more than once can deepen your understanding of its specific pantheon and culture, especially if you already work with members of that pantheon.

———

City magicians may want to delve into city spirits beyond their own in order to fully understand how group identities and structure change over time, as well as how climate and landscape change can affect a city spirit. Most of these ancient cities no longer exist or exist in entirely new forms with very different cultures from that of their original settlers. Exploring the history of these ancient cities and looking for their ancient roots can help you connect to the roots of your own city. What layers are revealed in these famous places? What layers lie beneath your own city?

The End of City Walls

After the fall of Rome, cities went through a strange evolution. The Middle East advanced while Europe endured the Dark Ages.[21] The Ottomans brought order to the former Roman Empire, and Byzantium brought Rome back as a major power, but this did not give Western Europe full restoration. European cities, for the most part, suffered from disease and war. Governments stopped building city walls. Between the popularity of sieges and the graphic pile of bodies outside city walls that the Black Plague caused, it made sense to allow humans more freedom to flow in and out. This period marked an in-between time for cities, where building technology remained primitive and new systems of government that expanded beyond cities rose and died.

While the cities of the Middle East continued to generate advancements in science and culture, the cities of Dark Ages Europe acted more as agricultural centers. Farmers came to cities to trade crops and livestock, sometimes moving to apartments in the city during the winter. Property ownership came with assumptions of human ownership, and land bought and sold included the purchase of people living on that land.

---

21. Smith, *City*, 35.

FIVE
URBAN DESIGN AS OCCULT ART

Some city magicians may find the theories and history behind city planning/urban design irrelevant. After all, a healthy city is a growing, mysterious energy in a constant state of change. The philosophy behind that design changes at a constant rate, changed by human consciousness and changing human consciousness as it comes into being. For those not privy to the political machinations of urban planning, the process can appear arcane and bureaucratic. Most can go about their magickal lives without this knowledge. But for those on the urban Priesthood path, understanding the mindsets that lays the map is essential. We workers already know that magick results don't happen by magick; neither do cities merely sprout from the ground. That candle in glass still takes someone pouring wax and centering a wick ... and how was that wax manufactured? That one-way street became so for a reason, as did the brick road hiding beneath the pavement on that street now.

The Occult Nature of City Planners and Urban Designers

In their current form, city planning and urban design involve the capture of an entire zeitgeist of a population, and from there building a physical city. The streets built then become pathways of unconscious thought for their residents for decades and even lifetimes. Think about the city where you spent the greater part of your life. Imagine the street in front of your domicile. Imagine the route you took to school, or to pick up groceries, or to visit the post office. You can likely recall traffic signs, specific landmarks, and quirks of the area, such as a mysterious shoe that has sat on the same curb for years. If you grew up in an especially large city, you may also have several void spots on your inner map. The city in your memory is wholly unique to yourself, as it is based on where you went and what you saw. Yet at the same time, part of your own mind was drawn by an urban planner.

While on the level of personal workings, we may connect to a city spirit, an urban designer, on some level, must continuously tap into the shared spirit and give it form and flow. The planner's complete maps overlap in spirit with our personal, incomplete ones. When we live in cities—simply by having an awareness and things to do—we become containers in that flow. Each resident of the city bears one of thousands or millions of aspects of the city spirit, even when the city spirits take specific godforms and symbols to represent the whole of a city. The city can't exist without its people. We would not have some of the thoughts that we do without the city. Urban planners manage our shared consciousness.

This is not simple work. Urban planners navigate the practicalities of cities and neighborhoods dying and rebirthing from decade to decade. Like the study of magick, urban design demands constant study and progress.

Some magicians aspire to the level of power of an urban designer. Those designs alter the way we walk, where we linger, and even how we think. We cross the street here, and not there—we even only jaywalk at certain points. We pull into the parking lot at the stoplight-regulated intersection, not over there by the back-loading docks. We subconsciously avoid the trees lining the edge of strip mall parking lots. Most of us feel a mood shift when we walk around a town square after relaxing on a train that stops at the city center. All living cities have some project going that is intended for the next era of city development, and the better magickal people understand that, the better they can predict energy shifts that might serve or cross them.

How the Industrial Revolution Changed Cities and City Spirits

In order to understand how urban planning became so necessary, we need to understand the shifts in culture that brought the practice from something maybe done at random to something universal to all industrialized cities. The city lost its agricultural rooting in human consciousness altogether as the Machine Age took hold, beginning with the invention of the cotton gin. This machine allowed for the mass production of textiles in England and made living in the city and working at millineries full-time a valid economic choice for young people. It also gave fresh economic incentive to the institution of slavery—with the slaves present, there was less need for all of the landowner's children to

stay on the farm to help.[22] This first invention led to other technologies that changed the nature of the city and altered the relationship of the city with nature. Rather than a place to go to sell
food raised on the farm, it became a place to go and earn money
with skilled work. Steam power begat electricity,[23] advances in
civil engineering led to improvements in water sanitation, and
new methods for creating metal alloys dramatically altered architecture and transportation. Options for long-term food preser-
vation advanced. Cities became sites of grand experiments in the
latest explorations of humanity.

The progress brought by these inventions still came with an
add-on tax to advancement bought with the blood of slavery: the
poorest in urban populations often died from the side effects of
industrial advancement. The increased use of coal increased inci-
dences of lung disease, and the lowest-cost housing was located
near railways.[24] While the unsavory side of humanity always
showed its face faster in cities as a direct consequence of population density, the Industrial Revolution began to highlight how
unprepared the brave new world was to help those who became
poor as the result of new technology. City conditions made natural and human-generated disasters worse, enough to force mon-
umental economic rebuilding whenever a city death count ran
too high.

These technological shifts, combined with mass tragedies,
forced a shift in human consciousness when it came to cities.

22. Mark Romero, "The Cotton Gin," http://score.rims.k12.ca.us/score_lessons
/cotton_gin/pages/reading.html.

23. Anthony Townsend, *Smart Cities: Big Data, Civic Hackers and the Quest for
a New Utopia* (New York: W. W. Norton, 2013), 93.

24. Neil Levine, *The Urbanism of Frank Lloyd Wright* (Trenton, NJ: Princeton
University Press, 2015), 7.

Society's shared inner map moved nature to something pristine and far away, and many moved the divine out with it. God, or Pan, or whoever held sway, now moved beyond the clouds of smoke, dust, and human crowding. Science and technology became the city magick of the day and those who still practiced rituals of spirit veneration in the Western world began forming magical lodges, in part to explore sexual and ceremonial advancements often deemed illegal in the late nineteenth and early twentieth centuries. Over time, all magick became cast as something innately natural and thus not urban, and all technology was viewed as replacing magick. Cities never lost their spirits or their souls, but humanity lost its awareness of those shared spirits.

In the face of this loss and separation of consciousness, urban design became necessary. Each new philosophy sought to answer the emergencies and ideals of its time. In some locales urban design movements with opposing ideals overlapped, sometimes manifesting within the city. From a magickal perspective, the history of urban design is the history of human cities slowly creating their own maps back to real connection with earth and Spirit.

The Garden City Movement (1890s)

The Garden City Movement began in Great Britain in 1898. Utopian science fiction of the era inspired Architect Ebenezer Howard to introduce greenbelts and greenways to British cities.[25] His idealized city, meant for a maximum population of 32,000, built residences around concentric paths of shared yards and gardens.

Howard believed that communal green areas created happy, peaceful communities. Architects and urban planners of his time

---

25. Levine, *Urbanism*, 898.

took up his ideas, but too-large populations and rapid technology advancement in the twentieth century made for mixed results. Even so, it had its impact on major cities. Garden City concepts of shared green space led to the creation of Central Park in New York City and to the practice of urban landscape design.

By the 1920s, as skyscrapers and more grandiose urban planning approaches evolved, the Garden City movement became other-than-city. As car-centric Modernism took primacy, middle-class people with jobs began driving to the city to work and then returning to their Garden Cities to live, creating with their traffic patterns the American suburb. This became a popular ideal, as families could enjoy the earnings of city jobs and the healthier atmosphere of Garden Cities. Few cities with populations exceeding 50,000 can sustain the level of green design Howard advocated—in part because he advocated such designs before cars made that type of shared public space infeasible.

Modern Garden Cities never existed as intended because of both the car and the population boom that came with the Industrial Revolution. The layout was untenable for populations of greater than 32,000. Garden Cities that might have grown beyond this were often paved around as local and national governments built highways and bypasses, often passing by these cities in the process. Most Garden City bergs can't form a city spirit because the population is too low. Genius loci and smaller nature spirits can exist in these areas, but often they must fight off the environmental pollution brought on from excess car dependence. These spirits usually demand an act of healing on the part of local magick workers to demonstrate good faith before they even consider forming a working relationship.

The Garden City is a Utopian ideal. While not sustainable in the physical world for city spirit work, it still has its uses for urban magick workers. If you are especially burdened by the psychic effects of population density, you can use this as a way of creating a happy place or even as a means of establishing a place in the astral to talk to your own city spirit. The ambitious might even use this method to establish an astral temple.

Ritual 2: Build Your Garden City in the Astral

Choose an image of a rounded labyrinth. Spend three to four nights just gazing at it, building it into your inner map. Make this experience as image-filled and sensory as you can conjure. Imagine building the walls out of shrubs and trees or favorite herbs. If you are more tactile than visual, try to imagine how the scents or the sensation of leaves brushing your skin might feel. Work your way through the path of the labyrinth, all the way in and all the way back, building up what you put in this space with every step.

You can add layers of whatever you like to the center of the labyrinth, whether taking inspiration from the 1986 movie starring David Bowie or placing a temple from your own spiritual alignment. For those sensitive to crowded and over-urbanized environments, this inner green space creates a buffer between yourself and the outside world. Go in to ground or to retreat for peace and strength when otherwise feeling overwhelmed by outside stimuli. If you invite spirits into the space, invoke the laws of hospitality first. For those on the city Priesthood Path, this establishes a safe space for the city spirit to take a load off and share.

The City Beautiful Movement and
Landscape Architecture (1890s)

While Ebenezer Howard put forth his Utopian ideals, American architect Daniel Burnham developed a philosophy of city design inspired by classical, grandiose architecture reminiscent of the temples of ancient Pagan cities. Burnham passionately believed he could inspire creativity and happiness by placing awe-striking architecture in high-traffic areas and creating paths that forced human movement around them in specific patterns. Burnham, through his urban design, found ways to control human behavior and emotions.

This manipulation had its shadow side. It inadvertently gave power to racial segregation. City Beautiful came as a response to the urban disasters of the late nineteenth and early twentieth centuries. Most of those disasters happened where the poorest lived, and so rather than rebuilding the neighborhoods, urban planners moved the poor to the outskirts of town and replaced the original neighborhoods with parks. This mimicked the organization of ancient cities, those who left their poorest outside the protection of city walls.

Integral to the City Beautiful movement was the growing discipline of landscape architecture, a profession founded by Frederick Law Olmstead. In the United States, public parks began replacing neighborhoods wiped out by fire and national disaster. One of the most famous of these park replacements that Olmstead designed: New York City's Central Park. Soon he brought his talent to cities throughout the United States, and his work formed a medium between Howard's Garden City/suburbs and Burnham's City Beautiful.

The legacy of these prior urban designs remains. Several cities in the United States still boast City Beautiful architecture. Washington, DC, in 1902 became the first place to carry out such a plan. Under the McMillan plan, the city limited building heights and placed structures to create a pleasing-to-the-eye symmetry when viewed on a map.[26] The city hall of San Francisco, and the Benjamin Franklin museum row in Philadelphia, all came from the architects influenced by this movement. The expense of City Beautiful eventually exceeded what most city budgets could tolerate, and thus the way opened for modernism and efficiency.

Exercise 3: City Beautiful Spirit Hunt

Cities descended from City Beautiful architecture often have additional spirits, deities, and collective energies. These energies are often attracted by what the city spirit projects and can change as the population changes over the course of decades. Discovering what other energies adopt such cities can show you additional pools of energy hidden amongst the fanciest buildings. It can also show you what your city spirit truly considers important.

Pick a building of grand design that calls to you. Spend time studying that building. If you can, look up its history. Often architecture from the City Beautiful era will have frescoes and reliefs of Greek, Roman, or Egyptian gods; other times the décor may use Victorian codes to indicate details about the building's original inhabitants. Some may go as far as planting statues. On one San Francisco skyscraper, the architect placed statues of the three Fates looking down on the city. Most architects of

---

26. Naomi Blumberg, Ida Yalzadeh, "Urban Planning: City Beautiful Movement" in *Encylopedia Brittanica*, https://www.britannica.com/topic/City-Beautiful-movement.

the era opted to keep their neoclassical Paganism subtle. Create a list of the symbols, the structure, and any
known intentions of the building.

If the building is open to the public, go inside. If not,
sit on the front steps or stand where you can see the
entrance. Bring a coin with you as an offering; deity-
level entities like flashier offerings, so a big half dollar
or a gold dollar coin works best. Drop the coin near the
door when you enter (or leave near the door if closed),
and then find a place to meditate. Depending on how
you process information, different things will happen.
You may find yourself noticing certain details about the
building—its shape, the tile, and so on. You may experience body sensations. If you're prone to visions, you may
see flashes of symbols or even historical events in your
inner eye. Sometimes there is no spirit and nothing at all
happens, although it's rare for public buildings to exist
without something inhabiting that psychic space.

As a caution, keep legal concerns in mind. Many public buildings have security officers or other people who
may inquire as to what you are doing while you practice
this exercise. Some cities go so far as to enact "stand, sit,
lie" ordinances that do not allow people to loiter. Often
a proactive approach renders the best results if you live
in such a city. If you feel safe enough doing so, approach
a security officer before you begin and just tell him/her
that you're waiting for a friend and will only be in the
space for a certain number of minutes. You may choose,
as you research the building, to examine how people who
work/live in that building dress and copy their style to
blend into the environment. People carrying briefcases

tend to attract hassle far less than those wearing backpacks. This can also help you connect more with any spirit inhabiting that building. As an extra magickal protection, keep poppy seeds or black beans in your pocket; they can help you escape scrutiny.

The City Efficient Movement (1890s–1930s)

While Frederick Law Olmsted's landscape architecture rounded out what made the City Beautiful movement, the approach to urban design came at too high a cost for most cities to sustain. The need to accommodate cars made maintaining grandiose architecture and parks all the more difficult. By the 1920s Olmsted's own son, Frederick Law Olmsted Jr., spearheaded more cost-effective approaches to urban design by dividing the city into intentional zones. While some mix from the days before zoning persist—corner bodegas and meat markets are holdovers from pre-City Efficient culture—most cities separate business, industry, and residences. These zones, while not necessarily aesthetically pleasing, can improve quality of life by isolating residential areas from the byproducts of nearby businesses and factories.

This City Efficient movement was developed to facilitate manufacturing in major cities, and by doing so often prioritized the needs of corporations over the needs of residents. One company in one city might produce iron and another nearby city might purchase the refined steel to use for manufacturing cars. This design philosophy used two models of city layout to ensure the support of this commerce: the concentric zone model and the sector model. In this model, the center of the city consisted of a central business district, ringed next by the industrial/production zone. Then designers built a transition buffer for mass transit, a working-class residence area for people of lower income who worked in factories, and then a residential zone for those who could afford larger domiciles and land. Finally, thanks to the ideas and values of the era, most City Efficient urban designers added a commuter zone, such as a highway ringing the city with highway exits to area suburbs/Garden Cities. The sector model for the most part expanded the concentric model by adding mass transit arteries from the city that ran parallel to railroads. Several cities still operate on these zoning models, including Chicago, Detroit, and the Twin Cities.

Leveraging the City Wheel

For an urban magician, city zoning fosters specific neighborhood spirits and energies. Retail districts generate social and commerce energy that aligns with attracting money and friends. Residential areas can cue rest and reflection, though the disposition of the citizens also affect that. Transit buffers act as an energetic whirlpool mixing all energy streams of the city.

Magicians living in cities with City Efficient designs have multiple giant rotating prayer wheels at their disposal. As traffic ebbs and flows, the power of any prayer attached to that movement may also wax and wane, but most cities with a population over 150,000 will see some degree of constant movement on all roadways. If you are working on a project where you need a pool of constant ideas, connect your consciousness to that continuous movement—but limit it to no more than a few times a week. (No one wants to be in a constant mental state where thoughts can't slow down—it's quite unpleasant.) If you need to banish something especially large that may take a while to dissipate, attaching it to a bus or truck that runs counter-clockwise through the city traffic loop can get the job done far more effectively than what you might manage burning black candles or using similar banishing methods.

Ritual 3: City Zone Prayer

Along with using transit loops to raise or banish energy, connecting to defined zones of a city can allow you access to pools of emotional energy needed for personal workings. The technique that follows might not end well for everyone; if you tend to suffer from anxiety or unmanaged empath abilities, skip this. Cleanse first. This magickal method requires standing in the midst of city energy and will cause a degree of psychic strain. As a precaution, smudge in lemongrass or lavender smoke and/or take an Epsom salt bath before and after this work. You may also want quartz crystals and tourmaline in your pockets to filter some of the psychic pollution.

Choose a city zone that aligns with your purpose. If you wish to experience greater tranquility, find a quiet neighborhood near a park or cemetery. If you want to increase income flow, pick a thriving business district. If you want to open communication with your city spirit, choose the most iconic building or sculpture near the busiest traffic hub of your city.

Choose a spot to stand just to the side of any foot traffic. Take a few breaths and make sure you feel fully present in your own body, noticing the sensations of gravity and the texture of air on your skin and on the top of your head. Imagine extending a cord from your feet down to the earth all the way below the buildings and concrete, greeting the concrete and road material along the way. Breathe into this and build this anchored feeling. This mental-sensory space will be where you store excess energy you may later use in home spellwork or release.

Keep your eyes open and really listen/feel the vibration of the traffic around you. Imagine a cord with a shovel attached (like a child's sand castle building kit) extending from your crown out into that vibration of movement. See the little shovel scooping up the energy and pulling back into you through the crown of your head, closing the door it came through behind it. Imagine that energy dropping through the center of your body and down into that cord beneath your feet. You may see a cloud of energy in your inner mind or feel the vibration below you. Muster in yourself the emotions you experience after accomplishing a goal. If you want to feel relief, or joy, or comfort, imagine how that feels in your body. Then visualize the energy you just gathered forming a film over your body and sliding that film off and into the energy gathered beneath. Imagine the two merging until each molecule intertwines. You have created an energy pocket that can now do the job. Silently explain to this energy what it does and when to stop. Communicate this by mentally riding the energy waves generated by steady traffic. Then, see yourself as a straw sucking this in and up through your feet, then projecting it out from your solar plexus. Push out as much energy as you can, dispersing it in tandem with the ambient traffic.

When finished, visualize a door closing in your solar plexus. Think of gravity claiming any excess energy, drawing it out from your feet. Release as much of this as you can. If you draw some energy back into your body, you may need to reopen your solar plexus before you release yet more of that energy. Always mentally close that door when finished. When you return home from your work, cleanse yourself magickally and physically.

Modernism (1920s)

In 1855, English engineer and inventor Henry Bessemer discovered a way to mass-produce steel.[27] This heralded the two hallmarks of city life in the twentieth century: the mass-produced automobile and the skyscraper.[28] This new approach to steel and its related inventions forced an entirely new approach to urban design, and along with that design, it permanently altered city culture. The former bedrock of city life, street culture, died to make way for the automobile. The people who once gathered to trade and gossip were dispersed, and some moved into the vertical city of skyscraper life.

This period of urban restructuring, called Modernism, not only changed the physical structure of the city, but who lived in them. Frank Lloyd Wright attempted to incorporate skyscrapers and cars into his dream of the Garden City of North America.[29] In his vision, people went to the city to work, then drove to a home outside of the city. In his effort to create Howard's vision, Wright invented the archetypal American middle- and upper-class suburb.

---

27. Mary Bellis, "How Henry Bessemer Made Skyscrapers Possible" https://www.thoughtco.com/henry-bessemer-the-steel-man-4075538.
28. Kate Ascher, *The Heights: Anatomy of a Skyscraper* (New York, Penguin Press, 2011), 12–13.
29. Levine, *Urbanism*, 46.

The rising popularity of the car and the consequent change in roads to accommodate this traffic led to the death of street culture. Before motorized vehicles held sway, streets served as places for social gathering.[30] Neighbors going to and from their homes and businesses stopped in the street to talk, even coming out with no set destination just to see their neighbors. "Word on the street" referred to literal local gossip people got by going out on the street. Vendors would weave their way among the chatterers with their wares. Many of these people did not care to give way to the automobiles appearing in their streets, and this contention of cultural change led to several vehicular deaths.

Wright did attempt to alleviate the destruction of those social connections. He and his modernist peers came up with two solutions to street congestion and public safety: First, Modernist designers created streets that favored the car.[31] Second, they built skyscrapers as part of the Modernist vision of the vertical city. They intended to move street culture and commerce above ground, out of the way of cars. Walkable neighborhoods disappeared from major cities, Chicago and New York first among them. Chicago had the first-ever skyscraper, the ten-story Home Insurance Building, quickly matched in height by an equivalent skyscraper in New York City.[32] Through the 1920s, the two cities raced to build the tallest structure. By the 1930s, suburbs belonged to the rich and cities belonged to the poor and the corporations that manufactured products in them. This ended the City Beautiful movement.

---

30. Smith, *City*, 86–87.

31. Levine, *Urbanism*, 117.

32. Ascher, *Heights,* 14.

Skyscrapers

While all city architecture has magickal aspects, the skyscraper, just by virtue of being a building only seen in major cities, is probably the most important iconic symbol of any city. While skyscrapers often house multiple uses, for the most part they fail to contain the full community and street culture of buildings with fewer than four floors. Research shows that people who live in buildings six floors high or taller are less likely to help a neighbor in distress, less likely to have interacted with their neighbors, and more likely to suffer from a sense of isolation and disconnection.[33] Architects of the late twentieth and early twenty-first centuries corrected some of the issues that make taller buildings more problematic places to live, including better lighting in individual homes, reducing the waste produced by these buildings, and establishing clear communal spaces such as swimming pools or rooftop gardens, but problems persist.

Urban magicians working with skyscrapers need to understand the history of the building, and how the building design at present affects the residence. For those on the city Priesthood Path who are trying to facilitate healing energy for an injured city spirit, the tallest buildings can present a resource, a symptom, or a necessary quarantine. The buildings tend to form a spirit rather rapidly because they receive attention from far more than just the people who use them. Often, they are the subject of news articles, architectural criticism, environmental protest, and real estate news/scandals. Even though a great deal of human spirit goes into the construction of such amazing buildings, human

---

33. Robert Gifford, "The Consequences of Living in High-Rise Buildings." *Architectural Science Review* 50, no. 1, (March 2007): https://www.tandfonline.com/doi/abs/10.3763/asre.2007.5002.

greed sucks it right out. Attached spirits/personalities in these buildings can form rapidly, although management companies can drain them of personality through poor interior design, lack of plants/greenery, and paints and carpeting that emit poisonous fumes. Sometimes if a building has a particularly messy history, you may need to cut a deal with the spirit of that particular building so that it leaves you alone and you leave it alone.

Spell 1: Skyscraper Word on the Street

Skip this working if you have a strong fear of heights. Even in a country as new as the United States, modern cities are still built on top of older cities. This spell, mostly spoken, draws on the energy of the hidden historic city, bringing it up from beneath the ground, from where the original information superhighway involved the baker on one block running across the street to say hello to the tailor and share the news about what happened after the banks closed last night.

The fundamental purpose of this work calls upon the city spirit to show you what you don't know you don't know. It works best when cast from an emotional place of humility, a way of grounding since you also cast it from a place high above the city. This state allows you to be open to whatever the city might have to say to you and shows you where the energies of the city spirit truly originate.

Visit the tallest building in your city that has an observation deck with public access. If you can visit at night, so much the better (but work within the rules of building management). Go to the deck and take a moment to really look at the city from that perspective. Close your eyes and listen to how city sounds echo differently from far above the ground. Imagine the soil beneath the building and imagine what the world looks like when a cloud floats through the building. Look down at the city and announce what you want it most to show you. Then speak this spell:

From here in city sky
Where I see all streets and lights
Show me hidden enterprise
Show me what the ground denies
Reveal shadows and delight

You may need to repeat the verse a few times to really feel its effect. When finished, thank the city for listening and enjoy exploring the world from the tall perspective.

Skyscrapers and observation decks come in handy for a lot of release/opportunity seeding in city magick, so becoming intimate with the building and any manifest spirit it might have can certainly help you.

The Radiant City (1930s)

Just before the Great Depression took hold of the world, architects and urban planners (among others) began noticing the negative impact of life on blue-collar laborers. While Modernist design moved people of middle and upper class into the suburbs and outside of the pollution range and consequent health issues of living in a city, laborer families often could only afford in-city housing. The affordability of the car meant more people owned them and the streets offered even less breathing space. Crowding continued as a serious city problem.

Architect Charles-Édouard Jeanneret, who went by the *nom de plume* Le Corbusier, believed he could resolve these social issues through his architecture. Taking up the cause of the proletariat—in this case, meaning low-wage laborers—he devoted his talent to improving their work and life conditions.

In 1926, Le Corbusier entered a competition to design the headquarters for the League of Nations in Geneva. While he did not win—the judges all opted for Neoclassical designs—he capitalized on his loss by giving lectures about what the League of Nations missed by passing on his design. These lectures earned him his first big commission: employee housing for a French industrialist. At the time, housing designed for the proletariat/working class was viewed as a progressive concern, not just because of what affordability in housing meant as a social equalizer, but from capitalist interest in improving the productivity of laborers. Le Corbusier believed that the design of a worker's home could produce a more dedicated, productive employee. As his ideas coincided with many of the new ideas brought about from the Bolshevik Revolution, he tested several of his designs in Moscow.

After World War II, the rising fear of Communism drastically changed Le Corbusier's priorities. He abandoned the concept of housing designed for a specific social class, opting to create family-centered housing that did not serve the interests of the companies that employed the common people. Despite the failure of his first projects to produce a happier and more effective working class, future architects aimed to learn from his mistakes and attempted to adapt those early ideas into affordable and low-income housing.

The one proletariat-inspired housing project that did not devolve into a bastion of sorrow is still present in Marseilles. The remaining Radiant City projects, however, became for the most part bastions of poverty and disease. Residents in these domiciles demonstrated escalating rates of depression and addiction. Lack of regular sunlight and a building design that increased isolation from social contact turned an attempted social solution into a social problem. While Le Corbusier succeeded in designing utilitarian housing, the results of his own projects thwarted his dream of a healthier labor class through urban design. Yet, there are those designers who still want to realize Le Corbusier's vision. This Radiant City, first revealed in 1924 and further detailed in a book of that title in 1933, presented a city designed with ample green space and sunlight while still honoring the inventions common during the 1920s and 1930s. Le Corbusier, like Howard, presented his design as a potential Utopia. While Howard's Utopia relied on social connection, Le Corbusier's vision relied on totalitarian rule.

Some urban magicians reading this may recall housing projects in their own cities, some from living in them. The Robert Taylor and Cabrini-Green homes in Chicago were descendants of Le Corbusier's Radiant City idea—and were affected by systemic racism and xenophobia, undermining the purpose of building the housing. While the buildings themselves are now mostly a memory in Chicago, the culture that created them and then made them tools of oppression remain. The wounds that result from this type of convoluted oppression can heal, with conscious effort. They can, with care, transform into sources of power and support for people who live in these areas or that still bear psychic wounds from their time in such neighborhoods.

Housing projects tend to develop spirits of their own, and when those projects are razed, the spirits linger. To city priests and civic magicians, I advise against exorcism. Erasure has already dug too deep into our shared magickal fabric. Instead, performing rituals of healing that reconnect the land and the neighborhood spirit or that reconnect the neighborhood spirit to those who fought for collective dignity are more honorable ways to handle these urban phantoms.

Ritual 4: To Re-Anchor a Razed Neighborhood Spirit

If you decide to do this work, expect it to take several weeks, even months. It is intense work that requires research, connection, and internalization. There is almost no way to do this without changing some aspect of your worldview, even if you lived in the neighborhood before someone knocked it down.

Inner Preparation

Before taking up the work of healing a neighborhood spirit, the healers must do some shadow work. This can involve deep meditation or shamanic travel, but often enough honest introspection does the necessary work of spiritual realignment. Total self-honesty and recognition of personal prejudice is paramount to a successful working.

In whatever form works for you, consider the following ideas. Cities are famously unequal places. We often mentally divide large cities into "good" and "bad" neighborhoods, without saying out loud what that division means or considering how a neighborhood came to have its particular label. Do you remember how, when, and why you found out a certain neighborhood was "bad?" What were the reasons for the application of that label? How important is it that you know why? Those on the

Hearth and Home Path may not need to know as long as home and family are safe, while city priests and civic magicians need to understand where these labels originated so they know how many layers of resistance they may encounter. This especially includes the magician's own resistance. Do not move forward until you have explored the history or the area and your own thoughts and prejudices about the neighborhood fully.

Once you do fully recognize where your truth lies in why you want to repair this spirit, you can move forward with the healing work.

Building the Relationship

Often the spirits of still existent housing projects from the Radiant City era respond well to the presence of green energy, because that's what they were most denied. The common thick cement blocks that limit circulation of air and give institutional boundaries need enlivening. Even if the building no longer exists, the spirit may need to feel free/broken out of all that cement. Waking up the cement—reminding the silica of its ocean or lake roots—and bringing in green, air-cleaning plants as an offering of friendship can improve both your daily health and the overall health of spirits formed by the collective consciousnesses that inhabited such constructions. For any holdover structures that might still be standing, a drive-by house plant left near a door is a good start (and if someone adopts it, even better.) The daring might even sneak in potted guerilla gardens throughout a site. This gives the original neighborhood spirit something that makes it feel a sense of freedom and reminds it that it has organic origins and life force in it too.

Spirits, even those created as a byproduct of shared consciousness, can be living or dead. When they come from demolished neighborhoods, you may need to bring people with you that are used to either—perhaps someone versed in fairy work/super living energy, and someone versed in ancestor and dead work. If this spirit is living, it will probably draw your attention to certain areas where it feels pain through acts of synchronicity, such as a wild animal appearing out of context or even a piece of paper with words printed on it appearing in a certain spot. If you determine the spirit of the place to be dead, you can reach that ghost by demonstrating a connection to its history. If you stand on the corner of where a housing project once was and tell stories from its time and about the specific people who lived in that area, you will draw the attention of the ghost of that place. Even dead spirits can receive healing. If you can gain its attention and cooperation, you can move forward more easily with your work.

Once you have the relationship established, if the spirit wants it, you can move forward with giving it a new anchor. The anchor lets the spirit care for the people who used to make it what it was, and lets those people also draw resilience from it when they tell stories about where they grew up and what they survived.

You will need:

- Preferably a partner or group that includes people who lived in the original neighborhood
- Pictures of the neighborhood when first built (you can often find these in online library archives.)
- Water from the closest natural water source (in this case, tap water is not cheating)
- A list of the neighborhood characters from "movers and shakers" to quirky characters
- A small table, flowers, cloths—anything for building a small altar

Go to the site of the original neighborhood. You may want to bring your country's flags with you, or all wear the same colored T-shirts to give the appearance of a civic rally. Stand either at what was the busiest foot path of the neighborhood or in the center of where the central building in the complex stood. Each person should say out loud the name of the complex and announce, "We honor your spirit and the memory of what once was and invite that energy to renew in the healthiest form."

The person holding the water should pour out a little, and then tell a short story or give a brief biography of one of the memorable neighborhood characters. Once finished, they should pass the water to the person on their right and continue until as many people as possible receive memorial. When finished, pour any remaining water onto the soil in front of the altar, and say, "While the buildings are gone, the spirit remains. All hail the neighborhood!"

If possible, bury the picture and take the rest of the altar with you. The act of burial invites that energy to remain and transform into the best version of itself. During the storytelling, you probably brought up many traits that came with living in that neighborhood. Keep these characteristics in mind. When you need those qualities in future magickal endeavors, come back to the old neighborhood site and soak up that energy, whether through crystals or a good conversation with that neighborhood spirit. Always leave a little something for that neighborhood spirit, especially anything that helps it breathe.

Urban Renewal (1950s)

The urban design movements that shifted the wealthiest to homes outside the city had a deleterious effect on urban centers. Most people in dense urban areas had low income; cities that relied on taxing citizens for maintenance of public resources had to work with a populace that did not make enough money to fill the city coffers. Often city living meant lower-quality public resources, while those living in the suburbs enjoyed nicer public resources. Sometimes city government's inability to maintain even reasonable street conditions led to major manufacturers relocating, further disrupting a city's tax base.

Cities managed this issue often by neglecting care of poor and minority neighborhoods, justified by arguing that because those neighborhoods paid the least in taxes, they merited less care. This led to several run-down neighborhoods, usually labeled as

suffering from "urban blight."[34] Most of these "blighted" neighborhoods had thriving minority communities that found ways
to make do without public support. Spurred by city planners,
the solution to this so-called disease was "urban renewal."[35] This
renewal usually involved tearing down entire communities and
replacing them with highways or with housing too expensive for
the displaced to afford. After World War II, some neighborhood
populations dwindled enough that abandoned housing posed a
serious public safety issue, although these were not where urban
planners turned their attention for the most part. Instead they
targeted areas with higher minority populations.[36]

The Urban Renewal movement brought into contention the
opposing forces of xenophobic greed and neighborhood loy-
alty. These forces, represented by city planner Robert Moses
and urban theorist Jane Jacobs, brought grassroots activism up
against corporate-influenced government interests. When Moses
advocated for the demolishment of Jacobs's Greenwich neighborhood village (calling it "slum clearance"), Jacobs led protests
that halted his project. Though the best-known of these activists,
Jacobs was far from the only woman who took up this cause. An
era of citizen activism followed her example as people fought to
save their homes. The neighborhoods that succeeded often did so
through the leadership of women-led grassroots organizations.

---

34. Roberta Brandes Gratz, *We're Still Here Ya Bastards: How the People of New
Orleans Rebuilt Their City* (New York: Nation Books, 2015), xii.

35. Roberta Brandes Gratz, "The Genius of Jane Jacobs, Who Changed the Way
We Think About Cities," https://www.thenation.com/article/the-genius-of
-jane-jacobs-who-changed-the-way-we-think-about-cities/.

36. Bruce J. Katz, Jennifer Bradley, *The Metropolitan Revolution: How Cities and
Metros are Fixing Our Broken Politics and Fragile Economy* (Washington,
DC: Brookings Institution Press, 2013), 48.

These women not only rallied their communities, they implemented changes without government oversight—sometimes to the point of civil disobedience.[37] Even in modern days, as disaster capitalists exploited the tragedies of Hurricane Katrina, women in New Orleans fought to wrest their city back from the opportunism. Resisting urban renewal became a foundation cause in grassroots politics in the United States and is a reason why some cities still maintain their own spirit and flavor while others have become bland. The strongest neighborhoods had citizens who were able to stand up and fight.

Gentrification (1970s)

Not every neighborhood won its fight against urban renewal. When they lost, those neighborhoods gentrified. The concept of gentrification has its origins in the United Kingdom. While the United States began addressing the so-called and mostly racially motivated urban blight, the United Kingdom birthed a very similar imbalance that the United States later adopted. Gentrification differs from the blight in that it places its primary focus on economic class division first, and then theoretically only targets race as a byproduct of economic fallout. To a magician, this difference is more than semantic because while blight/renewal in the United States was often race-specific, the origin of the issues of gentrification affected more populations, making it a far more intersectional issue.

In the 1970s, cities throughout England began displacing the working class/working poor in favor of wealthier citizenry. This practice, called "gentrification," took the work of the lower and middle classes and capitalized it to the point where the people

---

37. Gratz, *Still Here*, 163.

who built and improved their neighborhoods could no longer afford their own housing.[38] Those who benefit from gentrification favor it—cleaner streets, old businesses replaced with ones that suit their lifestyles, lower crime, and much more expensive housing that drives out the "problem" people, making neighborhoods safer. In England, this practice mainly affected laborers that developed their trade skills outside of a college education. When gentrification manifested in the United States, it often affected not only these blue-collar laborers but full-time artists who often moved into less desirable spaces, such as old warehouses. Developers and real estate companies began grabbing the lofts and warehouses that the original tenants had improved. These subculture havens started falling to condominium and coffee shop building plans all over both countries. These artists of all walks included occultists of various ilk, both in the UK and the US.

As technology progresses, gentrification takes new forms that can add layers to class division. Technological gentrification may be the best-known new form. Just as the car disrupted city social life, wireless technologies, fiber optics, and smartphones disrupt world cultures and industries in ways good and bad. As with the introduction of the car, the proliferation of smartphones has contributed to dramatic changes in human interaction that widen generation and culture gaps.[39] While this digital divide still affects mainly the elderly and rural populations of the United States,

---

38. CP Hellmund, Daniel Somers Smith, *Designing Greenways: Sustainable Landscapes for Nature and People* (Washington, DC: Island Press, 2006), 162–163.

39. Bryan Alexander, "When the mobile revolution and the digital divide combine," May 8, 2018, https://bryanalexander.org/technology/when-the-mobile-revolution-and-the-digital-divide-combine.

those restricted to smartphones for internet access in urban areas also struggle with the limits of even government-supplied phones. Many must fight with the expense of data caps and inadequate ways to submit documents and data from phones. This can limit their ability to find work. Because all such programs demand guidelines, this government provision also leaves out those in the ever-present gap where they make too much to qualify for smartphone aid but make too little/have credit limits too low to afford to pay for the phone itself. Efforts to make technology more accessible still have a long way to go before we reach universal access.

This means that even when someone does have at least limited internet access, they may lag behind on cultural shifts. Electronic communication changes language—nuances of those communication methods develop even as certain details of human expression and vocal tone change. Like any culture change, these transitions always leave someone behind.

Among magick workers, these tools create divisions in visible arguments online and off. Some magicians integrate technological tools into their magical workings, while others argue for a less internet-dependent society. There are still those who swear using an electronic device means that the magick worked comes solely from self-delusion. For those working with city magick, a smartphone offers many advantages to the work just because of the fast access to information. These phones can serve as magickal tools in and of themselves. They assist with navigation, research, and even placing secret sigils using only the element of electricity. That said, they, like any other tool, can be dispensed with in favor of other methods, especially when getting one may create financial or emotional distress. Depending on how you use them, they can improve your connections or divide you further from others.

Since a support system matters, it's important to have ways of cultivating friendships online and off.

Ritual 5: For Human Connections

It may seem odd to include a friendship spell just after a passage about gentrification. Those who have experienced either urban renewal or its descendant, gentrification, know well the importance of community-building and support. Support systems protects us. How those support systems function and who they include changes based on how we use technology. This spell is intended to improve face-to-face connections, but as an add-on you can then make it a point to introduce people you know online to people you know in-person, as interests and needs may connect.

To prepare:

- Make sure to have time and mental bandwidth for the possibility of interaction with another person.

- Seriously assess your personal interests and the things you do for frivolous joy. This spell doesn't bring you bar friends; it brings real ones, and that requires opening to connections that go a bit deeper than what alcohol allows.

- If you suffer from social anxiety, general shyness, or "er, what do I say next?" conditions, you may also want to prepare yourself by reading some good old-fashioned self-help books or watching a few YouTube videos about building rapport. Susan

RoAne's *What Do I Say Next?* really does help with that awkward brain-blank when trying to connect to someone signaling that they welcome connection.

- Establish a routine of attending events related to your interests.

Once you've opened your path with these preparations, you are ready to set the energy of this ritual in motion. While here it works as a means of attracting friendship, you can adjust it to attract money, information sources, and even random moments of luck. You can perform this working anywhere, but adding in some soil from specific parts of the city where you want to spend time with other people can increase your odds of success.

You will need:

- A table or tray to maintain the altar for this spell; the power of it accumulates over time
- Images of groups of people having fun together, preferably engaging in activities you enjoy yourself
- Images of places you enjoy spending time around the city
- Dirt from your favorite places in the city [40]
- Two pink candles
- A box of passionflower tea bags

---

40. When you collect dirt or botanicals of any kind, always leave an offering in exchange. Loose tobacco and water usually satisfy North American land spirits.

- Cloves

- Anise

- An image of the First Pentacle of Venus, which draws friends to the possessor

- Attraction oil (This is common at most occult shops, but you can make your own by putting a very small magnet in a glass vial with anise, clove, and lemon rind and then adding olive oil.)

This is a ritual to perform continuously until you feel you have a large enough social pool. Before you begin, make the attraction oil and have a bottle ready on the altar. Next, prepare yourself a cup of passionflower tea. When you finish steeping the tea, set up your tray or altar, first by covering it in the images you selected. In the center, place the First Pentacle of Venus. Set two pink candles dressed with a little bit of the attraction oil on either side of the pentacle. Surround the candles and seal with a ring of anise and clove. The anise makes your endeavor more successful, the clove protects you from predatory people disguised as friends. Add the dirt to the center of the pentacle and place your attraction oil in the center of that. Set your tea cup so that it touches the ring of herbs.

Cast a circle or declare sacred space however you see fit. With the altar built, light the candles. Imagine the pentacle growing and spinning and waking up the herbs, the candles, the oil, and you. Imagine it drawing in exactly the right people for you in your life while the clove acts as a strainer to hold out those wrong for you.

Then slowly and thoughtfully sip the passionflower tea. Meditate on friendship and what good friendship and good boundaries mean to you. When you finish the tea, set the cup down and anoint yourself with the attraction oil. Then snuff out the candles and take down any circle you cast.

You may want to perform this ritual during waxing moon cycles or on every Friday, if those rhythms speak to you. You can also perform it before you attend an event. Wear the attraction oil daily, and trust that it filters out the wrong people while drawing the right ones closer. Once you feel you have enough happy connections, you can let the candles burn all the way down (while standing in water for safety) and save the images and pentacle for when you might need them in the future.

The Green City Movement (1970s)

An environmental awakening happened at the beginning of the 1970s. Multiple discoveries about the negative impact of modern industry's practices on earth's resources changed people's view of city living, especially since the actions of major companies damaged wildlife and public health. Cities of the era were determined the worst of all pollution generators. Acid rain, poisoned rivers, and animal mutations found in nearby water sources became serious concerns. Response to this newfound crisis varied, in part because it depended on the response of the corporations whose practices led to the toxic crisis.

Embargoes on the sale of crude oil in 1973 and 1979 disrupted life and manufacturing in the United States and several other countries. More companies in countries outside the United States began mass-producing affordable automobiles, some of whom did not have oil embargoes working against them. In an effort to stay competitive, car manufacturers mainly located in Detroit began moving corporate operations to other states and outsourcing productions to other countries, thus destabilizing the Modernist Motor City. The decline of Detroit—including the population falling from roughly two million at its peak in the 1950s to roughly 673,000 in 2017—marked the end of what the Modernist era of urban design could serve.

Some cities took it upon themselves to alleviate the damages, instituting recycling programs, reducing waste generated by city-owned buildings, demanding factories make an effort to offset CO_2 emissions, and increasing housing density to reduce the collective carbon footprint. More visionary city governments attempted to entice sustainable businesses to establish industries in their cities.

Technological efforts began to focus on improving communication and solving the environmental problems caused by the Industrial Revolution. These advancements made recycling and offsetting greenhouse gas more feasible. Grassroots organizations encouraged creative reuse and reduced consumption. Urban designers, ever using their science and art to address social problems, turned their attention to creating Green Cities.

The premier Green City in the world as of 2018 is Cutriba, Brazil. Since 1972, the mayor has closed six blocks of the city to cars, introduced a fuel-efficient bus system, and been building residential areas close to transit hubs. Cutriba is notable in that the mayor of the city initiated the effort long before any global call for change. Other Green Movement cities include Amsterdam, San Francisco, Copenhagen, and Stockholm.

An urban magician living in a Green City has the best of all worlds, whatever path this person might walk. Green Cities tend to have larger safe zones for pedestrians, allowing for less worry during meditative walks. While housing tends toward higher population density, reduced pollution makes close proximity with others less stressful. Most notable is that Green Cities find ways to keep their dense populations connected to nature, not only through parks but by making sure commonly traveled paths have plant life on them.

Green Cities also usually have a clearly identifiable place where the city spirit likely "lives." While in most cities a city spirit has an immanent quality, spreading from border to border, certain places in the city might emanate more of that presence than others. In New York City, for example, Times Square clearly holds the spirit of the city closest. Minneapolis's Loring Park, located in a zone between Uptown and Downtown, is clearly a settling place for the city spirit. Green Cities tend to have these spaces clearly defined. They are usually at the intersection of a transportation nexus and a historic space. For instance, in Amsterdam, the city spirit clearly dwells in the palace at the end of the downtown zone.

Working Magick in a Green City

It might appear that a Green City spirit has fewer needs than a city spirit still laboring under a different design. This may not be true, and you can only know by making contact. One thing an urban magician might open with when working with such a city is the question, "Where does it still hurt?" Ask both city spirit and land spirits. Sometimes the city will direct you to places where energy pools and stagnates. It may show you the site of a recent human or animal tragedy. Land spirits might direct you to industrial zones where perhaps not all land reclamation has succeeded, or they may point to strip malls where land spirits might suffocate under the weight of concrete and tar.

The solutions to these common needs, at least in concept, are simple. For instance, if the city spirit points you to a stagnant spot, you need to find ways to get that energy moving and keep it moving. Creating a tunnel of energy from places in the city with constant motion to those where the energy doesn't or can't move can stir a sense of life in those stagnated areas.

You can do this by going to the park or other space that the city spirit most obviously inhabits. Mentally connect to the motion around you, asking "Where does it hurt?" After you receive your answer, ask, "Where feels too active?" You may receive a mental image of a street or neighborhood or a sound familiar to a specific area of the city—or you might simply know that a certain set of cross streets has what you're looking for. If it is safe for you to go and stand in the area with too much motion, do. But if it's in the middle of a highway, stay where the city center/city spirit is—urban magick does no good if you get hit by a car.

Imagine a tunnel forming beneath the motion; see the excess vibration fall into the tunnel and travel all the way to the place of stagnation. You may ask the city spirit to plug the tunnel into itself like a tube directing energy from one place to another, or you may visualize a map of the city, as though you're creating an astral subway that redistributes energy into places that need a feeling of movement or oxygen. If you are a Hearth and Home magick worker, this seemingly broad magick can also work for your personal dwelling, especially when you are feeling a sense of stickiness around career and creative projects. If you keep a garden that seems to be languishing, a small amount of this energy (making your tunnel very narrow to control the flow) can revive it, especially if you live in an area where the soil is still recovering from pollution. If you only want to do this for your home, simply make the tunnel very small.

If you engage with the city spirit with the intention of caring for it, the spirit will often show you how to move energy in ways that it needs. It may work with your own perceptions and inclinations—and do similar work using totally different methods with another person it chooses to assist with its care. Don't sweat not knowing how to do something. Your city spirit will show you what it needs and how to make that happen.

The New Urbanism Movement (1980s)

The New Urbanism movement differs from the Green City movement in that it aims to directly affect human behavior. Green Cities take systems already in use and improve them; it's an innovation. They still rely on influencing humans on a subconscious/acculturation level. New Urbanist cities alter how people can move around the city in ways that make them fully conscious of the changes to their own behavior. Rather than adding buildings and roads, these cities promote initiatives, such as walk-your-child-to-school programs, that create a more active population—and as a byproduct bring back pre-Modernist street culture.

New Urbanism also attempts to disrupt one specific technology: the car. It may seem obvious to state the issues, but within these issues are the foundation of New Urbanism tactics: cars cause air pollution, sedentary lifestyles, traffic congestion, lowered quality of life, and raised stress levels. They also increase a sense of isolation.

In many ways, New Urbanism addresses the common factors that can weaken a city spirit. The fewer pockets of connection for the residents, the less power a city spirit has. In the 1990s, as environmental and lifestyle concerns began to peak, urban planners formed an international organization called the Congress of New Urbanism. This group established the following principles as their core design philosophy, many of which also apply to practices of magickal urbanism:[41]

1. Cities should be walkable.

2. The street grid should decrease driving and increase foot traffic.

3. Diversity in community is valuable. People of diverse cultures, worldviews, and lifestyles should be able to share a neighborhood, and their presence and differences should make the neighborhood better. These neighborhoods should also be mixed-use, meaning businesses and residences intermingle.

4. Public spaces should also function as civic art.

5. The landscape and architecture of a city should celebrate its history.

6. Landscape should honor its climate.

7. Neighborhoods should have centers and edges—and the center should always be public-use space.

8. Public transit should connect towns, cities, and neighborhoods, while the design of these neighborhoods should encourage walking.

---

41. "10 Principles of New Urbanism: Michigan Land Use Institute," Michigan Land Use Institute, http://www.mlui.org/mlui/news-views/articles-from-1995-to-2012.html?archive_id=678#.WSuQ0Ma1vIV.

9. Sustainability should be strongly encouraged. Use ecologically friendly technologies whenever possible.

10. The design of these neighborhoods should uplift and inspire the human spirit.

Principles of Magickal Urbanism Based On New Urbanism

Many of these principles resonate with the Civic Path of magickal urbanism. Adopting a similar code (and allowing for it to change when calcification makes the solutions become problems) provides a map of where to concentrate activist magick. If the above ten principles were rephrased into a creed of magickal urbanism it might look like this:

1. Walk whenever possible and strive to make your city navigable for those who can't walk.

2. When reasonable to do so, choose driving last rather than first as your method of transit. If you have to own a vehicle, if it is within your means to do so, balance your household transportation needs with ways to minimize exploitation of non-renewable resources.

3. Value your neighbors, especially those who differ from you. Magickal priests and civic workers learn about their neighbors by greeting them with kindness and listening to them when they talk about their lives.

4. Public spaces and public art are energy pockets containing both the intention of the artist and the collected intention of those who use that space.

5. A city's history matters just as much as the folklore about a deity matters in divine-centered practices. The history shows you what created the city spirit's temperament and what energies the city might call to itself. A deep aware-

ness of a city's history can also reveal the hidden treasures of magickal opportunity.

6. Cities affect nature because they are part of it; any personal landscaping, gardening, and water use should happen with current climate conditions in mind. Honor nature and consider the condition of the climate in all actions.

7. Advocating for a city that serves all your neighbors serves the city spirit. Good city magicians learn their neighborhoods well and uses their natural inclinations and skills to make it a better place for having them in it.

8. Public transit is an important purveyor of not just people, but of equal opportunity and redistribution of energies. Magicians should strive to overcome any internalized stigma held against using mass transit or against those who do use it.

9. A sustainable city is a magickally strong one. All efforts should be made personally and on a civic level to push forward environmental wellness. Magick can improve environmental sustainability when practiced with that intention. Holding a view of sustainability that includes the greater good of your neighbors, even those you do not personally know, is key to establishing a long-term healthy environment. Working personal magick to make the personal parts of your city life easier helps just as much as large rites, public service, and volunteerism. Sometimes simply taking steps to reduce stress on yourself and your loved ones also improves your city by adding happier energy to the city spirit energy mix.

10. Magick that uplifts the human spirit benefits everyone.

This list does not serve as dogma. Cities constantly change in order to thrive. This means that values may end up shifting in order for those who practice them to thrive as well.

Tactical Urbanism (2010s)

Tactical Urbanism is less a philosophy of urban planning and more a philosophy of urban living. While New Urbanism still does some building and restructuring, tactical urbanism takes what is already present and subverts it. This approach likely speaks to the heart of every anarchist-DIY-bohemian who ever built a wooden bench for the highest good.

Tactical Urbanism as a movement began around 2010 and has gained global traction. This approach encourages citizens to drive urban design and urban living to the point of civil disobedience. For example, instead of waiting for city government to clean up a street or repair broken playground equipment, city residents might step in and do the repairs themselves, sourcing scrap materials or providing their own funding for the new equipment. Detroit, New Orleans, and Mumbai all have high profile Tactical Urbanist movements. In Mumbai, a website titled The Ugly Indian posts pictures of city projects the local government has ignored. Often the people who post also go clean the sites up, badger government officials to bring supplies, and if local government still refuses to do its part, the citizens do the repair work and beautification themselves.

Magickal urbanism pairs well with Tactical Urbanism. For example, Detroit's guerilla gardening movement transformed urban agriculture—and many a magician dreams of an herb garden. Guerilla gardens are gardens grown on public land or on land that does not have a clearly identifiable owner. These gardens began as a means of beautifying roadways while offsetting air pollution. Now they correct food deserts (urban areas without access to fresh food).

Witchy types might want to grow their own herbs in these plots of land—and why not grow some veggies to feed yourself or to offer to local schools while you're at it? Another civic project now popular: chair bombing. This practice removes waste dumped in public areas and transforms the salvageable parts into public seating. Often this added seating helps the homeless population. In San Francisco, carpenters and artists began building these seats as protest of a sit/lie ordinance passed in 2011 that banned people from sitting or lying on city sidewalks. The city responded to this protest by creating parklets, miniature parks just off public sidewalks, usually located in front of coffee shops and restaurants, to extend public space where people could sit for long periods. Since these parklets also eat up parking spaces, this means a fewer people in the city drive, again reducing air pollution. Pop-up shops and restaurants, now usually endorsed by cities because they give life and use to languishing space, allow smaller businesses to find their footing and provide a novel shopping experience for people nearby.

Several public initiatives have come out of Tactical Urbanism's rule-breaking grassroots efforts. The Open Streets project, where a different well-traveled street is shut down to car traffic for one Sunday, is now a popular event in cities throughout the United States. It began when neighborhoods throughout the country began having guerilla street shutdowns. Park(ing) days converts single parking spots to public park spaces. The de-fencing movement removes unnecessary fences and expands enjoyable green space.

Tactical Urbanism is itself a reminder that, at least in democracies, the ordinary citizen *is* the government. These acts of protest and creation of rebel spaces often force cities to respond in kind—and establish people over corporations as priorities to city planners.

Tactical Urbanism for the Urban Magician

Any magician with the slightest sense of civic-minded mischief can recognize many opportunities for spirit work awaiting a tactical urban flair. For example, someone who has always dreamed of running an occult shop of their own might participate in a local pop-up project. You might create your own chair charm and invest it with healing energy or much-needed good luck for any homeless person who happens to sit on it. Along with urban foraging, you might improve the relationship between land spirits and the city spirit by seeding a few pollution-negating plants near a busy street or quietly create an oasis in a food desert near your home. Some of this may rely on how you define magick—it's far more than just chanting and visualizing; it's also about putting change in motion. Sometimes magick involves ragged fingernails and sweat. Tactical Urbanism is all about claiming personal power to collaborate for a greater good—and that can get sweaty.

Urban Design Movements and Magickal Thinking

By now we recognize that a well-planned city reduces the bumps of daily life that, when the basics aren't available, can impact our physical and mental health. In a healthy city, the water is clean, the waste invisible, the transit easy, and the neighbors familiar.

City design serves on a grand scale what magicians attempt to do on a small scale: improve happiness, distribute prosperity, and create protective boundaries. They also demonstrate structures that can support or inhibit long-term growth. For those who prefer magick that follows the path of a tradition, such structures assist everything from composing a ritual to determining how energy flows along a certain path, whether modeled on an urban design philosophy or rooted in folkloric tradition.

Just as one tradition of magick can't apply to every person, one uniform approach to urban design can't work with every municipality. Each incarnation of city planning reflects the ideals and assumptions of its time and place. Those ideals have inextricable history, politics, and technology influencing them. These factors lay the framework for how the energies of the city interact with the energies of the land. These tensions and memories all form threads in the hand of the urban magician. Careful urban planning can drastically alter a person's lifestyle and thinking—as seen with the example presented previously about cars leading to the demise of street culture. That these alterations happened without total awareness on a mass scale is both frightening and informative about the power contained within an urban design. It is the subtle power some magicians aspire to, while others prefer the forced consciousness of New Urbanism and Tactical Urbanism.

SIX
URBAN ART AND MAGICK

One of the greatest problems in cities is how the value placed on art has shifted since ancient times. In the ancient world, one of the first things humans embraced once relieved of farming was creative activity. Once the city temple was built and the water supply and housing established, they turned to creating art pieces that praised the gods and memorialized the realities of their time.

In modern times, art, while pervasive in our lives, is treated as frivolous. Because it isn't making a product or enforcing specific aspects of society, it is treated as if it has little or no value. Yet artists are among the first people governments and grassroots organizations turn to when they want to make a change. Artists are the emotional body of a city spirit, and when it's necessary to change public feeling about something, it always takes the work of someone versed in the arts. Those arts may be dubious—spin doctors have as much creative skill as painters—but all the same, the results of the work lie in the emotive.

Arts, in city magick, fall into four categories: the art you make for your own pleasure, the public art you witness, the art you create through interaction, and the art placed in your path to cause changes. That these aspects align with the different paths of city magick is no accident; the occult is, after all, referred to interchangeably as an art and a science.

Artists, scientists, innovators, rebels, and witches all gravitate to cities—and have since long before it could possibly be good for your health. They did and continue to do so because by congregating there, they give each other a pool of creative energy. This creative energy may appear in strange forms: New York has its theater scene, Amsterdam its museums and civic mind, Warsaw its cussedness, San Francisco its tech innovators, and London its rich history. Magickal people tend to be cross-disciplinary sorts, who often have more than one interest and thus drink from more than one pool of city creativity.

To practice the occult arts, most magick workers need to develop a few—or even several—skills. A Hearth and Home witch often evolves the arts of cooking and gardening—and along with it learns soap and candle-making. Many chaos magicians pursue psychedelic experiences and then must evolve the painting, drawing, and writing skills to share and process their experiences. City priests, along with having to evolve and maintain strong city connections, must become expert researchers, map readers, urban explorers, and frequently, extemporaneous poets. Even those with introverted preferences benefit from being close to the energetic-creative pool. The amassed interests make everything from occult shops to craft and hobby stores more easily and immediately accessible, and with that, face-to-face subject matter experts who can help perfect and evolve arts based on where and how magickal people are living.

While the internet has bridged a significant part of the distance gap, not everywhere in the world has easy access, and the best of internet communications can't replace the synergy of a face-to-face meeting. Cities are creative centers, and that makes them magickal centers as well.

Working Magick with Public Art

The next time you go to a coffee shop, take a look at the art hanging on the wall. Observe what energy it emanates. Do you feel sad or happy looking at it? What does it make you think about? If you brought it into your home, what energy or changes might it generate? Expand this consideration to public art. Most major cities have epic graffiti murals—some installed legally, others not. Focus on the ones that visibly took some planning. What emotional read do you get from them? How does that emotional reading connect to the canvas for the graffiti (usually a building) and the neighborhood it's in?

Most major cities also have public art projects scattered throughout their neighborhoods. Find the one closest to your neighborhood. You might already know it because it is a landmark for you. If not, some cities keep maps of the public art on the city government website; others may be more scattered and left to local bloggers and urban explorers to share. While most people think of a mural or a sculpture when they think of public art, more cities have started including interactive art displays such as musical instruments in playgrounds, auditory history pieces, or even staged areas that invite the public to come and make art.

Exercise 4: Finding the Spirit in Public Art

For the sake of this exercise, let's assume that the art you locate nearby is stationary and static—a sculpture or a mural that won't be going anywhere. Before you visit, try to learn the name of it, who created it, and the history of the piece. Look into what was happening in the story of the city up to five years before installation of the piece. Create the best picture in your mind of the intention of the piece, the moods and energy of its creator, and what zeitgeist the art contains within it.

When you visit the art, really think about what you learned for the piece. If it's a sculpture, walk all the way around it if possible. Take in all the dimensions and angles. If you're working with a mural, stand back and see what details jump out at you—and check your emotional response to those details. If you are an art student or have an arts degree, try to step away from the part of yourself that analyzes form, technique, or movement. This art isn't about art history; it's about city history, something here, now, and considered by many too trivial to acknowledge.

Bear in mind that most magick travels along emotional circuits; when you ask a spirit inhabiting an art piece what concerns it, you may receive strong feelings or messages about the emotions that prompted the art creation and what feelings people have invested in their reactions to the art piece over the course of years. Even in the case of abstract art, ask it, "Who are you?" before you ask it, "What do you mean?" The answer that comes to you will tell you what you can draw on that artwork for—

whether it's a mouthpiece to the manifest neighborhood spirit or a repository of other energies.

The emotional states you pick up from the art can have many applications. The following is a general guideline; as your own practices evolve, you may begin to identify subtler emotive pockets in artwork and find more applications for them.

- Anger—justice work, change, eradicating stagnation
- Sadness—healing work, cleansing, revealing secrets
- Joy—healing work, creating stability, growth, prosperity work
- Pride—grounding and centering, ancestor work, land spirit work
- Fear—protection work, transformation, transmutation, alchemy of chaos and ancestry
- Love—nurturing energy/feeding the masses, family or romantic love working, neighborhood stability, especially for families
- Ecstasy—destruction, creation, transformation, resurrection

When you wish to apply these energies, your mind has a go-to symbol in the form of the artwork. An abstract sculpture can operate as a three-dimensional sigil. If you want to move that emotional energy into your own space or into a different public space, simply imagine it occupying where you want that energy to manifest. If working with murals, especially those who show the faces of humans and animals, you can call on different characters in the image for wisdom or guidance. But keep in mind, if they get a little too connected, they will on occasion become a peanut gallery.

Working Magick with
Personal Art and City Energy

One of the reasons creative people flock to cities is because creativity demands feeding. While some smaller communities do a great job of supporting the arts, many have other priorities. Just as the first cities came about because fewer people needed to contribute to farming, major cities are growing in the United States because fewer people are needed for agricultural operations and smaller cities lack the variety of opportunities that larger cities contain.

You may have grown up in a given city, or you may have lived in a rural area and moved to the city for a job or other personal opportunities. While you might not plan on a full engagement with the city spirit, by living in the city you are part of the energy that makes the city spirit. When you create something, anything, you are in a small way taking a little of the city's energy for yourself. As Julia Cameron writes, "creativity is God's gift to us."[42] While interpreting city spirit as deity might be a stretch for some, the possibility of an energetic/creative symbiosis that you can bring to your home or to your creative projects is tough to resist.

It truly does not matter what you create or how you go about it so long as you create. If you would like to get a little extra zip from your city spirit in all of your personal projects, consider making a shrine to it in your home. In and of itself, this is a creative act. If you do not have a flat surface to add items to, consider

---

42. Julia Cameron, *The Artist's Way*, (New York: J. P. Tarcher, 2002), 3.

converting a shoebox into a diorama-style altar. It takes relatively little room and is built for storage if you need to tuck magickal objects away when visitors come by.

A city spirit creativity altar might include symbols unique to your city, plants that grow near your home, and maybe a map or a photo of your city skyline. Find items that speak to you about your life in the city, especially what you like best about it. You may want to add a little dirt you pick up from creative centers. Museums, libraries, schools, and theaters often carry a little bit of an extra creative buzz. If using a shoebox shrine, mix the dirt into any glue you use to paste photos/images. You can also simply keep the dirt in vials or mix them with living plants kept on your altar.

Maintain the altar in whatever way speaks to you. You might want to light incense once a week and just before you start a creative project. You may offer wine or water. If you move to another city, you can keep the shrine to maintain your connection to that city's energy or bury it so that the city can consume it and give that creative drive to someone else.

Art As Healing Tools for City Priests

City priests often perform healings on the city spirit itself. Those wounds happen just as much from natural disaster as they do from human catastrophe. For example, a city that sees a sudden increase in gun violence develops psychic wounds that embed themselves in the fabric of the city. While the tools of conventional healing magick can work for some of this, at times it is like trying to use a standard size bandage on a giant wound. It might work for a paper cut, but if you want to make a difference, you need something bigger. But this can be complicated by the city itself. You might be able to get away with a large ritual work-ing in a city like New York and San Francisco, but the culture of most cities will demand something a bit more covert. How do you make something large enough to heal a city spirit wound that is covert enough for the public to shrug it off?

The answer is art, whether it's a visual installation or a per-formance. If you sense that the spirit injury is something that could affect future generations, your best option is to create (or recruit someone to create) a public art piece that addresses the pain and offers the energy of resolution within it. What is specif-ically appropriate will depend on the city and the situation. For example, if there's a riot, the art should acknowledge the causes of the anger while communicating—either through symbolism or through the emotion the piece is charged with—wishes for the health and prosperity of the disempowered party.

You may feel yourself moved to do something more active that falls in the performance art category. Don't worry if you're shy; you're not required to act out a full skit on a street corner! In areas of wounded distress, you may do something much sim-pler, such as asperging rose water down a sidewalk as you move through a place that recently saw death and tragedy. Often the specific city will tell you in visions, sudden knowing, or strong emotional responses what it needs. If you are a musician or singer, you might purchase a busking license and sing or play to an area that needs healing energy. Adding positive sound vibra-tions can have a healing impact and boost the collective human mood, furthering your energetic effort.

One of the more complicated aspects of using art or public performance as a healing tool is that most city governments reg-ulate it in some way. If you believe that working through the red tape benefits your city spirit, do it, as you'll receive permission to paint large murals and city support to keep them around this way. However, this is also an area that can fall into the realm of necessary civil disobedience. You may find yourself drawing on the principles of Tactical Urbanism and going ahead with your project without permission. It may be that you only need to create this healing art piece once and if it ends up destroyed, it will stimulate a replacement because it highlights a city need.

Balancing Urban Art and Urban Green

Most city spirits need help balancing between the arts and the usually green (in the environmental market sense) markers of prosperity. Often a city may be "green" or it can be "creative," but it rarely manages to be both simultaneously.[43] Wonderful innovations such as green roofing and water cleanup make cities safer, cleaner, and healthier to live in, but also come at significant costs to taxpayers—and the resultant increase in property values drives out the artists who prompted people to want to clean up the city in the first place.

This is one place where the practice of tactical urbanism combined with magick can help, and those in the Priesthood Path and the Civic Path might feel especially compelled to work on this balance. Cities benefit from a thriving art movement because it brings in money from cultural tourists and improves the quality of life for full-time residents. They benefit from greening the cities because the overall health of the citizenry improves.[44] When

---

43. Miles Orvell and Klaus Benesh, *Rethinking the American City: An International Dialogue* (Anthology) (Philadelphia: University of Pennsylvania Press, 2014), 93.

44. "How Art Benefits Cities" Project for Public Spaces, https://www.pps.org/article/how-art-economically-benefits-cities.

these factors are well-balanced, you get a thriving city spirit that feeds the people who feed it.

For those who wish to bring about this balance—and the emphasis is indeed on balance—this spell, repeated over seasons, should help. A tip: Whenever you gather dirt from a place, leave a small offering behind. Pennies are okay; tobacco or mint is probably better. Be sure you label the dirt. Glass vials are best for dirt collection, but most people end up using a plastic bag.

Spell 2: Art-Environment Greening Spell

You will need:
- Dirt from the largest park in the city
- Dirt from the largest art museum in the city
- Dirt from near any especially well-done graffiti art
- Dirt from an area of the city that is either art poor or greenery poor—or both
- A glass of water from a municipal water supply
- Two empty containers with lids

You may be tempted to add salt, the chemical of equilibrium, to this spell. *Do not do it.* Salt purifies by killing. It's good for washing off energetic and physical parasites, but not for trying to stimulate growth in any area.

While invoking a deity is never required for a spell to work—if you put enough of your intent and energy into it, it can go a long way on its own—you will likely benefit if you call together spirits and energies known for what you most need balance in. Since this addresses an imbalance between city greening and the arts, you need to appeal to representatives of both energies—or find the spirit of someone who fairly represented both. You could also work art with planetary energies for this balance, if you feel you have a nuanced understanding of them.

Since ancient Rome already had citified aspects to its religion while still finding ways to venerate nature within the city proper, the Roman deity Venus, along with her Greek counterpart Aphrodite, are good to call on for this work. Venus had several groves dedicated to her throughout Rome while she was also propitiated as a lover the arts and of refinement. Aphrodite, while often treated as the same being, came from something wild and primal. In Hellenic myth, she was born from the castration of Kronos on the sea foam. We only associate her with graceful delicate things because of patriarchal views on womanhood; in truth she had a wilder nature than what we've been taught. Aphrodite has in her the punk-rock nature of a city arts movement and the appreciation for the forces of nature herself; Venus is about formality, refinement, graces, and privilege. You need both (and regular redistribution of that privilege) for a healthy, high-functioning city.

While this spell works best in a public space, some cities are friendlier to open occultism than others, so you can also perform this spell in your own home. Just make sure you do your follow-up at the end, as you will need to deliver remixed waters to places where the energy needs to spread. You likely will need to repeat this spell a few times until you begin seeing and sensing the rebalancing of city energies.

Set the glass of water in the center of your working altar or table. Flank it with the two resealable containers. Have one dish for each dirt. If possible, have some incense burning for the deities—Aphrodite and Venus both respond well to rose or jasmine—or float flowers in a bowl of water.

Enter your sacred state of consciousness and declare your space sacred in whatever way suits you best. You will likely have your own words of invocation for how your city speaks to you; the following is simply a suggestion to get you started.

Invocation:

Aphrodite and Venus, Venus and Aphrodite
Goddesses of love and grace,
Goddesses of beautiful space
I call upon you to bless and rebalance the
green and the art of (name of your city.)
Bring together the love of nature
with the love of all creation
and let these pleasures mingle, spread and grow!

Drop the soil from the arts space in the water, along with the soil from the green space. Mix them together in the glass of municipal water, saying over it, "Blend and brighten, soil enlighten, and now in these spaces let your energy enlighten!" Hold them in your hands and state your purpose again: "Let the energies of creation and creativity mix and balance, that (name your city) has a balance of both, that creatives may live here amidst the green."

Pour half the water in each of the sealable containers. Close the circle. As soon as possible after—preferably during a full moon or on a Friday during the waxing moon—pour half the water in the arts-poor area and half the water in the green-poor area, repeating your purpose of rebalancing both.

Artists, whether conscious magick workers or unconscious shamans, have a way of manifesting a shared consciousness with their work. This is one way you can check on the health of the city spirit. Also, art in and of itself can be used to manipulate and direct human consciousness, which is one reason that so many artists throughout history have been employed to spread propaganda. Where they express themselves can significantly affect your community. Any city magician, even those on a personal path, can find themselves affected by the energies emitted from artwork placed throughout the city. For instance, a mural on an otherwise drab street can give the place life and make it looked cared for. The very presence of that art signals that block is cared for—and often a community making a mural will prompt the people nearby to keep it clean.[45]

Magicians already function as artists. We call occult practices the "ritual arts" because they involve writing, theater, and assignation of meaning to symbols. These practices integrate with city arts that extend beyond museum pieces and graffiti tags. We can take our art, our language of symbols, and encode new languages and

45. Sarah Plake, "More Murals & Public Art Decrease Crime, Increase Pride," 13WIBW, http://www.wibw.com/home/headlines/More-Murals-Public-Art-Decrease-Crime-Increase-Pride-262129391.html.

thoughts into our local ether. The outcome, like much art, might simply be to change the overarching mood of a geographic area. This can be done by tapping public art pieces—as described at the beginning of the chapter—or by creating one of your own.

Spell 3: Mini Mural for Uplifting a Depressed Area

If you notice an area of your city becoming run-down and wish to give the neighborhood a lift—and you feel you have the creative energy to do so—you can create a miniature mural to seed the energy and care that community murals attract.

This idea of magickal people in the city affecting the city isn't new. Ancient city temple priests performed magick on behalf of the city, and often the spirit inhabiting the temple represented the spirit of the city. When the spirit made demands, it often reflected the needs of the people. In the nineteenth century, esoteric ritual orders kept temples in major cities. It was easier for people who already lived in cities most of the year to come together in a clubhouse to work occult experiments (and yes, engage in sexual experimentation) than it was to travel to the countryside. Some of these ritual experiments had to have some effect on overarching city spirit, for good or ill.

Magick workers of all walks can benefit from engaging with the art scene in their cities. People on the personal path can visit for inspiration in their own creative practices. Museums tend to imitate temples either through direct appearance or through the experience intended by the architect, allowing you to access spiritual energy and mental states in secular spaces. One year during a spiritual crisis, I attended a city art crawl and through a series of synchronistic images and conversations wound up with marital advice, self-care advice, and a new avenue for my spiritual practice.

There are several ways art, even art created by others, can serve as a magickal tool. Also, seeing art increases your own ability to create art—and for much magickal work it matters more that you create than that anything you create be particularly good.

Divination with Public Art

When you walk the city, pause to really look at graffiti, sidewalk art, murals, and even signs posted on telephone poles. These seemingly random images make a powerful divination tool. Choose a neighborhood you don't visit often. Hold a question in your mind as you walk. See what draws your eye: someone's lawn statue, a mural, or possibly a graffiti stencil. As you walk, pay attention to what images you see repeat and the moods and energies those images emit. Look for images that inspire wonder and mystery—these are portals you can open to bring in the good. At the end of each block, close your eyes and see what images or feelings come to you. Apply those to your question.

If you see an image repeat—for instance, an elephant graffiti stencil or an unusual number of garden gnomes—look up the symbol in a dream dictionary. These are handy for interpreting symbols you see in waking life and for helping you determine ways to respond to those omens and symbols. The repeating omen may come simply as a color. You might suddenly notice more blue cars than normal or an image of a bear just as you're feeling especially vulnerable. These images are a way the city spirit and the universe can talk to you.

This divination style comes in handy for people who feel like they have weak clairvoyance/clairsentience (or are having a down day psychically). The intentional receiving of image can become a way to invite the city spirit to speak back to you after you make a request. For example, if you're looking to move to a particular neighborhood, ask the city spirit what you need to do to live there. It might show you an image of green (money) or an image of yellow (electricity/connection), meaning that you need to network with people who live in the area to find a place. It might draw your attention to dry grass—there just isn't room at the time you want to go there or what is there isn't good. Think of it as a moving meditation, where you simply allow the city spirit to guide your attention.

Ritual 6: Spirit Evocation with Memorial Statues

Many cities, it seems, like to place statues of their founders and other historical heroes in high-traffic areas. While some are unfortunate (civil war "heroes") and others more lighthearted (Minneapolis's Mary Tyler Moore statue), most appear quite solemn. These monuments create a permanent city-connected channel that goes through someone designated as a city ancestor. Working with founders and indigenous spirits as city ancestral energy is complicated work that goes far beyond tapping city statues. However, working with the statues can be a way of seeking advice, finding out about secret resources in the city itself, and learning to reimagine the possibilities of a place you may have lived in for decades.

A statue spirit evocation can be tricky because it's difficult to perform with subtlety. Unlike city divination where you can go for a walk, you usually need to talk out loud to the statue. Also, be polite! It's good form to bring an offering. Statues are usually located in public places that are monitored by police or are someone's sleeping spot/safe place at night. What I have crafted here is a way to be relatively low-key in your approach. You will need a partner to sell it because, if you do this, you're going to have to convincingly behave as though you are engaging in an act of performance art.

You will need:

- A partner—it's a lot easier to sell this as theater with another player
- Chalk or cascarilla
- Flowers
- Water
- A poetry book, hymnal, or something that sounds lyrical when read out loud
- A knowledge of the person that the statue honors, and if you can find it, why it is located where it is
- An incense stick and holder, if you can get away with it (Public fire codes may prevent this.)

Go to the statue at a low-traffic time and draw a circle around its base that's large enough to include yourself.

Your partner should remain on the other side of the line as a spotter (and to grab things for you since once you draw a circle it's near inevitable you'll have forgotten something). Say the name marked on the statue plaque three times. Pour out water at the foot of the statue and place the flowers in front of it. Say, "I brought you some water and some flowers, and I have some questions for you."

If you can, light the incense stick. Incense historically carried prayers to the gods. It also allowed easier communication between magicians and noncorporeal entities. If someone asks about the incense, you can simply say it's a convenient way of minimizing bugs. The incense can act as a sort of pendulum. It can blow in certain directions for yes or no, toward you if the answer lies with you, toward a part of the city you need to explore, and so on.

Introduce yourself. State that you are a resident of the city and explain why you're interested in the personage of the statue. Make a few comments about what you know about that figure, and pause to ask, "Is this true?" Look up at the face of the statue. You may notice subtle changes of expression that can also answer your questions.

Depending on what city magick path you work, you may have wildly different questions. These suggested questions apply to city priests and people on the Civic Path; personal and chaos workers may have other concerns and request more personal assistance. The better you know the history of the statue and its model, the better you will know what help might come from it.

Suggested Questions for City Statue Evocations

- Are you happy that you are memorialized here?

- Does your spirit still live here?

- Does your spirit dwell in this statue or elsewhere?

- Is the city how you remember it? (This response can come with images, sounds, and smells.)

- What part of the city do you feel needs attention?

- What part of the city do you feel needs rest?

- What would you like to still be able to influence? How? (This is why it is so important to know the character of the memorialized. Not all statues memorialize heroes, and you may be looking to excise that influence.)

- Are you willing to help restore justice?

Once you finish, thank the being you evoked, pour out a little more water, and say goodbye. You may have to take the flowers with you because of city cleanup regulations. Smudge the chalk circle and release the energy that calling a spirit raised.

You may have noticed that I left the Chaos Path out of this chapter. That's because much of chaos magick already takes what's around and distills it into new forms or takes it as is and works it into a cross-disciplinary symbolism. Chaotes are already enacting art.

Art is a wonderful expression of a thriving, well-balanced city. There are as many ways to work with it spiritually as there are people living in a city. While this chapter focused on public art as in outdoors art, art kept indoors can be worked with in much the same way—and in a few additional ways because of its relationship to architecture. As you work with art on a spiritual level, you may find yourself more connected to and conversant with the city spirit.

SEVEN
NATURE MAGICK IN THE CEMENT JUNGLE

To review, after the Industrial Revolution, the definition of nature transformed from meaning "oh, here's this plant on the sidewalk" to a distant, pristine ideal.[46] Until then, people met nature where it was: in cities, farms, and distant wilderness. Even now, urban designers and landscape architects struggle with city residents failing to recognize the nature already in their environment. For the magickal urbanist, it is time to re-meet that nature.

Rather than looking around a city block and dismissing it as unnatural at the first sight of concrete, consider the origin of material. Think about where cement comes from: it is made by mixing minerals including iron, silica, sand, and others. All those minerals originate in the earth. The telephone pole began as a tree and as metals found in the ground. The car's tires most likely

---

46. Hellmund and Somers Smith, *Greenways*, 162.

began in the sap of a rubber tree. All the synthetics around us have an origin in nature; we just need to remember them.

Pure, unsullied nature—what we call *life*—also exists in the city. As famously said in the 1993 movie *Jurassic Park*, "Life finds a way." The first instinct of any species, plant or animal, is to survive. The next time you walk through your streets in warm weather, take a close look at the sidewalks. Observe what grows in the cracks and on the sides. Dandelions and other tap roots have a way of eating at and overcoming even the firmest of concrete blocks. Mints regularly appear at the edge of parking lots. Roman chamomile shows up everywhere moist enough for grass.

Urban wildlife extends far beyond plant incursions. Larger mammals adapt to the urban, including mountain lions, bears, and coyotes.[47] It's common to see foxes, deer, and even rattlesnakes move into sectors of dense population.[48] The way the animals see it, we're just using the inside of the building; if they have a reason to get in, they will. The outside is fair game.

Understanding the origin of the material that makes the chair you sit in connects you to the nature in it. This applies to all the material, alive and not, that makes a city. If you wish to tap into the energy of nature while in an artificial environment, recognizing the origin of the material and its elemental alignment makes that possible. We reshaped nature, and in a few places made it unhealthy, but we haven't separated from it—not at all. We never will.

---

47. Smith, *City*, 288.

48. Janet O and Katie Marzullo, "Two Children Bitten by Rattlesnakes within Week in Northern Ca," https://abc7news.com/news/2-children-bitten-by-rattlesnakes-within-week-in-northern-ca/775850/.

You may not even need to leave your house to spot nature where you live. Do you have house plants? That counts as natural energy. The disturbing fungi that grow in corners also count as nature, even if it's not the fun and pretty version. Looking at the spaces around where you live and asking yourself, "What is natural here?" can shift your perspective. For instance, if you visit a public park with a playground, explore the grounds. The playground equipment looks machine-crafted, but what about the cultivated garden? What about the woods along the edge?

Does the process of cultivation change the energy of the plant? Can cultivation of a space produce a desired energy you might not get without the practice? Look for these areas around apartment buildings and public buildings, too. Does the location of the plant make it any less natural? Yes, chemicals sprayed on a plant may alter its makeup, but does it stop emitting oxygen or engaging in photosynthesis?

Exercise 5: Elemental Awareness

One of the greatest struggles certain magick workers have with city life is that they feel separated from nature. This exercise puts you in touch with nature even when surrounded by synthetic objects. This understanding will make certain spells easier to perform, especially when surrounded by manufactured material.

Choose a synthetic object. Pick anything that speaks to you—a bus bench, a patch of sidewalk, a public sculpture, a car, a telephone pole. Break down your understanding of the object into its components, such as wood, sand, iron, and so on. Assign each of those components an element. For example, iron belongs to earth. Wood goes with earth, or fire. Imagine how each of the separate elements combine to form the object before you and think about what the object becomes when you use it, are near it, or in any way alter it. How does your energy fit with its energy? How does the energy of hundreds or thousands of passerby affect it? How does the shifting energy of weather and season affect it? What does that object contain because of all that exposure? When you imagine the ripples this object sends out when you use it, what or who do you see it affecting first?

Exercise 6: Connecting Your Home to the Elements

When looking for nature connections, begin before you leave your house. Nature finds its way into human habitats—even yours. What plants do you have growing? What critters have managed to gain entry?

Next, look at the convergence of the five elements in your home. If you are unsure what element something might be, think about what natural materials went into making it. For example, a wooden desk with metal parts would be composed of the elements of earth and air. The tree took sustenance from both earth and sky to grow. In addition, account for the raw materials for all the screws and fasteners that came from deep within the earth.

Walk through each room in your house. Take note of the most important features and assign one or more of the five elements to each one. Your fireplace contains the elements of fire and earth. Your sink may contain the elements of water and earth. Some tools may have three elements—

or, at times, embody all five. Where would the spirit energy of your home reside? What is your reasoning?

Touch one object you use often that contains multiple elemental alignments. Try to call only fire or only air from it. Picture it in your mind's eye or feel how its vibrations change. Notice if any pitch or color you associate it with changes as you focus on that elemental alignment. There will be more you can do with this later, but for now, practice focusing on the different elemental layers.

Now, use this exercise outdoors. As you walk down your city block, first identify natural material such as trees, grass, gardens, animals, and so on. You may want to take this to a deeper level by learning the genus and species of the plants that grow nearby. Visit a business district where cement becomes common and green areas rare. Look for wildness combatting the encased environment. Look for how other people introduce nature, using sidewalk planters or their own guerilla approaches for greening an area.

In this cement area, shift to identifying the elements in the material around you. Practice on the cement, on the paint on buildings, on windows and doors, on old public phones. Pay attention to the differences in feelings and impressions. What does the earth-and-air combination of a public telephone feel like? If you reach deeper, can you spot the fire or electricity? Compare that energy to the feeling of your personal phone. How is it different?

As you expand your explorations through the city, you will find elements in broader forms. Earth, air, fire, water, and yes, spirits have all visible manifestations in cities. Before you can decide how to use that energy, you need to learn how to identify it. And to identify it, you must both acknowledge the obvious nature and expand your mind to include drastically transformed nature.

———

The following exercises will walk you through the five major elements as you may encounter them in an urban environment. The exercise groupings are not perfect; sometimes mastering one skill in one element is what you need to do something specific with another element. Also, the climate and culture of a city may change how much of this might work. You may find features unique to your city not mentioned here, features ripe for elemental exploration. Those are opportunities for you to work with the energy and share your discoveries.

Urban Earth

Cities begin with land. Usually this land is a patch of earth that people gather on and form a communal identity over. The land itself can absorb energies from those who live on it and in it, and these form subtle energies. You can fully connect to these subtle energies by literally getting your hands dirty.

Exercise 7: Connecting to Urban Earth

For this, you need a very small jar, a water bottle, a garden trowel, and somewhere you can dig that won't upset your neighbors. Unless you know how to identify poisonous plants, you should also wear gloves. Choose a spot you frequent (and can dig in) and spend a few moments observing what happens on that patch of dirt.

Do you notice any insect or animal behavior? Do you recognize the plants growing in that patch? Sprinkle a little water on the soil and then dig down as far as you reasonably can with just the garden trowel. Take a close look at the soil. Notice any differences in color, texture, and critters at the different levels. How does it smell? What animals and plants do you find as you dig? Take a pinch of the soil and put it in your glass jar. Replace the dirt in the hole, pour out the remaining contents of your water bottle, and thank the soil.

Carry the vial of soil with you as a small neighborhood talisman. You may want to take it out and compare the feel of it with the soil in other neighborhoods. If you were to dig into the dirt on a different city block, what would you find that's different? The next time you take mass transit, imagine one of the things you found in the soil following you. How does it get from point A to point B? How does it see the city from the perspective of living in soil? What happens when that bit of life gets encased in cement? Does that energy change?

Digging in every garden you encounter will get you arrested or worse, so only take a literal pinch of dirt from other locations. Keeping a pinch of home soil on your person also gives you a grounding touchstone. You can use this as a way of comparing the subtle energies of the soil near your home to the soil in other areas of the city. You may notice that the mental impressions you receive from your own pinch differs from a sample from even a block away.

Exercise 8: Mapping Urban Earth and Nature

Pick five parks inside your city limits and meditate in each one over the course of six weeks. Keep a notebook observing each park, how you experience each, and the changes you observe as you visit them. Use these meditations to cultivate a relationship with the earth and the nature spirits within your city. When you visit each park, bring a little water and pour it on the ground as an offering, and then introduce yourself. Let the land spirits know you want to connect with them. As you practice this, you may receive visits from animals (insects included), or find random items related to your spiritual work as you move around the city visiting the parks. You may start sensing that one park is good for one type of magickal work, while another park offers something different. At the end of six weeks (roughly the space between Sabbat cycles) look over your notes and reflect on the relationships created.

Exercise 9: Finding the Roots

You may want a smartphone or tablet handy to look up information as you do this exercise. If those are not available to you, have a pen and notebook on hand to write down questions for library research later. Sit in front of a window and name objects in front of you. "Street, car, house," and so on. Now name the object—for instance, street—and name what material constructs the street. For each material named, assign it one of the five Western elements. Some material falls under multiple element categories. If the road is made of cement, cement is made from sand. Sand is a natural material found near water. The road may represent both earth and water. If made with tar, it may represent both fire and earth. When finished, move onto the next object. Cars come from specific metals. What natural processes result in the minerals that form those metals? Now look at the tires. Practice this in a few locations around town—what are stoplights made from, or newspaper dispensers, or the table you sit at? What was it and how did it get here? What will it become once it breaks down too much for use?

While you will learn—or reaffirm—that artificial products come from nature, this process of identification and categorization also adds a new form of visualization or imagination to your magickal toolbox. When you need to imagine fire energy, you can look at the objects around you and recognize how they already contain fire (or any of the other elements) and call upon them. If you believe yourself to have some astral nastiness on you and you don't have a candle or smudge stick handy, call on that latent fire energy to send it packing.

Exercise 10: Calling Out an Element from an Object

This extends a little bit beyond just connecting to the element of earth, but at this point you should have enough understanding of how elements combine to try this. To call an element from an object, you only need you, your ability to concentrate, and a willingness to talk out loud to an inanimate object. Place your hand on the object you wish to change the balance in. For instance, if you're struggling with a cold apartment, place your hand on a wall. Imagine the atoms shifting underneath your hand as you focus. Picture the wall as four walls: one made of air, one of fire, one of water, and one of earth. Pull the walls together mentally and slowly draw the fire element wall to the top of the "stack" asking that it gently warm your apartment for a specific length of time and, at the end of that period, fade back to its normal place.

You may use this method in other ways, such as turning each wall into a protective ward or using a specific elemental layer to alter the general mood of your space. This practice connects you to the natural components in any space, no matter what it's made of. You may want to practice connecting to layers of elements with objects outside your house—the sidewalk, telephone poles, even the outside of utility boxes. Remember to only move these layers temporarily, and always restore them to their original condition when done. It's just the neighborly thing to do.

Exercise 11: Connecting to Urban Plant Life

For this you may want to bring a plant and wildlife identification guide, or download a plant identification app on your phone. If able, walk or otherwise explore about a half mile of city sidewalk. Count the number of different plant species you see growing either in the sidewalk cracks or in the curb. Do your best to identify those plants. When you return home, catalog them and learn about each one. Find out how they spread their seed, what they do to the soil, which are toxic, and what medicinal virtues the nontoxic plants carry.

Then, as much as you can, look up folklore associated with each plant you identify. Learn of any superstitions or stories associated with each plant. Categorize them by use: protection, cursing, healing, good luck, and so on. This gets you started on your own magickal herbal practice, but also shows you what tools the city and land itself produces for you to use in your communications with it. Smudging with sage is lovely, but what if your city honestly prefers the scent of dried dandelion root?

Urban Water

The two most important elements for building a city are land and water. The first people needed a way to grow food, and they needed fresh water to live. Even though agriculture has advanced so much that a few can feed the many, the need for water in a settlement never disappears.

In ancient cities, wells and fountains served as community gathering centers; by ancient Roman times, community pools acted as social centers similar to modern night clubs. The need for water connected everyone, affected everyone's health, and when droughts happened, the water shortages could hurt everyone. City spirits form from shared group identity and socializing around a water source can build that energy. When droughts and famine happened, the spirits suffered too.

So well-known is the effect of that communal energy that it has a place in folklore. Tales abound about spirits living in fountains and wells, helping or harassing different communities. Collective water spirits could grant wishes, spread disease, or take on haunting vendettas of their own.[49] Haunted wells and alien kidnappings at popular swimming holes have become something a storytelling trope. In modern times, the richness of fairy lore has given way to mild urban legend. Now, instead of a well-spirit invading our kitchens, we hear sketchy stories about creatures living in the sewers beneath our homes.

Communal water as gathering places in major cities has not disappeared, but it engages a smaller percentage of the population. Public fountains and pools still beckon people to gather in hot weather. It's difficult to imagine a placid wading pool holding the magick of a water spirit, and more difficult to imagine a water spirit surviving chlorination. Yet despite our own chemical alterations, our remixes of the natural for unnatural results, water keeps its magick. The magick is different, yes, but it takes far more than a human sterilization to stop water from giving collective sustenance.

Exercise 12: Reaching the Communal Water Spirits

Visit a public water source, whether it's a public pool or a nearby lake, and watch how people interact with each other and the water. Examine the color and clarity of the water. How do you imagine the water and inherent water spirits feel about the people? What is the collective spirit/mood of the water space?

Next, watch how people act around public drinking fountains. Is there a shared spirit there? Think about

49. Rustom Pestonji Masani, *Folklore of Wells Being a Study of Water Worship in East and West* (Mumbai: D.B. Taraporevala & Sons 1918), 1–8.

where the water comes from and how it gets to the fountain. How is the energy changed by moving from one source to another?

When you look at the water you drink at home or the water used to fill a pool, ask yourself: What about the water is altered? Drinking water and pool water have added chemicals. Do the chemicals alter the function or energy of the water? How so? How would this affect its magickal potency?

Water spirits inhabit any source of water. Just as water itself flows to fit any container, the water spirits themselves do the same. You are just as likely to find them in a shopping mall fountain as you are playing on the banks of a river. Like many spirits, they have adapted and even found ways to incorporate the chemical additives we put in our water supplies into themselves. While the presence of chlorine does dissuade certain water spirits, if the location sees enough human traffic, water spirits—especially fountain and well spirits—will opt to overlook the inconvenience so long as the water has continuous attention, as the attention strengthens their presence.

While wells almost all have their own inhabiting spirits, they rarely interact with city energy, even when built inside of city limits. However, fountains and artificial waterfalls appear often in city architecture. Even if they only flow for a few hours a day, that flow creates enough energy and movement to call an inhabiting spirit.

While the following exercise demonstrates how to reach one type of communal spirit, a fountain spirit, you can also connect to water spirits of your municipality through your indoor plumbing. Just keep in mind that water spirits are made of the liquid but have enough sense of self that they don't particularly enjoy some-one swallowing them. (A few do; there's always that one eccentric …) You can take a bowl (preferably black enamel), fill it with water, hold the bowl, and drop a penny in the bottom. Then turn on a faucet nearby for no more than two minutes. Say out loud, "Spirits of the water of (your city), come and speak with me!" You will know a spirit has arrived when the bowl suddenly feels heavier. Make sure you have some questions to ask the spirit—they usually have a lot to share about the general mood of the city and whether the living water sources are healthy enough.

Exercise 13: How to Communicate with a Fountain Spirit

Fountains in modern day are popular for beautification, and sometimes offer relief for people stuck outside on hot days. They hark back to the fountains and wells of ancient cities, where people once gathered as they drew water for their homes. While public swimming pools and indoor plumbing have displaced fountains as places of collective social energy, a large body of folklore about the spirits that dwell in these wellsprings lives on. The super-stition of throwing a penny in a fountain and making a wish persists, although many have forgotten the specifics of the spirits that lived in those fountains who granted those wishes. The spirits themselves live on—and much like other wild creatures, adapt to—urban environments.

If you wish to meet and work with a water fountain spirit, do so from a place of community appreciation. These spirits are all about community connection; your personal wishes will affect your neighbor, and to these beings, all energy ebbs, flows, and comes back around again. All beings on this planet are partly made of water, and the fountain spirit will expect you to have that awareness. Also, choose your words with care. Most water spirits take promises very seriously. If you say you will do or give something to that spirit in exchange for an action by that spirit, make sure you do it! You are much too dependent on water to mess around with false promises or forgetfulness.

Water spirits can do what water does: flow over everything, erode solid objects, and saturate porous objects with deep energies. Have one of these aspects in mind before approaching a fountain spirit. In ancient societies, offerings of local crops to the fountain spirits ensured good crops and healthy people. Now, as we spend more time producing abstractions as products, abstractions in physical forms work for the spirits as well. Thus, the penny in the fountain—or at the edge of it—serves as an adequate offering to spirit. Because water spirits operate on emotion, the feeling of truly parting with something (a feeling we often get with money) is the energy that they will respond to.

Choose a public fountain that resonates with you. You may respond to the location, to the design of the fountain, or just have a general feeling about it. Stand in front of the fountain with your penny, kiss the penny, and toss it in *without making a wish*. Say as you toss it,

"This is for you, fountain spirit!" After the penny falls in the water, proceed to introduce yourself and wait for a response. The spirit may refuse to respond on the first try, especially if you do not live in its city. Water spirits are sensitive to energies from outside their environment. It will want to know why you dare intrude on its domain. If you don't get a response on the first try, repeat this procedure and introduction two or three more times. Wait for a few minutes. If the water spirit responds, you will feel it and sense it before you see or hear anything—and what you do see and hear may not come from the fountain but could still be a communication from it.

Once you have contact with the fountain spirit, build a relationship. A few good questions to ask at the beginning:

- What would you like me to call you?
- What offerings would you like?
- How do you feel about the people of this city?
- How do you feel about the city spirit?
- If I took a little of your water home, what would you prefer I do with it?
- Is there anything you need?

You may feel or know how to do something, rather than hearing a clear voice in your head. If you work the Priesthood and Civic Paths, pay close attention to any sense of dissatisfaction from the water spirits. If they aren't happy, they can take a whole city down fast! Resolving the issue may be as simple as placing a protective talisman to keep drunk people from peeing in the fountain, or it may require repairs that involve the city, or performing a rebellious act of tactical urbanism to repair the fountain. If something especially untoward happens to the fountain spirit, always bring it flowers. No one wants an angry spirit loose in the water supply.

If you work with a fountain spirit for the Personal Path, be sure to bring it an offering that comes from the essence of your home and you. Your work falls into the line of protecting the harvest—your own harvest. If you have a garden, bring nontoxic plants from what you grow. If you knit, create a cozy that fits around something attached to the fountain or bring a bit of salt to allow the fountain spirit to improve its equilibrium.

If the fountain agrees, take a very small vial of its water home. You can use that water for making potions that relate to cleansing and community-level movement. If you find your book club has taken a sudden catty bent, creating a spritz of fountain water with a little bit of orange peel, cinnamon, and spearmint should shift the atmosphere from spiteful to convivial. You may take it to another part of the city that appears depressed and sprinkle it on a spot that feels especially heavy to inspire a sense of movement. For chaos-minded folks, this same water might be a way of saturating new ideas into rigid institutions—perhaps spiking the holy water somewhere.

Urban Fire

The relationship between cities and fire is, at best, an uneasy one. Out of all the elements, fire presents the greatest potential for immediate devastation and yet also protects humans in the harshest of weather conditions. During the Industrial Revolution, San Francisco, Chicago, and New York all experienced devastating fires that started from simple, common incidents like the wind blowing a gas lamp into something dry. While it's less likely for a home to burst into flames out of nowhere these days, there is always some risk of a fire. We hide most from view now, mediated into electrical connections and gas furnaces. But it is still there, pulsing beneath our homes and businesses, a wild energy disguised as tame for our convenience. All elements have the potential to sustain or destroy us; fire destroys the fastest.

Exercise 14: Fire of City Spirit

Skip this exercise if you have any kind of allergy, lung disorder, or claustrophobia from even thinking about closed spaces. There are always other ways to learn and connect to these energies; you may need to create your own.

If your city incinerates its garbage, you can connect to urban fire energy firsthand. Since most dumps and incinerator sites are located outside the city and away from most traffic routes, I make the assumption that those of you who can will drive. If you can't drive, make sure you have a mask designed to filter poor air quality on before you do this. Find out the day and time the city sanitation department burns garbage. At this time, park near the landfill area—if you can see the incinerator from outside the dump, great, but if not, just watch from where you can see the plume of smoke. Even if you remain in your car to observe the incineration, make sure you have your mask on, because incineration fumes are unavoidably toxic. Imagine the fire closing in on the objects in the incineration chamber and imagine how the molecules all slowly turn to carbon and become porous as they burn. Imagine the smoke that rises from the burning, and how it flows back into the city. If your consciousness goes airborne with the smoke, imagine scanning the city for areas that match the energy. Look for sources of light and heat, sources of destruction and decomposition. Garbage incinerators do this to make room, and fire is a way of clearing a path. After you finish this visualization, think about the ways, both good and bad, that fire has cleared paths in different neighborhoods in your city.

Not all cities use incinerators, and the climate of a region can also change the outlook on fire. If your city doesn't burn garbage, look for other ways to connect. One way is to look for the places that use the most fuel. Identify buildings that likely have the highest heating and electrical bills. Look for the byproducts of that energy, such as large plumes of smoke from a chimney. In most cases, this leads to the industrial zone of your city.

Fire represents both excess use of resources and the necessity of survival: While fire may provide heat, it also casts shadow because of the fuel that it consumes. Even in well-kept green cities, the industrial areas tend to carry a lot of shadow energy. They are often neglected aesthetically and become the night-abandoned places where questionable activities take place. These activities, sometimes violent ones, come from the shadow of urban fire.

You may be tempted to try to clear this negative energy. I advise against it. Cities consist of a delicate balance of light and shadows, and if you remove something large, even if negative, you must have something to replace it with immediately. At a city-size scale, you must take into account what energies the organism requires to prevent collapse. If you cleanse a factory until it shuts down, you may end up replacing it with an even more oppressive mood as people who were barely getting by now fall below the poverty line.

Fire and fire's shadow demand a willingness to dance. What is the right amount of fuel to sustain survival, and at what point does the smoke of pollution exhaust all resources? The city spirit itself can often guide you to the best ways to help with that balance.

Urban Air

Most people who work with the elements report air as the hardest to learn. This is because of all the elements, results are the hardest to perceive. Although air absolutely has physical presence—we definitely know when it's gone—its lack of visibility to the naked eye makes working with it an often-theoretical abstraction. Contrasted to the real feel of earth, fire, and water, air requires vision to take a backseat to sensation and inner knowing.

The element of air in an urban context has an added concern: pollution. The more visible the air, the more likely it's in trouble. An entire population can suffer a nasty mood change on a poor air quality day because literally everyone is gasping for clean oxygen!

Exercise 15: Connect to the Force of City Air

To prepare for this exercise, spend one season observing air quality and wind patterns. You may find marking these shifts and trends in a calendar or datebook helpful. Pay attention to when winds shift or pick up speed. Notice what weather conditions contribute to a worsening of air quality. You may, as a byproduct of this, end up taking an interest in your city's plans for carbon offsets, such as green roofing.

Next make a master list of all the things people use that travel through the air: wireless signals, radio waves, music—all the nonvisible things that we consider part of concrete reality. When you feel like you understand the winds, air quality, and shifts enough, visit the highest open point in your city. This may take you to the top of a hill, or it may take you to the rooftop of a building.

When you visit, come prepared with something to read or sing to the city. This serves as your offering of connection. At this point, imagine you can see all the things in the air around you and how busy and full and possibly dirty they are. With that connection placed in your mind, read to the city spirit. Feel that connection build. After this, whenever you speak directly to the city spirit, it will be able to pinpoint you a tiny bit faster than perhaps it did before.

Exercise 16: Bird Watching — Meet Your Neighbors

Bird watch at a minimum of four different locations, all within your city. Choose at least one busy city street to watch from. Watch from a window of your home. Watch from inside a park. Pick your fourth spot at random, maybe walking out into the city and then stopping where your intuition calls you to do so. Pay attention to the different species of birds you see. Is it all pigeons? Is your neighborhood crow-versus-blue jay territory? Do any birds appear to have a street war going against the squirrels? Notice how the societies of animals within the city behave around each other. Also find out what birds migrate in and out of your city and when.

After identifying the birds that you watch, learn about their folklore and symbolism. How do the common birds and their migratory habits align with the story and the spirit of the city? As you learn which birds signify what omens, begin to ask the city spirit questions and request it send birds in answer to them. If a new bird appears, learn about it and how it might fit into the overall history and self-perception of the city.

You can expand this bird watching to other animals of the city. As you develop a profile and understanding of animal behaviors, you also begin to understand how they too contribute to the city spirit. Suddenly intrepid bees building a hive on a stoplight hanger makes sense; when you see coyotes, you recognize that they bring an energy to the city that the city spirit itself needs to balance another energy usually brought by the human population. Working with the animal energy gives you a next step for engaging the city spirit. Using material left behind by the animals, you can build shrines to the nature energy of the city.

After performing these exercises, you should have a deeper sense of relationship to the city and its rhythms. This should help those who do feel nature as something entirely too far away—and also help the city spirit sense you and what you're about just a little bit more. All these exercises should improve your perception of energies, and by the end you should have a posse of urban spirit friends.

EIGHT
SPIRIT WORK AND THE CITY

One of the terms used for more fluid and less culturally anchored magickal work is "spirit work." Most people who use this phrase mean it in very broad terms—it is about working with spirits. Those spirits range from smaller beings to named powers and the effort of those relationships exists outside of named traditions or religions. While some aspect of spirit work exists in every culture, in the US the term gets used most often by people who practice magic that neighbors on African Traditional Religions and Native American practices, often without actually being those practices.

A city spirit worker, in terms most used at the time of this writing, is likely the urban equivalent to a hedgewitch. Wicca, ceremonial magick, and syncretic faiths also rely heavily on spirit work and divine/genetic relationships, although often those center around specific deities, demons and angels, and ancestors.

Some magicians may even create their spirits or just work with abstract energies.

Created spirits tend to fall into the realm of those on the chaos and/or ceremonial paths. City spirits fall in a strange grey area, because most were not intentionally created, but certain city spirits and neighborhood spirits exist as a byproduct of collective human consciousness.

Those on the Priesthood Path and those who practice the path of the Hearth have a need—if not a requirement—to form cooperative relationships with the both land spirits and the spirits borne of city. In the Hearth Path, spirits are neighbors, and neighbors require some accommodation for harmonious living. For those on the Priesthood Path, spirits are fellow citizens overlooked by the city-as-government-entity. These beings are vulnerable to human decisions, especially since they often have little direct say in what humans do to land and resources. It's the job of a city priest to allow their energies in—or shut them out, in some cases—to allow for fair and equal influence.

City Spirit versus Land Spirits

Land spirits, fae, and nature spirits continue to live in cities, and are different from city spirits and neighborhood spirits. Someone building on their territory without so much as a hello can lead to serious consequences such as hauntings or worse. Urban designers and landscape architects may not consciously keep those spirits in mind when crafting their designs, but those who do tend to fare better because they work with nature rather than against it. For those serious about working with city energy, it is important to understand both city spirit/spirits and land spirits as much as they will allow themselves to be understood. Both veneration of land spirit and veneration of city spirit go back to early civilization; only since the late nineteenth century have we come to see them as oppositional forces. Fortunately for humanity, these spirits do not hold the collective human view of themselves. Most (not all) cooperate. Those who don't usually have some very busy city priests.

Just as early city settlers deified city spirits or found an existing deity to venerate, agrarian cultures often did the same with the land itself. Some societies named those land spirits. For example, in Celtic tradition, the goddess Danu represents the soil itself.[50] So deep was the relationship to the land that Celtic tribal kings ceremonially married the land as part of coronation. If he was a true king, people believed that land prospered. If a false king took the throne, the land rejected him, and famine overtook the land.

Not all land spirits are overarching, civilization-influencing entities. Land wights are small-scale land spirits. They can include spirits of animals that remained on the earthly plain and gained power or fae-like creatures that once enjoyed worship by local humans.[51] In some cases, the spirits of land include immigrant spirits—beings that traveled with human families that resettled in new places.

These smaller land spirits vary in individual strength and in their tolerance for humans. Some have adapted to cities, others have not. Some are quite pleased to share their land and see themselves as ancestors who tend to our families; others less so. A land wight could hang out in a backyard or in a bedroom closet

---

50. StormPhoenix, "Danu" Sisters in the Goddess Tree, http://thegoddesstree .com/GoddessGallery/Danu.html.

51. "The Landvaettir or Land-Wights of the Asatru/Heathen Religion," http:// www.norsegodsasatru.net/land-wights.html.

just as well as it might on the back thirty acres of a family farm. Many now take up residence in city parks or private gardens.

These land spirits can and do interact with city spirits, and that interaction can have resounding effects on the human population. We are all neighbors, and it behooves us to have an awareness of our neighbors. This good-neighbor policy, harking back to early human-fairy relationships, informs many of the rules of working with spirits within a city spirit context.

Working with the Land Spirits in Your City

How you work with the innate land spirits of your city depends a great deal on your own energy and inclinations. Your path of city work can affect who wants to work with you, as can all sorts of odd influences ranging from past lives to ancestry/genetics. Whatever path you practice, the initial procedure for this type of spirit work remains the same. Try to identify the spirit, make an overture, make an offering, listen, and develop a relationship.

Certain situations arise when you open up to spirits. You may encounter a land spirit on land you're already using—or as happens more often of late—you may find land wights acting as house wights, cramming themselves into garages and basements after someone built over their territory. If psychically sensitive, you likely already know something is there. You may receive images of animals or even plants in certain areas of the city or your home. You may also receive more humanoid impressions, but most land spirits don't bother with that affectation. They aren't here to make us feel comfortable. If you have the sensitivity, check on its emotional state. This tells you quickly whether it's friend or foe, whether it sought you out for help, or if it's just hanging out. You need to figure this out, so you know whether to make friends with the spirits or evict them.

A few precautions can ease awkward moments in spiritual cohabitation. It's good form for any magick worker to approach the spirit of the land and related spirits and ask permission to perform workings. What humans do, even metaphysically, can disrupt their environments. Giving the spirits a heads-up and a small peace offering can smooth the path. If you wish to work directly with land spirits, you can do this as an introduction for yourself, but you still need to demonstrate ongoing interest and concern. You can't just show up at a park and do a fly-by ritual. You have to keep coming back. Also, if you show up and say "Hey, I need to do this working," it gives the spirits a choice about their exposure to you.

Building a strong, co-creative relationship with a land spirit can take years. On the other hand, gaining a basic tolerance if you employ courtesy takes a little less work. Unless you rely heavily on land magick as part of your personal tradition, or if the land spirit is damaged and thus less than friendly, you can generally operate with basic acknowledgment, much like how you nod to the neighbor you encounter in your apartment hallway. The requirement for deep, intimate relationships falls on kings and priests. For those on the Priest and Civic Paths, deepening this relationship with land as much as city is imperative.

Seeding change in the magickal can foment change in what we perceive to be the practical and this spreads fastest when spirit of land and city come back you. Putting forth healing energy or an offering to a piece of poisoned land can send out a ripple effect that inspires those living on the land to engage in small acts of care that over time improve its health and their own. One hidden act can spark spontaneous human mimicry: perform a healing and suddenly several other people perform healings in their own spaces, not always knowing why or even that they're doing so. These healings can win you a good relationship with land spirits. You can also demonstrate good intentions by clearing trash away, or bringing medicine to injured trees, or possibly planting spells in the soil to help fend off predatory humans.

Ritual 7: The Rite of Three Visitations

If you want to connect deeply to a land spirit, make three visits to a place of your choosing.

On your first visit, share your water with the land spirits by pouring it into the soil. While we take sustenance from the land, the land takes sustenance from water. Sharing your water shows them that you understand where you intermesh with them. This gives you your common connection by which to bridge conversation. Since many land spirits communicate through emotion, and water carries emotions far better than any other element, this also helps build a sort of liquid phone line that, over time, increases the ability to understand true intentions, both on the land spirits' side and on yours.

On your second visit, bring two gifts. Preferably choose items that benefit the ecosphere. Land spirits respond well to loose tobacco, sage, water, and ashes from hearth and camp fires. Sometimes at the second visit, the land can sense your seriousness in forming a relationship and it may offer you a gift at that time. Take nothing with you from the land unless it asks you to. You will know if it has a gift because you will see an item and have a sudden sense that it belongs to you. It may appear in your path as you leave, when it was not there when you first came that way. If you do take something, as soon as you can, leave an additional offering to replace what you took.

On your third visit, bring both water and tobacco. Make the offering, and then sit and listen. In this case, receiving means not just listening, but watching, smelling, and touching; if possible, bare your feet. Take a moment to focus on what the land communicates to you through each of these senses. Depending on how you receive information, you might hear something, or get a certain taste in your mouth, or find yourself thinking about something incongruously.

These three visits open the path of communication. You did learn the land and the land spirit … and the land spirit also took this time to learn about you. You may want to perform these three visits again—water, offering, and listening—over the course of each season. If you spend time on the land more often, you may not need to as the relationship evolves. Once the land spirit opens to you, honor it. While these three visitations establish a relationship, whether the land spirit grants you access to its gifts depends on that spirit. Just like people, some open up with ease and others do so only over the course of years and many demonstrations of trustworthiness. One thing is universal to all land spirits, however: If you violate their trust just once, they are done with you for good.

During your visits, the land spirit may ask you to bring specific offerings, and some requests might seem strange. Usually they just want something cleaned up or may point you to an injured animal or tree. Sometimes, however, they may ask for children's toys or pennies. Often the reason for the request may appear in the next few days. For instance, the soil may have needed an infusion of some mineral in the coins.

A good relationship with land spirits can do much to negate the impact of city living on the sensitive. For those on the Hearth and Home Path, the land spirits can create thriving areas that seem to defy common city pollutants. You can tell when a happy land wight lives somewhere because all the houseplants thrive, and the grass looks lush even if the rest of the neighborhood is limping through the driest heat of summer. For those on other paths, nature may appear in odd places to send messages or give help—that wild turkey plopping itself into that parking space until you come along or that tree planted on the city sidewalk may suddenly appear more huggable than it does on days when work doesn't exhaust you.

Please note that land spirits respond poorly to domination. While ceremonial magick (including some aspects of the Chaotic Path) sometimes has a tradition of showing the spirits who's boss, this is unwise with land entities. First, most have an emotional understanding of humans that practice religious dominionism and they universally have negative feelings about that. Second, *nature always wins.* If it looks like it's losing, assume it's playing possum. Mother Earth hasn't swallowed us all and called for a redo because she hasn't quite lost patience … yet. Even those spirits with gentle appearances are nonetheless forces of nature that can and will cause devastation within their own understanding of the laws and cycles of the earth.

Take a co-creative, gentle, receiving approach with all of them. Some, especially ancient animal spirits, may challenge you, and in those cases, stand your ground. But do not ever assume that land spirits serve you. You'll fare far better if you assume that you serve them as thanks for all that they provide you. These spirits are the ones that can make sure you have food, healing, and water in a crisis, and while they don't make guarantees, they can choose to go a little easier on you during catastrophic weather events.

Land spirits can acknowledge and interact with city spirits, but not all do. When land and city spirits have aligned intentions, all residents of the city enjoy relative safety and abundance. When those intentions do not align, you can see the unrest in certain areas of the city. While the obvious places are where crime and poverty affect the human population, areas of extreme wealth and excess consumption often also show signs of land/city spirit misalignment. Sometimes city priests and civic magick workers can combine efforts to settle these differences, but sometimes those grudges run deeper than human conception.

Named Spirits of Place and Personified City Spirits

City dwellers have acknowledged city spirits since shortly after they began moving into walled settlements. Acknowledging them and recognizing their sentience has slowly come back in vogue. How city spirits form, however, is still a mystery. The prevailing theory: collective beliefs form literal entities when enough people share identity. In ancient times, people either invoked a spirit to be the city or found an inherent land spirit and propitiated it until it became the city spirit. Now it involves almost no conscious thought.

In earlier chapters, we discussed Athens, the most famous example of propitiating an existing divinity to operate as city spirit. India boasts many modern cities that still engage in this practice, including its most populated city, Mumbai. Named for and dedicated to the mother goddess, Mumba Devi, the 400-year-old temple sits where city walls have long gone derelict. Worship of this mother goddess still thrives in this city, while the British fort behind it turns to dust. To me, this suggests an active and ancient goddess who can outlast empires.

Thanks to the prevalence of Abrahamic religions in much of the world, modern cities do not always have such clear-cut spiritual establishment. While separation of church and state is indeed a very good thing for freedom-loving people, it makes the work of an urban magician a little bit harder. How do you find your city spirit in order to interact with it when you don't necessarily know where it hangs out or how it manifests? While some city spirits are immanent, others function more as hard polytheistic entities. That means they move around and sometimes decide to go invisible. They sometimes inhabit physical bodies. Sometimes they just get weird.

While you might find one with a map and a pendulum, there are several factors that might pose blocks: the city spirit doesn't want to be found, the pendulum has a broader interpretation of "city spirit" than you do, you're trying to find it in the middle of an Independence Day parade. On occasion, the spirit died. Until you know the sensations or images that come with meeting a city spirit, divining for it can be highly unreliable. How do you figure out the who, the what, and the when in order to ask the why? You look for clues, of course!

The clues you find are often in the names and histories of the city itself. If you grew up in your city, you probably already know the founders and the major industries and can recognize the names of families and companies that show up in charity works and public events all the time. You may know the park everyone visits every summer or where everyone gathers to see Christmas lights. City spirits tend to hang out in—or form from—places that gather collective human attention. Somewhere out there someone has quantum theories relating to mirror neurons taking form and maybe forming spirits because of all this human attention, but I leave that to the quantum enthusiasts. If you prefer a less complicated approach, I encourage you to look for name repetitions in streets and buildings and to go to your library or look online to find out how those names garnered importance. You may find even more clues by visiting local cemeteries and taking in the most-repeated names you see on the gravestones.

For those who have lived in a certain urban area most of their lives, they have an advantage in that they innately know the stories and legends of the area. Kids whisper spooky stories at school, and weird little scandals pop up that build a narrative about an overarching personality of place over time. At the same time, being a lifelong local can create a blind spot. You may be unaware of certain cultural traits, or you take certain traditions for granted just because you've been around them your entire life. As you grew up, all these area quirks were your norm, and unless you've had the good fortune to travel, you may never discover these quirks. It also can make the location of the city spirit more invisible to you. It's been part of the oxygen you breathe (metaphorically) and has been for your entire life.

Some city spirits become so clearly defined that they take on the faces and stories of historical characters and monuments.

San Francisco most famously has Emperor Norton, New Orleans has Marie Laveau, New York has Lady Liberty.[52] Other city spirits may choose a non-humanoid entity or not take form at all. Sometimes these entities are the city spirit embodied, and other times these characters form a sort of pantheon of spirits unique to the city. Urban legends, street names, and institution names can reveal who belongs to your city pantheon. For example, Dale Carnegie, Martin Luther King, and Malcolm X might be part of a national pantheon in the United States. Cities and townships may have founding families that are part of their local spiritual pantheon. Knowing the history and burial location of members of these specific pantheons can especially help urban magicians on the Civic Path. These are the spirits that had a vision for the development of your city, just as you do. Venerate them and accept their guidance. These spirits all have stories to tell.

Connecting to Your City Spirit

In *The Urban Primitive,* the authors suggest city dwellers visit a park or any other place of human gathering that seems quintessential to the city itself. After making a silent connection, ask: "What's going on?" This is an excellent practice, especially since the answer that comes back usually is, as the authors say, "Life!"[53]

This meditation practice is a great opening to meeting your city spirit, and it also serves as a touchstone as you deepen the relationship. It may not immediately reveal its name or preferred persona to you (and it may simply go by the city name); it will,

52. "Norton I, Emperor of the United States," The Virtual Museum of the City of San Francisco, http://www.sfmuseum.org/hist1/norton.html.

53. Raven Kaldera and Tannin Schwartzstein, *The Urban Primitive: Paganism in the Concrete Jungle* (St. Paul, MN: Llewellyn Worldwide, 2002), 189.

however invite you further in to its secrets on most occasions. As you explore the city, you may discover hidden streets and byways, or even find yourself led to lesser known nature areas. The more you explore the city—neighborhoods outside your beaten path, parks in odd little corners, lingering over art on the street and in the art gallery—the more you'll recognize the overall feel of your city spirit.

As in all things, different people experience the same things differently, and discussing the different ways the city opened its energy to each participant makes for a fascinating discussion about the city spirit and how it operates. This knowledge is worth exploring and repeating annually or even seasonally. Each time you practice the city spirit meditation, pay attention to the tone of the city—is there an emotional timber to that answer? Do you feel the impact of population density in one area a different way than you do in another area?

I expanded the meditation from *Urban Primitive* into my own version. For several years, I visited Minneapolis city hall on the first warm day of spring, and as I sat on the steps with other urban magicians, I led them through a variation of this city spirit meditation. Adjust it for your own city and see how it responds.

Meditation: Your City Spirit

Close your eyes.
Listen to the sounds around you.
Just receive them
Free of labels.
Accept the buzz of traffic,
The cacophony of voices, maybe languages,
That fill up the space around you.

Turn your attention to the sidewalk.
Feel the movement, or the stillness,
The sun-captured heat or the nighttime cool.
Pause on a cement square.
What drama played out on this scrap of sidewalk today?
See yourself in your downtown,
Pick a tall building,
Lean back against it and look up, up, up
Reach high with your mind,
Enter through a window. How doesn't matter.
Walk around that floor.
Peer in stairwells.
Punch the elevator buttons.
Think—who else goes here every day?
What is their daily routine? How do they get here?
When they eat, where do they go? What do they eat?
How do they leave?
Lean out the window.
Look into the sky above the buildings.
What goes through the sky every day?
Pretend you are one of the waves of sound,
Information, a radio signal, a television signal
Bouncing off walls and hurtling through sky.
Some of you land at an airplane, others, an antenna,
A few land at last in the grass and sink.
Look at the road in front of you—
the cars that travel it every day.
Imagine the buses, trains or trolleys
That roll by either side.
Think about the stories contained
In each and every passing car.

Stories that bring them to this part of the street—
Some only once, some every day.
Now stop, and ground and center yourself.
Think about the city around you—
And just be in it.
What is your place in this creature?
How do you fit?
What piece of your personality
Do you give it?
Now pause and listen.
What does it have to say to you?

Your Neighborhood Spirits

While most cities with a population over 100,000 have a defined and unique spirit, that is not the only human-generated urban spirit that can exist in such a place. Smaller spirits may appear, usually over neighborhood boundary lines. You may already know the sensation of entering a new spiritual territory. When walking in your city, you might cross a certain street or pass a certain stoplight and it feels like the air pressure changes or like new eyes are watching you. The houses might look exactly the same as those the other side of an intersection, but somehow the area is ineffably different.

You can likely still sense the overarching city spirit, especially one of immanent manifestation, but you might also notice another thread. That feeling suggests the presence of a neighborhood spirit. Like city spirits, neighborhood spirits are generated by collective human energy, but on a much smaller scale in specific subdivisions or even building complexes. Neighborhood spirits often have their boundaries marked by at least two crossroads/intersections, one as you enter the neighborhood and one as you leave.

Working with this spirit is much the same as working with a large city spirit. If you live in a city with a population under 100,000, you will still have at least one or two neighborhood spirits to work with. You can view building a relationship with them both as a way to serve your home and community and as training should you end up in a larger city later in life.

The condition and general demeanor of the neighborhood can indicate the health of the spirit. Standard visual status markers don't truly tell you whether a neighborhood has a strong community; people with nice cars and houses can still contain strife, and those in rundown areas may still have close-knit communities that make for a happy neighborhood spirit. The only real external indicator of neighborhood health is neighbors that interact in positive ways. If people feel motivated to, for example, shovel their walks and their neighbors' during winter, there's likely a strong and nourished neighborhood spirit.

The ways you might work with a neighborhood spirit depends on your preferred path of urban magick and your own priorities. The balance and variety of spirits by neighborhood allow residents in each section to determine what way to adjust energy flavors that prevents the main city spirit itself from becoming too bland. Those on the Chaotic Path might well want to remove a little chaos energy from one neighborhood and move it to another. Those on the Civic Path might connect to a neighborhood spirit to help them find out what that neighborhood explicitly needs. Those on the Hearth and Home Path often just want to know how to keep the peace with their neighbors while living comfortably and quietly in a home they can afford.

Identifying Your Neighborhood Correspondences

When working with city energies, it can help to know what design movement has the most influence over your city and to look for neighborhoods from prior urban design movements. In the largest cities, you may see a mélange of City Beautiful, Modernism, Urban Renewal, and Green City architecture and landscape designs. Catalog your energy sources; spend a day taking mass transit across as many different routes of the city as you can. Create your own table of correspondences for the neighborhoods within your city and identify what workings you might want to perform in those areas.

The following chart serves as a template. Design your own based on considerations unique to where you live. These considerations can be as narrow as "this neighborhood is close to the river and this one is farthest from it" or as specific as "this neighborhood has a lot of No Turn on Red signs because of a fight in the 1970s between two members of city council." If the city built its industrial zone along the river, that stream likely has fire and air energy. The No Turn on Red sign neighborhoods might serve best for resolving disputes or for when you want to bind and confront cultural or personal pettiness. As you spend more time working with city energy, the possibilities and understanding of each neighborhood can expand.

This chart uses examples from San Francisco. Your own chart may expand to include historical incidents, plants common in that neighborhood, the era it was built, and even the way the historic population has shifted through that part of your city.

Neighborhood	Urban Design Influence	Element	Intent
Outer Richmond	Earthquake Proof City Efficient	Water and Earth	Healing, calm, introspection
The Mission	Garden City/ pre-Urban Renewal	Fire	Communication, sub-verting technology, friendship/socialization
The Castro	Garden City/ New Urbanism	Air	Communication, sub-verting technology, friendship/socialization
Visitacion Valley	City Efficient	Fire and Earth	Blending nature and city energy, releasing the old, banishing

You can get a sense for the personality of several different neighborhoods and notice where they transition by noticing what people board and unboard buses and trains. For those working the Priesthood Path, this helps identify places of trauma. For the Chaotic Path, it helps identify places that might bene-fit from minor disturbances. For those on the Hearth and Home Path, this can help you understand your own neighborhood bet-ter and lets you see how the city's direction of change might affect your own life. For all paths, taking the time to create this set of correspondences can assist in crafting all your own spells and workings. You may need to update this chart every few years to reflect city construction.

Urban Animals and Animal Spirits

Most people think of cities as human habitats. While humans may make most of the mammal population, they are hardly all of it. Other creatures, both from nature and from the astral dimensions, find ways to adapt to city structures. Most people have had the experience of a housemate leaving out food only to find lines of black ants (or, more disturbing, red ants) marching in and gathering whatever crumbs they may. Anyone who has ever taken out trash has at some point had to wrestle with the persistence and creativity of raccoons, or dealt with a squirrel, emboldened by the indulgence of too many humans, that turns hostile at the refusal of a potato chip. In Chicago, coyotes have started breeding and living in dense urban areas. The San Joaquin kit fox has found ways to live off human food discarded in parks and golf courses. Mountain lions in California have reduced their territorial range from 370 square miles to 25 square miles to allow for human population density, and more than one hiker in San Jose, California, has discovered the uncomfortable way they equal the size of African lions.[54]

These animals, especially those where adaptation is a trait of their species, often come to represent spiritual forces present within the city. It differs from city to city. In many municipalities, for example, racoons are somewhat cute and friendly symbols of foraging and survival. In San Francisco, they are a totem of violence and organized crime. The crows and ravens that flock together on Ocean Beach represent the death of an era in literal and figurative ways. The coyotes symbolize change and survival. The koala bears in Golden Gate park represent the stoner culture associated with the city since the late 1960s.

Dense environments draw more of all types of life, and this includes life in the invisible worlds. These invisible worlds may

---

54. Christine Dell'Amore, "How Wild Animals Are Hacking Life in the City," *National Geographic*, https://news.nationalgeographic.com/2016/04/160418-animals-urban-cities-wildlife-science-coyotes/.

arrive through physical means, or collective belief can conjure them. Neil Gaiman's *American Gods*—the stories of how different gods came to North America—to some degree resembles the real process. Even though the Sidhe and other members of fairy lore originated in Europe, the Americas have their own fairy folk, intermingling with the spirits of indigenous people. In places with high immigrant populations, the dragons of one continent live next door to the djinn of another. These meetings can produce strange events that become stories that join the pool of human metaphor. These interactions contribute to the pool of urban legend. The longer a city exists, the more these stories happen. We as a collective culture tend to bill them as ghost stories or odd occurrences, but sometimes our neighbors are just weird, human or not.

These new spirits and entities still interact with the indigenous spirits, and just like anyone dealing with neighbors, intercultural dustups may occur. Sensitive people can pick up on this, and when it happens in a city it can be hard to avoid. Even in the spiritual world, ecosystems and apex predators need something to maintain a balance. All things that come onto the land must interact with the land, and that dirt under your feet will always be the oldest thing around. The land—and the city spirit—may not always like these smaller spirits. It can create a sense of tension or discomfort where these smaller-scale spirits (in comparison to the city and land spirit) live.

Those on the Priest and Civic Paths may feel called to identify places where these conflicts happen and try to calm the energy. Those on other paths may sometimes encounter one of these spiritual conflicts in or near their homes. When this happens, there is a process to follow to go about establishing peace.

Ritual 8: Calm Conflicting Spirits

First, cleanse the space in whatever manner best suits your own practice, whether you prefer to smudge, burn candles, spray, or simply recite prayers for cleansing. When finished, set the rules. Stand in the center of your home or the place of disturbance and announce what spiritual behavior you allow and what you do not. It's good to add in certain jobs for spirits dwelling in your house—protection from intruders, bans on certain spirits, and so on. Once finished, ask the spirits to stop fighting in your space. Give them guidelines for handling their disputes.

If your perceptions allow you to see and hear spirits, two-way communication should be possible, even if it doesn't feel the same as a full conversation. For some, sitting and listening opens enough of a communication channel. If you need a little more help, using a pendulum or similar device can help you narrow down the issues between the contentious spirits. In some cases, the conflict between them exists for reasons beyond human conception. When this happens, give them somewhere else to go. I often choose vacant lots or abandoned buildings and set strict rules around how to handle humans and animals that might cross the fray. Sometimes I direct them to a river and ask the river spirit to take them to the ocean for rebirth. Not all spirits can resolve their disputes, but for the most part they do appreciate the opportunity to try.

Architecture and Building Spirits

Architects might be identified as the microcosm to the macrosmic work of urban planners. Structures focus on a single purpose, a single project, and sometimes the architects work on them in the context of their neighborhoods, but sometimes they focus on the buildings as experiences unto themselves, utterly separate from what neighbors them. Architecture itself has been pointed to as a possible solution to social issues, and as evidenced by everything from big box stores to segregated neighborhoods, architecture can also create and reinforce those very problems.

Like cities and neighborhoods, buildings can develop their own spirits in addition to those who move into the space when an opportunity presents itself. This happens often enough for it to recur in pop culture. Stephen King's short story "1408," John Bellairs's *The House with a Clock in Its Wall*, and Poppy Z. Brite's *Lost Souls* all tell tales of buildings and rooms that formed their own personalities. In the real world, many buildings do have a spirit designed to evoke emotional and behavioral responses that, over time, generate a building spirit. Usually the intention is benevolent—and the exceptions are well-exploited by television programs such as *American Horror Story*.

A strong empath need not do much to determine if a building has its own spirit. Most empaths can feel sentience while merely standing in front of a building. Psychics may have direct visions of the history of the place or "see" the image the building spirit projects of itself. If you practice magick without psychism, you can use a divination system and old-fashioned research to make an educated guess whether a building has its own spirit. If you use tarot cards, the Ten of Cups and Temperance may show up in answer to such an inquiry. If the Devil shows up, do a deeper reading, as this card can mean a lot of things, but generally indicates minimizing time there if possible. If the Tower card appears, get out, unless you came in to correct an energetic imbalance.

You can learn the history of a building by typing the address into Google or calling your library reference desk and asking how to find out more. Most large public buildings have a cornerstone bearing the year the building was built; this information can help pin down whether you have the right building when researching the address and the lot where it stands. Some cities raze and rebuild so often that the original buildings lie underneath what is now standing. Most of these spirits die when the building falls. Look at the history of the lot, not just the building: energetic twitches can come from phantom buildings as much as they can a haunted house.

Misbehaving building spirits seem to annoy city spirits the most. If you serve as a city priest, the city spirit may call you to adjust its horizontal and vertical alignment because of this general brattiness. The people in tall buildings can emit collective energies that conflict with those closer to the ground, creating unrest. The lucky can pinpoint an identifiable cause: a tragedy that happened while a high rise was under construction, a market shift that made housing more competitive, or a sports rivalry between cities that shifted from friendly to ugly. City priests, often enough, must invent ways to cleanse and heal these issues.

In cases where the building is affordable housing/tenement housing, you may need to surround the building with justice energy. If threatening incidents happen at street level, you may need to draw the energy of the higher floors of the building down to meet with the land spirit trapped beneath the concrete to even out the energy so that people crossing that area feel a sense of equity that reduces the need to act out in violence.

Iconic Buildings and Structures

Every city has unique buildings, works of public art, and memorials. The appearance of each of these gives a hint to the nature of the city spirit: what mattered to the original people who formed the city, what those of the present day wish to preserve, and sometimes whether the populace shares a sense of humor. The national monuments in Washington, DC, often reflect on aspects of the national spirit—which is also very much the city spirit.[55] The pieces revolve around history, war, painful evolution, and the intellectual movements that led to the Declaration of Independence and the Constitution of 1787. In many ways, these places are temples to secular concepts. The Abraham Lincoln Memorial speaks to the divisions of the country and the sacrifices necessary to keep it united; the Washington monument declares a single unified sense of direction … from a specific patriarchal perspective.

In cities that are state capitals, most capitol buildings resemble palaces.[56] Often the flow of traffic around these buildings is circular, creating the revolution of power in much the same ways as the princes of ancient cities designed the flow around their own palaces.[57] In county seats, the courthouses may have a palatial look or be moved to the edge of the city, where they have

---

55. "Monuments & Memorials," Destination DC, https://washington.org/topics/monuments-memorials.

56. Hunter Schwarz, "State Capitol Buildings That Don't Look Anything Like State Capitol Buildings, Ranked," *Washington Post*, https://www.washingtonpost.com/blogs/govbeat/wp/2014/11/20/state-capitol-buildings-that-dont-look-anything-like-state-capitol-buildings-ranked/.

57. Christopher Marcinoski, *The City That Never Was* (Princeton, NJ: Princeton Architectural Press, 2016), 64.

often had utilitarian appearances.[58] The design and location give you a sense of how strong the county/regional identity is in that area. Some people may identify more as part of their state, others as part of their city—the further to the edge of town a courthouse sits, the more liminal the collective city identity of that county seat.

Museums, libraries, and churches all also add significant identity flavor to a city. Often these buildings also have temple-style designs,[59] sometimes in ways that compete with nearby capitol/ government buildings for attention. For example, in St. Paul, Minnesota, the Cathedral of Saint Paul sits at the edge of the downtown grid atop a hill. Churchgoers can see the state capitol from the entrance to the church, just before the streets begin to circle the capitol. It is a visceral example of the pull between the temple at the edge of the city and the ancient prince-built palaces. The iconography within, on, and around these buildings can in some ways give a sort of structure to the city spirit. Minneapolis's famous *Spoonbridge and Cherry* is a psychic key to the city. A museum may offer a skyline perspective on city and history; a library is not just access to knowledge but access to the energy of that knowledge. These places are often simultaneously secular and sacred—a church with a labyrinth open to the public or a museum that also houses sacred objects from several other cultures. It is in this liminality that city spirit manifests, holding in that balance a sense of room for all.

Following are a few ways to work with public buildings and space:

---

58. Bruce Katz, Jennifer Bradley, *The Metropolitan Revolution: How Cities and Metros Are Fixing Our Broken Politics and Fragile Economy* (Washington, DC: Brookings Institution Press, 2013), 18–19.

59. Smith, *City*, 8–12.

Libraries	• Contact deities of spirits and wisdom • Seek out the history of your city • Use bibliomancy for personal questions and to converse with the city spirit
Museums	• Connect to sacred objects on display • Walk through different entryways; notice the emotional impact you experience moving from one doorway to another • Observe the way people interact; what about a work prompts a meditative or outreaching response?
Public Parks	• Connect with the genius loci; see how it gets on with the city spirit • Refresh and renew personal energy • Cultivate a spirit of play
Iconic Skyscrapers	• Easy visual when wanting to connect to the city spirit • Anchor, when doing other work, especially involving astral travel • Transmitter using the roof of the building to send an idea or energy out over the city
Theaters	• Connect to specific pantheons; city-to-city communication • Encourage visions and improve visualization • Tap into collective consciousness of the city

Churches	• Connect to source and mystery energy • Take sanctuary from more volatile energies • Seek out saints and similar members of city pantheons for conversation
Schools/ Universities/ Colleges	• Connect to wisdom entities • City-within-a-city energy if you need to obscure larger work

The Spirits a City Attracts

Cities with governments that take care to maintain clean air, abundant greenery, and well-fed creatives tend to attract adaptive nature spirits. Often these deva and pixie energies operate communally, moving into parks and cultivated gardens. These beings recognize the benefits of sustaining human community as symbiosis. It's good to take an attitude of cultivation with them, knowing that those who move into human cities see us as what *they* cultivate and care for.

If you want to work with these symbiotic nature spirits, get a houseplant. Often pixie-type spirits prefer flowering plants, but any plant will do. In denser cities they especially appreciate plants that put out lots of oxygen, such as ferns, peace lilies, or chrysanthemums. Set the plant in your home where it gets the amount of light it prefers and put a few crystals in the soil. These spirits tend to respond well to iridescent and pastel-hued stones such as moonstone or watermelon tourmaline.[60] A deva will let you know it's there in its own way.

---

60. "Attract the Fairies with Our 3 Must-Have Crystals!" *Soul & Spirit Magazine,* http://www.soulandspiritmagazine.com/attract-fairies-3-must-crystals/.

Ghosts

The spirits of the dead are everywhere, and now that ancestor veneration has returned to the Western world, we see more of them than ever before. If you live in a large city, you automatically increase your odds of a ghostly encounter that you don't actively seek out. Because of this, nearly all major cities now offer some variation of a ghost tour. Ghosts are common, and their stories are dense.

While things that go bump in the night—or day—may not necessarily be ghosts (and might be fae, land spirits, demons, your neighbor on the way to the toilet, or your cat), when we hear/see unearthly phenomena our human-centered minds tend to guess first that the noises come from either living humans, plumbing, or disembodied humans. Usually looking and listening can rule out a mechanical or living cause. Determining whether you have a ghost, and whether you need to do anything about the ghost, is a little trickier.

We don't fully know how ghosts happen. Many people still disbelieve that they exist at all. The common wisdom is that ghosts stay on the Earth plane to complete unfinished business. Most I encounter do stay around to care for family and friends, or they're just annoyed that they're dead and refuse to leave despite the considerable effort it can take to stay here. Most ghosts manage to stick around through food offerings, or by draining energy from light bulbs and similar electrical devices. Ghosts are hell on the electric bill. The exception to this rule is people who died while undergoing a significant trauma. The trauma, especially if it affected many people, contains enough emotional energy to sustain ghosts for decades.

Some ghost hunters have reported that some spirits expressed other causes for hanging around, including fear of the afterlife, atheism on the part of the ghost, stubbornness, or bad priorities. What this suggests is that ghosts are not the helpless victims of their own stories, as is often presumed, and that death still comes with choices. Those choices can include selecting your apartment to hang out in … rent-free.

There is a second common opinion that violent ghosts—particularly poltergeists—usually originate in living energy.[61] This is now more complicated than in the past because of the availability of how-to information about spellcasting and the occult on the internet. Before the internet, poltergeist energy often came from an adolescent or adult under constant physical and emotional duress. All too often the activity manifested as a sideways outburst from sexual and physical abuse. In modern day, people get upset with each other and often look online for ways to attack those who offended them. Psychic attack and hiring out demons for psychic attack has become all too common. Many of these attacks manifest in ways that look exactly like poltergeist activity. Sometimes a spirit really is hired to stir trouble. This creates a cycle where a household removes one poltergeist only to have another show up, and the inhabitants end up convinced their house is cursed. It is, but not because of ghosts—because of living people who keep lobbing them.

If you determine you have a ghost and that the ghost's behavior is unacceptable, the following house preparation and ritual can help. This can also cover most random spiritual entities. In the case of psychic attack, you may need to seek out a psychic, demonologist, or theistic Satanist to help settle the matter. If your

---

61. John Sandiopoulis, "What Is the Source of Poltergeist Activity?" https://www
    .johnsanidopoulos.com/2011/05/what-is-source-of-poltergeist-activity
    .html.

house does not settle down after this working, find someone who practices divination that has a solid community reputation to determine what is really happening.

Ritual 9: Ghost Banishment

In this case, a banishment differs from an exorcism. In an exorcism, you release the spirit to the plane of existence it belongs on. It often requires the cooperation, capitulation, or overpowering of the spirit. In a banishment, you essentially say, "You don't have to go home, but you can't stay here." If you can't find the items listed here in your local supermarket or occult shop, check at halal and East Indian groceries. Most major cities have stores specifically to serve these communities.

You will need

- A broom
- Sea salt
- Witches' black salt
- Camphor chips or cotton balls with a few drops of the essential oil on them (If you have pets, skip this.)
- Sage smudge or spray
- A white candle, seven-day glass preferably
- Incense, or if you have smoke allergies, the herbs thyme, rosemary, and lemon peel in a pot of boiling water
- A spray bottle filled with lemon juice, apple cider vinegar, and garlic juice

- Chalk or cascarilla
- An address, picture, or recommendation for where the ghosts might go

First, declutter your home as much as you can. You don't necessarily need to do a deep clean (although it helps), but clear enough of a path that you won't injure yourself. Starting at the back of your house, walk home with the broom. Ritually sweep out the house, touching every corner and opening every door including cupboards and refrigerator doors. As you sweep it out, announce "Out! Go to (the place you decide they need to go)." Next, walk through your home and drop a small chip of camphor or the cotton ball in every corner. If you have pets, skip the camphor. Instead, mark any protection symbol you like in those corners with the chalk. Next, smudge or spray your house while chanting a prayer, intoning sounds, or enjoying music that makes you want to dance.

After you have done the perambulations through your home, take the cascarilla or chalk and draw a line around the frame of every door and window in the house. You may also wish to do this on all TV sets, phones, electrical outlets, and computer monitors. The cascarilla is a line ghosts can't cross. It is made from powdered eggshell, so it shouldn't stain or do lasting damage to your walls. Across all doorways and windowsills, sprinkle just a pinch of black salt and sea salt. While certain TV shows always show long lines across the window sills, in real life it only takes a little bit.

Set the candle in a bowl of water on your stovetop or in the place that members of the household spend the most communal time. Light the candle and pray your house remains protected and ghost-free. You may also at this time request that certain spirits move into your house for protective purposes. If you do this, announce your rules and be mindful that many spirits love to exploit a good loophole! Allow the candle to burn down completely so that its energy intertwines with the energy of your home.

Over the next few days, spray your walls, door handles, and fixtures with the vinegar mix and wipe them down. This cleans while also building up a steady "anti-ghost" and general clearing energy. It has the added benefit of serving as a decent all-purpose cleaner.

While we may think of ghosts as indoor spirits or even as beings tied to one place, plenty also haunt the streets. Many stories from my clients who hire me for clearings begin with, "After I went to this emotionally charged event…" People attend rallies, or visit memorials, or go to a bar, only to have something follow or even ride them home. City ghosts are often quite happy to blend in with the citizenry; you may notice an oddly dressed person in passing on the sidewalk as a chill rolls through you. And every so often, one of them wants a change of scenery and uses someone with strong sensitivities to do it.

The best way to deal with something following you home is to take steps to prevent it from doing so. Simple shielding can hinder spirit hitchhiking because some spirits simply ride the bubble you project to their next destination. Carrying camphor keeps most astral pests away.

Most spirits can't cross running water or lines of cascarilla. Rubbing some cascarilla chalk inside the bottom of your shoes sends a message that wherever you go, the spirits can't cross your line. If you live in a city near a river, crossing a bridge on your way home may shake off all but the most persistent of entities. You may enjoy researching this; there is lore on ghost management going far back into recorded history.

Some Final Thoughts on Spirit Work in the City

Magicians, especially early in their practice, often get reminders of the ripple effect, where one magickal action sets forth a series of actions. Studying what works and what fails in urban design and city planning is a good object lesson in how far ripples can reach. In both urban design and magick, at some point you must let go … and take responsibility for all the possible consequences.

There are those who see this rippling as reason not to practice magick at all. Even without magickal intent, our most trivial acts set off chain reactions, so many and some so minute that they are simply beyond the range of our consciousness even at its most expanded. To own the ripples and direct them is simply to surrender to the reality that if you're going to make ripples anyway, you might as well consciously pick a few of them. Spirits can tell you what happens with your ripples first, making it well worth the time to cultivate those relationships.

The step beyond meeting your city spirit is meeting the individual spirits and ancestors tied to your city. These individual beings, when well propitiated, can become guides that lead you to hidden energetic treasures, keep you out of danger, and yes, some do help you avoid the occasional traffic jam. It is most likely that those on the Priesthood or Civic Path will need to engage with these spirits—these are the beings that point out areas that need repair or where the literal or metaphorical bodies are buried.

If you try to learn more of your city's history, you will also turn up both ancestors to the city and city spirits borne of folk legend. Some of these spirits already have their rituals—such as those in New Orleans that circle Marie Laveau's tomb and leave a chalk X—or they may want you to develop some. In cities borne of more formal cultures, the spirits and city ancestors tend to want more ceremony; in cities with more casual cultures, ceremony may even offend some of them. (They all, however, appreciate good manners and sincere offerings; just find out if they *want* you to light a candle and perform that dance.) If you actively work with city spirits and run into a social crisis on some level, you may need to work with multiple city spirits at the same time, or anchor relationships by performing rituals on anniversaries and celebrations significant to the city. While many of these may parallel the Pagan practice of honoring the seasons, often the core of them is about human invention and survival, overcoming the challenges of nature, or celebrating new freedoms. It is well-nigh impossible to give an exhaustive list of such events. The "[slot spirit here]" approach to ritual is almost guaranteed to offend spirits and lead to disaster.

If you feel a call to perform a city holiday working and need to find the right spirits, you can put out a call for the right ones to show up.

Rather than offering a generic ritual for your use, following is a list of common holidays and historic events. Every major city has some version of these stories, along with a few urban legends that also might hint at the presence of city-connected spirits.

Holiday/Event	Examples
Independence Day	July 4 (USA)
	September 16 (Mexico)
	Australia (January 26)
Labor Celebrations	Labor Day
	Cinco de Mayo
Veteran Celebrations	Memorial Day
	Veterans Day
Harvest Festivals	Harvest Home
	Thanksgiving
	Oktoberfest
Ethnic/National	Saint Patrick's Day
Specific celebrations	Chinese New Year
	Constitution Days for various countries
Agricultural	Garlic festival
Festivals	Tomato festival
	Tulip festival
Beginning/End of	
School Terms	
Popular Religious	Christmas
Holidays	Dia de los Muertos
	All Saint's Day
	Easter
	Mardi Gras
Music, Art and	Fringe Festival
Theater Festivals	Sundance
	Art fairs
	Art and craft fair seasons

City spirit work can mean working with city spirits, plural. For most of us, what we can handle on a spiritual level comes to us as we can handle it. This remains as true in city work as it does in initiatory traditions. As your relationship with your city grows, your pool of spirits and allies grows as well. Make sure you take care of it then, and in turn they will take care of you.

NINE
LIFE IN THE CITY

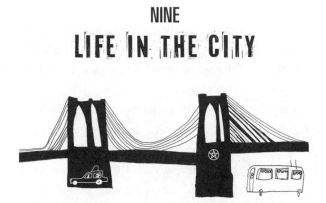

Think of your home as a sacred space that reflects your inner self. As the poet Kahlil Gibran wrote: "Your daily life is your temple and your religion. When you enter into it, take with you your all."[62] In other words, when you enter, your home's condition shows the inside of your mind and heart. When you enter, it may appear cluttered, bland, neat, or minimalist. The décor may have bright colors or muted shades. Ultimately, your dwelling reflects your values, what matters to you most when all your duties to the outside world are done, and it sets the tone for your emotional state on a daily basis. Having a well-managed home within a large city gives you a strong place of power in the midst of a large body of communal power. When you make your home in a city, you

---

62. Kahlil Gibran, Brainyquote, https://www.brainyquote.com/quotes/khalil _gibran_386479.

are also creating a space of stillness for yourself within constant motion.

What you do in your home can affect the city spirit, your neighborhood spirit, and your immediate neighbors. For example, if you have a stubborn ghost in your house and you exorcise it without giving it a specific destination, it's going to haunt the least resistant place nearby. It could land on your neighbors, the street outside your house, or even a local park.

For those who share homes with roommates and/or parents, managing this energy can present a challenge. First, you have less privacy to practice spiritual workings. Second, allowing your energy to interact cooperatively with those in your living space takes continuous effort and having more people around can increase the difficulty of that. Third, just as you risk catching a cold when exposed to germs while taking public transportation, you can also catch small unwanted metaphysical visitors—sometimes despite the best quality magickal shielding. Just as the world now has antibiotic-resistant bacteria, it now has shield-resistant astral parasites.

Meanwhile, neighbors have their own energetic happenings, and sometimes when they move energies in and out of their homes it also runs into your energy and boundaries. While psychic attacks happen more than they once did, much of this energetic bumping is the same as the neighbor that plays music too loud: most of the time it's not malicious, someone just forgot to consider who else their actions might affect.

Use of Space on Magickal and Practical Levels

Your entire home can serve magickal purposes. Just as each room in ancient temples served a purpose, the entire space of your home can draw energy into your home or project a desire outward into the city. If you plan to use your home this way, it is important that the interior have fortified protections both on a practical level (smoke detectors and quality locks) and on a magickal level (wards, room purifiers, and deactivated mirrors.)[63] The larger the population of the city, the more wards—practical and magickal—you need.

Routinely rearranging your furniture—and regularly changing that plan—can improve your daily life in all its aspects. Think about how you really live your life in that space. Make a list: things you must do and things you should do. On the things you should do, also write down what stops you from doing them daily. Strike through anything self-judging, like "I'm lazy" or "I am bad at it." (Everyone is bad at everything for a little while.) Now look at the more practical reasons: You don't exercise in the morning because you don't have floor space, or you can't meditate because the clutter distracts you. Pick one of these "shoulds" and plan your space around fixing the issue.

Revising your home may take months, so best to plan one room, or even only one corner, at a time. For those of you with only one room to yourselves, this should be relatively simple. For those with larger spaces, it may take a few months to clear out the excess junk—and then you can enjoy all the goodies a clean home energy flow can bring.

Most homes, like most cities, are constructed on grids and/ or around a central space. Rooms usually fall into squares and rectangles. In rare cases, a triangular shape may work its way into a dwelling space. The box equates with containment. Treat

---

63. You can deactivate a mirror, rendering it useless as a spiritual portal, by washing it with ammonia and then drawing on it with graphite.

each room as a container for the specific energy and overarching mood you want it to hold. Much of this concept of magick is rooted in an understanding of Platonic solids—you can start with your understanding of how this works with your own home and furniture and over time extend to buildings and sculptures you encounter in the city. The chart that follows gives a few correspondences you can use when deciding how to configure your furniture to tap into certain energies and purposes.

Platonic Solid	Magick Association
Triangles (tetrahedron, octahedron, icosaheldron)	Attacking, trapping, or banishing
Squares (hexahedron, cube)	Containment; boxing something in, energy storage
Pentagons	Incorporating five elements, bringing nature energy indoors
Hexagons	Extreme protection, combining offensive and defensive methods; block off most interdimensional intrusions
Circles	Storage for later; energy batteries and prosperity work

You can rearrange your furniture into these geometric configurations in order to create containment or direction for a given purpose. If you do not have enough furniture to rearrange, you can post art inspired by these geometric concepts to produce similar results.

Once you declutter enough, you can use your home grid to direct an energy current through your home, making the energy feed your work continuously. Necessary actions like laundry and housecleaning can raise energy toward your goals—all that elbow grease can feed into the shapes you set up for containment. Treat your home as sanctuary and battery; this can ease all other aspects and experiences of city life.

A common mistake of people first practicing shields or casting circles is that they limit the spread of their energy to the physical space they see. The circles stop at the walls. Their shields stop at the floor. But energy is not limited by walls; it can push through solid objects. It does not have the same atomic density as that chair or that table. You can cast a circle that pushes through the walls or create a shield that pushes into the ground underneath you. If your neighbors below you have a fight, you are going to hear it, and you may even feel that oppressive after-fight energy in your own space. Adding wards and shields that push through the walls and floors and stop just inside of your neighbors' ceiling (for example) can blunt that intrusive energy without intruding on their space.

Magickal Thinking for City Traffic

Think back to high school physics classes. Do you remember the difference between kinetic energy and potential energy?[64] You may even recall using the car stopped or in motion as an example of potential (unused) energy and kinetic (in motion) energy. Most short-commute magick follows these rules. It also travels most easily on straight lines, can be affected negatively or positively by inertia, and can (once in a great while) explode.

---

64. "Kinetic and Potential Energy—Difference and Comparison," Diffen, http:// www.diffen.com/difference/Kinetic_Energy_vs_Potential_Energy.

Cities' most visible—and arguably dirtiest—pool of energy comes from traffic. Many magick workers tend to look at the pollution generated by typical traffic and deem it entirely anti-magickal. While they're absolutely correct to express concern about the pollution, dismissing the opportunity to leverage that energy seems like a significant oversight. Any mass transit center, with a well-set and well-maintained intention, can serve as a living prayer wheel. The larger the city, the thicker the traffic, the larger the pull of kinetic energy.

The Energy of Roads and Highways (Curves)

Street layout affects energy flow. When you're trying to accomplish a small change, like a stoplight change, or a big change, like a rolling mood shift, you usually need straight lines. A curving road, a stoplight with multiple timers, or a hard turn left or right can break up energy you try to build.

Despite the difficulty of making a spell continue to work once you have to turn left to get to that parking lot on Maple, you can use your car to do short-term works. Just assume that the energy releases once you make that turn or hit that pothole. Despite the imperfection of roadways for magickal work from beginning to end of a trip (unless you can only travel in straight lines) you can still work some magick while driving. While perhaps not as satisfying, traffic jams do respond to a good energetic nudge. For instance, when dealing with a traffic backup on the curve of a road—especially during Mercury Retrograde—I like to imagine the road forming a rainbow path, the prism gently breaking up the traffic. Sometimes it does lessen a traffic jam (as does giving the driver in front of you plenty of room). Other times it relieves the mental pressure of being in a traffic jam, depending on what caused it.

Sensitive drivers may notice rolling energy patches. They may drive through a spot and feel a chill or a vibration. Do not stop to explore this unless spirit explicitly calls you to. If spirit does call, make sure you take backup.

Crossroads

The importance of crossroads goes far back into human history, when people first began building roads and traveling for trade.[65] In modern times, we think of crossroads as four-way intersections. The ancient Greeks considered any traffic passing a doorway as a crossroad[66] and the Celts considered the shore of the ocean a crossroad.[67] American folklore in the nineteenth and twentieth centuries had many tales of people calling the devil at the crossroads and trading their souls for a deep-seated desire.[68] "At a crossroads" now means choosing between desire and duty. To be at a crossroads is to have enormous power even when you feel the most powerless.

While country crossroads get the attention in folklore, all crossroads hold power sufficient for magickal work. A crossroad can be a major, high-traffic intersection or it can simply be a cross street. You can make a crossroads negotiation at any intersection, even at a four-way stop at the exit of a cul-de-sac.

---

65. "Crossroad," The Mystica, https://www.themystica.com/mystica/articles/c /crossroad.html.

66. Cara Schulz, Paganicon lecture, March 2011.

67. Shauna Aura Knight, Pantheacon, January 2015, (personal conversation).

68. "Blog Post 127—Summoning Devils," *New World Witchery,* NewWorldWitchery .com, 2011.

Spell 4: Planting Pennies at the Crossroads

Meditate on something good you wish to bring your entire neighborhood. Once you decide what that is, pick an intersection and four pennies, preferably minted on a leap year. Imagine the pennies forming a grid between themselves, as though each one transmitted energy to the other pennies in the batch. You may also want to anoint the pennies with mint oil, as mint brings about qualities of cleansing, protection, and prosperity. Plant one penny at each of the four corners of the intersection, preferably near streetlamps or at the base of telephone poles. State out loud what you wish the penny to do and remind it of the location of the other pennies. Leave a little water and a dime (also from a leap year) for the crossroads spirits as a thanks for their indulgence. When finished, go home without looking behind you. Keep an eye out for any differences in behavior from your neighbors. You may need to go out once a year or so and replant the pennies if you wish to maintain the spell.

Magick by Mass Transit

In this case, the frame is planetary energy. Even magicians that don't subscribe to astrology sometimes draw on the planets as a means of cataloging spell intentions or as a way to imagine a source of energy to feed and regulate their workings. In matters of communication and travel, most imagine the planet Mercury in its fast-spinning orbit as the place from which to take their needs for movement and speed.

While Mercury rules all transit, that planetary energy brought to earth has to combine in some way with the chosen vessel. For instance, a bus will almost definitely have a different, less targeted effect than a car, just because it carries a dense population. Before using the motion of any vehicle in a spell, spend time reflecting on the nature of each vehicle and its exposure, perhaps even developing your own magickal correspondence chart to explore the best magickal applications for each vehicle. Draw on what you know about analyzing the elemental makeup of different objects.

For example, if you want to perform a banishing on a large scale, you will need something that gathers energy, stops, and releases that energy. While not always necessary, the best practice in banishing is to call in a desired energy to replace the energy you don't want. A bus picks up speed and then stops, opens its door, releases passengers, picks up new ones, and moves on. Since in most banishings you also need to replace the energy you banish with fresh positive energy, a bus may be the perfect instrument. It picks up fresh energy every time someone climbs aboard.

The Magick City Bus

For some reason, buses tend to form their own universe. The mix of people combined with the massive size makes it a complex resource for applying energy. Buses aren't smooth, fast rides like cars and trains are, nor do they have the full commitment required to ride a ferry. (You can get off a bus before it gets to your destination.) They start and stop. They jerk. They rattle. People end up packed together tightly. They are, at rush hour, the experience of dense, uncomfortable flow.

On top of this, the population density inherent in any mass transit—but especially the bus—makes it necessary to do more personal protection than you need in other modes of transportation. When you travel by car, you mainly protect yourself from accidents and possibly carjacking. When you travel by bus, you need to protect yourself from the hazards of other passengers. Even with all these drawbacks, the bus can do one thing quite well: pick up energy that needs to shatter.

Spell 5: Bus Stop Banishing

In most cities, the bus may travel two blocks, or four, then it stops, and the door opens, and it closes. This means that momentum builds for a minute—and then abruptly halts. This happens over and over as the bus runs its route. This makes it the perfect vehicle for any situation where you want to disrupt momentum.

To perform this banishing, it helps if you can sit down on the bus the first few times you practice. As you gain more skill in shifting focus, you might do this standing. Choose what you want to banish, whether a person, a habit, or an entity. Assign it a simple image, fragrance, or texture that you can hold easily in your mind. For instance, you might imagine the silhouette of a crow, a simple triangle, or the scent of lemons. Keep this assignment held in your mind as you shift into energy work with the bus.

While most magickal manuals advise you to ground and center, in moving vehicles, the order of center and ground works a little bit better. Find your center, and then ground by extending awareness of the feeling of gravity on your body, especially where you feel yourself pulled into your seat or into the floor. From your center, imagine tendrils of energy attaching to each wheel of the bus.

As the wheels turn, each tendril gathers force. When the bus brakes or stops, gather the force of those sudden movements and shift your focus to the opening and closing door. Imagine a tendril gently collecting gas from the atmosphere above and below the cabin of the bus. This is the ambient energy of the other passengers.

Choose a stop with an evocative name, such as 13th Street or Liberty Avenue (if your city has such street names). When the bus stops there, gather all the tendrils together into the image/symbol of the thing you want to banish. Imagine giving it a giant push out the bus door, through the outside, through an imaginary door, into outer space. As the bus door closes, it cuts off the connection it had to you. Immediately after the moment of release, take a deep breath and muster how you want to feel when you experience the energy that replaces it. As you exit the bus, mentally ask that the bus cut off any residual energy to the old thing you might have missed. With each footstep to your destination gather up fresh energy to renew yourself.

Train of Mystery

Trains cover longer distances than buses, often underneath major city corridors. They also tend to cost more to ride and are often preferred by those who stigmatize riding the bus. Trains are more energy-efficient than buses (usually) and are the trendy commute for people with more money. Yet buses came about because of the limitations of trains. Trains must stay on a rail. A bus can go off-track and still function.

The limitations of trains are what make them magickally interesting. Trains must follow a specific path every day that they cannot deviate from. Its travel path consists of straight lines, allowing for a larger undisrupted build of energy. They often pass through shadowy tunnels that few can visit after they are built; yet somehow, someone always gets into those spaces and makes cave art even in the face of an oncoming train.

Commuter rails capture shadows of the city, literally and figuratively. Because it's the more acceptable method of mass transit for a city's wealthier denizens, the dichotomy between them and those of lower income on the train becomes starkly visible. They go underneath the streets—literally speeding through seedy undergrounds. The underworld qualities alone can make a magician's head spin.

Exercise 17: The Shadow of the Train

Trains are especially good for two types of shadow work: the inner work of the dark self, and wider shadow work. When you are on a train, who do you look at and think, "This person doesn't belong here," or "I wish this person would leave?" Ask yourself why. If it is because you have a reaction of disgust to a certain person, ask yourself about that several times as well. The smell? The style of clothing? What else? Now ask yourself, "Is this person harmful to me in any way? Is this person in any way dangerous?" If the answer is no, revisit your disgust and keep asking yourself questions. Sharing space with others can show us ourselves if we simply observe our thoughts critically. Once you complete this work, look at these people and ask yourself what role they take with your city and

with your city spirit. Do not try to concoct a label; instead,
let the answer come to you.

Meeting the Ferryman

Ferries bring their riders the simultaneous experience of stillness
and motion. You move steadily toward your destination but there is
no option to end the experience until the ferry arrives. There is no
pulling over or getting off at an earlier stop. It also brings together
two elements rarely combined: air and water. For those who practice magick with elements, the median between water and air is a
perfect space to work magick for situations where persistent mis-
understandings occur. Combining air—the power of communication—with water—the power of emotional depth—and anchoring
it to earth, in the form of the metals on both the boat and the cars
it carries, can bring to surface hidden feelings and address them in
a way that keeps a situation afloat.

Spell 6: The Ferry Bottle

This spell brings peace to a frustrating situation. Carry
an empty bottle with a cap onto the ferry. While glass is
ideal, sometimes it isn't allowed, so a plastic bottle—even
a used water bottle—is acceptable. Go to the deck of the
boat and uncap the bottle. Ask that the water particles
and the air particles come together, as you concentrate
on the way your feet feel connected to the boat. Say,
"Meet each other here." Talk into the bottle, telling about
the situation and what feelings you would like both sides
to have when all is finished—for the greatest good of all.
Save the bottle. When you get to your home or office,
open the bottle in a place where people from both sides

of the conflict will be. You may want to use the bottle as a vase for a flower, particularly one that is in bud and about to open.

There are many ways to get around a city, more than can fit here. You may find yourself on a motorboat taxi, wishing to talk to some fish. You might find biking connects you to nature and city or that a rickshaw comes in handy with attempting kairomantic divination. You can even work magick using the wheels as prayer wheels that generate your purpose wherever you go.

If you employ transit magick, whatever method you use, please use caution. Mass transit involves shared spaces—your actions always affect other people (especially people sitting near you) as you move from one place to another. Make an effort to learn the transit etiquette of your locale and pay attention to the people around you for your own safety and theirs. Life in a city can get stressful, especially as the psychic and physical noise comes at you. But this noise consists of the energy that you can leverage to achieve your personal goals. Make the most of your daily activities, no matter how simple, and build up that battery of energy you may draw from later. Whether you use it to fortify your defenses and peace or bring about some major change in your city, you will have tapped into a beautiful subversion of all the frustrating things in a city and make them into something that empowers.

TEN
SPELLS FOR URBAN LIVING

Most of these spells address situations that happen more frequently in major cities than other places, or that use material common to cities as symbolic anchors. On the one hand, city life demands enduring congested traffic, competitive housing, inappropriate strangers, and the possibility of getting lost even in a place you have lived for years. These inconveniences are balanced by the benefits of city life: the chance to find treasures unknown and to stumble upon a magickal evening by exploring a little out of your territory is likely to happen in a major city. All your chances of grabbing the benefits of city life increase when you consciously work with the spirit and rhythm.

Urban Spellcasting Foundations

The following spells delineate the baseline of any urban magick worker: safety, peace, and intuitive awareness of space. Since much of this book looks more into Priesthood and Civic work, most of spells in this chapter aim to enhance working with city spirit at a personal level. This means considering the common pitfalls of city living: crowding, crime, and noise. Using energy to handle each of these issues establishes the strong boundaries needed for any other type of magick.

If you want to make city spirit work a central magickal practice, develop an approach that adapts easily indoors and outdoors. While some of these spells influence those who live near you, they are not spells on people per se. Most spells emit a mood into the environment, something likely to affect people's mirror neurons and encourage (but not guarantee) them to fall in line with that energy. The more peaceful the energy promoted, the less chance of unintended consequences.

Ritual 10: Divine the Best Places to Work Magick

Alas, Atlas Obscura has no category named "Good places to light a candle, NOT set a fire, and NOT get caught." You are instead left with the old-fashioned option of using a map, a pendulum, and any local knowledge you might have or that you can get.

You will need:

- A map of the city, preferably in book atlas form
- A pendulum
- A list of clear criteria for your search

While this divination can work successfully with electronic tablets, screensavers and locks can make map dowsing with these devices a hassle. At the same time, almanacs and roadside maps are becoming much less common in the face of GPS. Do what works for you—whether it's paper or plastic.

After you calibrate your pendulum (saying hello, asking it to show you yes or no, and asking it to show you how it answers "where"), hold it over the map and ask your question. Often the way you phrase the question makes the most difference in the quality of answer you receive. "Where is the best place to bury my witch's bottle?" might be in a cemetery… with a lot of cameras installed to prevent vandalism. So, you might want to ask, "Where is the safest place to bury my witch's bottle?" You may need to hold the pendulum over a few different neighborhoods and notice stronger or weaker responses to similar questions.

This method can also open a path for the city spirit to communicate with you. The pendulum may guide you to neighborhoods or parks that need some care or to locations in need of spiritual cleansing.

Establish Communication with the Spirit

City spirit work, like any spirit work, over time aligns communications and relationships between the physical world and the unseen one. The divination method above allows the city spirit to show you where it needs you to go. Even the most psychic and tuned-in people often struggle with what can feel like a terrible phone connection. My preferred method for sparking a clear two-way conversation uses Kairomancy. In this divination method, you put forward a question and then walk through a crowded place, listening for conversation snippets. Ask the city spirit "What do you need?" Walk for about six blocks. By then you will have received your answer.

Dial Down the Signal

Empaths and other sensitives often struggle with the high noise-to-signal ratio in cities. Since wearing a tinfoil hat can work but comes with social consequences, the following practices can help you tone down the flow of information:

1. Wear a hat or scarf.

2. Wear any of the following stones: obsidian, tourmaline, citrine, and amber.

3. Add salt and a few drops of lemongrass oil to your shampoo or to a hairbrush. Brush your hair with it twice a day.

4. Drink teas from the following herbs: holy basil, yerba matte, or spearmint. You may also want to take a class of herbs labeled nervines that support the nervous system and reduce overall mental and physical stress.

Hearth and Home Magick for the City

The earliest magick involved protecting home and crops. City magick only extends that. The spells remain the same but must raise the level of power to match the surrounding energy. If you practice protections, you need slightly more protections than you might in a small town. If you need abundance, you need a little more drawing power to get past signals competing for attention. Folk/low magick has a host of power amplifiers in the form of botanicals and traditional charms. You can also take small charms to the city spirit and ask it to calibrate your work.

The following list of amplifiers are easily obtained from witchy shops, crystal shops, and herbal suppliers. Some you may even find in your local grocery store.

Magickal Amplifiers

- Dragon's blood
- Benzoin
- Myrrh
- Alum crystal
- Peppers (all kinds)
- Rare earth magnets
- Quartz crystals
- Gold-colored coins, any nation, any denomination

In addition to these baseline amplifiers, the city spirit itself may direct you to certain places where ordinary, common-to-your-city objects may amplify your work or better align it. Who better than the city spirit itself to show you where to get what you need?

Spell 7: To Settle a Household or Neighborhood Disturbance

Neighbors can fight like siblings, often acting out the worst of their childhoods on each other. If you're lucky, you're just the neighbor that observes the fight—but we all have healing to do, and because of that, you just might be that neighbor and not realize it. You can contain and banish the negativity for the sake of everyone, although if there are unresolved issues in the home, you may need to repeat this spell daily.

You will need:
- Chalk or cascarilla
- A shared wall, sidewalk, or pathway to draw on, all the better if your neighbors walk over it

On the shared wall or the ground, draw a square with a circle within it. In the center of the circle, draw a simple flower with seven petals. Concentrate on the square pulling the negative energy into the circle, and the circle spinning that energy into the flower that then emits peace back. You may wish to add colors or speak prayers to deities or to the city spirit itself to assist in promoting and transmitting this peace.

Spell 8: Eviction Prevention

Major cities are prone to economic waves that can make it hard to keep a home. Some cities address these insecurities through rent control, or tenants themselves buy their apartment building and make them cooperative living situations. These protections can't help in the face of major family illness, job instability, or pay cuts. While working prosperity magick and living frugally can offset some loss, when a big shift happens to a city, even the best-prepared sometimes struggle with the basics of food and shelter as the financial wave comes crashing through.

In American conjure, driving a railroad spike into the ground of the property you want to keep symbolizes putting down stakes. This method may not work as well in an apartment. You may be able to put the spike in a potted plant, and if that works, great! Barring that as an option, this spell is a smaller variation of the railroad spike spell.

You will need:

- Four iron nails
- Olive oil
- Garlic
- Iodized salt
- A pinch of dirt or pebbles from your apartment building
- Wire or twine
- A wire cutter
- Wall hanging hooks

Place a wall hanging hook over your bed and on the front or back of the entrance door of your apartment. Fill a bowl with about ½ cup of olive oil and add the garlic (doesn't matter if it's peeled), the salt, and the pinch of dirt. Soak the nails in this mixture overnight, setting your intention that they absorb as much earth-grounding protection energy as possible. The next day, remove the nails from the oil and wipe dry. You can bottle the remaining oil and save it for other home protection workings.

Take two of the nails and form a cross. Bind these together with the twine or wire. Leave a loop on the wire so that it can hang easily from the hook. Hang one on your front door hook and one over your bed. The iron creates a grounding protection and the dirt or pebbles from the property gives it a geographic point where the energy can anchor. The cross itself represents protection from all four directions.

Continue to Prosper in Cities

The twenty-first-century upsurge in technological gentrification has created an additional urban issue that increases homelessness. Most cities affected by technology booms are single or limited industry towns, and this includes major cities that affect finances throughout the global economy. Both high interest and obsolescence in tech products can lead to mass displacement and city disruption that can cause rippling job loss and evictions. Examples of cities in the United States with economies that depend on single industries include New York (finance); San Jose, San Francisco, and Austin, Texas (technology); and Detroit (cars). These places, called "monotowns" by economists, are also a huge part of the Chinese urban boom and have already led to increased economic insecurity throughout Russia.

Because we are human, urban magicians can only focus on so many issues at a time. Often the town's economy gets overlooked in the trivia of daily survival. It makes sense that many people might take a "Let's cross that bridge when we come to it" stance on limited economic opportunity in their own city. There is one reason to address this concern from a magickal standpoint. Out of all the issues most likely to affect you personally while living in a city, it's this one. If it does affect you, you might end up scrambling for a place to live—or worse.

The issue of cities being sustained by one industry only is a serious concern to anyone wanting to see everyone have an opportunity to thrive. Using the United States as an example (because I live here): for the first time in US history, more of the population is urban than rural. As of 2015, the US had 2.1 million farms—97 percent of them were family owned, but only 3 percent of farms provided 64 percent of vegetable sales and 66 percent of dairy sales in major supermarkets.[69] Food distribution remains the challenge.[70] Yet, according to Census reports as recent as 2010, more than 80 percent of the US population lives in cities with populations of 50,000 or more.[71] In the United States overall, 49 million people struggle with food insecurity.[72] People who live in cities with tech booms still suffer from food and housing insecurity—and when the boom becomes bust, that strain on local resources and distributions limits doubles or even triples.

For those on the Hearth and Home and Chaotic Paths, you may wish to shift your energies to protecting yourselves. Plenty of spells already exist for finding jobs, protecting your home, and for preventing eviction. Any magick that ancient city priests used to maintain citywide prosperity, if it hasn't disintegrated, may still be waiting for a translation from ancient Sumerian. Those likely included a lot of weather magick. This is an area of concern where magick needs invention, and because the breadth of economic change expands so large, it demands community more

69. "Organic Standards | Agricultural Marketing Service," USDA, https://www.ams.usda.gov/grades-standards/organic-standards.

70. Mike Lydon, Anthony Garcia, *Tactical Urbanism: Short-term Action for Long-term Change* (Washington, DC: Island Press, 2015) page. "The Next Generation of New Urbanists," Planetizen, https://www.planetizen.com/node/99/next-generation-new-urbanists.

71. Nate Berg, "U.S. Urban Population Is Up ... But What Does 'Urban' Really Mean?" CityLab, March 26, 2012, https://www.citylab.com/equity/2012/03/us-urban-population-what-does-urban-really-mean/1589/.

72. Elaine Waxman, "How food insecurity is adding to our health care costs" Urban.org, August 25, 2015, https://www.urban.org/urban-wire/how-food-insecurity-adding-our-health-care-costs.

than individual work. It also must be unique to each city. Even a general template for economic change could be the wrong fit.

Since magick doesn't multitask well, a general spell to "fix the economy" might result in a swing in the wrong direction. When you frame your purpose for the entire city, you need to follow the same rules that apply to weather magick.

1. Name and highlight the geographic boundaries of your work. Failing to name the boundaries can dissipate the magick. Trying to send the energy from one physical location to another a few hundred miles away simply doesn't work.

2. Name, in as clear and measurable terms as possible, how much is enough and how much is too much.

3. Identify clearly how you want the economic shift to manifest. Do you want to see a new company appear in your city? Do you want to see a sudden upsurge in art and creative production, linked to an upsurge in tourism? Do you want to see an already fading company leave and minimize the impact of its departure?

4. Have a way of breaking the work and allowing things to reset quickly if it becomes obvious that unintended consequences are spiraling.

5. The center part of the magick needs to involve physical movement. Economic and weather work must always move—static energy brings about death.

How a city priest or group of city priests/civic workers proceeds with these rules in mind is up to them. Some people work with direct energy constructs; I prefer the comfort of symbolic systems. However you choose to do it, make sure you can keep tabs on your progress.

While magickal people often identify themselves as the financially disadvantaged, the reality is that we are spread out across all socioeconomic classes. The advantages we take for ourselves usually involve a disadvantage given to someone, somewhere, including to people we consider part of our tribe. This give-and-take isn't because the universe has limited resources. It is because life demands movement, and that movement includes who has what resource. Living in a city only makes us able to see how those ripples of action affect our lives and the lives of others at closer range.

Spells for Safety

When you live in a dense urban environment, you will need a little more protection just because more people and more spirits involve more risk. Magickal work that promotes peace, calm, and prosperity for all can ameliorate some of that risk, but sometimes you either have to take a proactive stance or just block trouble before it happens. As always, the best indicator of a protection spell working is the most boring. If a protection works, nothing really happens.

Spell 9: Drive-By Magick for a Safer Neighborhood

This is a neighborhood/communal safety spell that is intended, by use of positive infection, to bring a neighborhood back to a healthy baseline. It is important to note that this spell works through accumulated effect; tossing out one penny makes a small movement. Over time, the effect compounds, and larger changes take place.

What the neighborhood spirit deems healthy may differ from your definition of it and consequently it's especially important to add a "for the greatest good of all" rider to any magick you may work for this.

You will need:

- Thirteen pennies[73]
- Mint oil
- A cloth bag

Mentally connect to the metal within the coin, imagining the penny come alive. Visualize the copper conducting energy along any ley lines in the street or even bouncing light and energy across cement into homes. You may want to imagine a conversation with Abe Lincoln as he takes your request to heart.

Anoint the penny with mint oil. You may want to speak a charm or make nonsensical intonations. I like to say, "Infect the all with tranquility." Place the pennies in the bag and put them in the center console of your car. (Stick them in your glove compartment or trunk if your city has an issue with car break-ins.) As you drive through your neighborhood or trouble spots, toss a penny out the window. As it touches the earth it spreads goodwill, and if some passerby picks it up, they might find themselves feeling a little bit healthier and stronger ... or at least a penny richer.

An easy alternative to this spell in spring and summer: blowing dandelion fluff after informing the seeds you wish them to spread peace is an innocuous-yet-

---

73. If your pennies are precious to you, loading a water gun with a few drops of mint oil makes a reasonable intentional substitute, but only if you are also unbothered by the use of a gun, even a "toy" one.

insidious way of infecting your neighborhood with positive energy. While people with allergies may not love this, the dandelion was already doing its thing and was going to spread energy already—so why not direct the spread?

Spell 10: Street Protection from City Predators

Folklore is filled to the brim with spells and charms to prevent theft and violence from strangers. These fall into two categories: the type you carry on your person and the type you affix in your home. You may be as subtle or overt as you wish in your choice of symbols. You may need to adjust your approach based on where you live or where you work.

You will need:

- Sage or Florida water (cologne water)
- Any item that you carry with you—I favor keychains and keys
- Any protection oil, preferably one with garlic in it

Smudge the keychains or wash them in Florida water, imagining any negative energies picked up fading away. Anoint each key on your keychain and the chain itself, while saying:

I awaken earth to keep me safe and strong
I awaken air to hear a warning song
I awaken fire to keep trouble at bay
I awaken water to sweep ill intentions away

Repeat this spell on your keychain every new moon, including the cleansing.

Home Protection

When I lived in Minneapolis, someone robbed the neighbors living on the end of my townhouse row. My neighbors went to bed in the upstairs of their home one night and in the morning found their front door jimmied open and everything on the first floor gone—including the carpet! The crime spree had spread through the neighborhood. Someone was picking homes and observing the habits of their inhabitants to rob them.

Even though it happened to my neighbors, I felt violated too. What if they came back and worked their way down the townhouse row? Unacceptable! This was not helped when one afternoon I sat down to read in the living room, looked up, and saw a man peering through the window at me. When he saw me get up and move toward my door, he ran away.

After I called the police, I washed and sprayed the inside of my windows with four thieves' vinegar (but not the outside, as that attracts wasps) and dug out some Crayola window markers.[74] I drew the following symbols on the windows: the glyph for the planet Mars for protection, the glyph for the Sun for exposure and observation, and the glyph Saturn for punishment of thieves. I went outside and asked the city spirit to lend a little energy to make my home appear threatening to thieves and other intrusive beings. You may want to choose from a variety of other protective symbols, sigils, and runes. Whether it's their own magick or the tendency of

---

74. Four thieves' vinegar is an herbal vinegar popular for protection spells, rooted in British/Medieval European Witchcraft.

those who steal to be superstitious, leaving obvious occult symbols can scare off many intrusive predators.

If it is not as safe to be so obvious, you may want to charge window decals (especially bright blue ones) or place more subtle symbols along your windowsills and over your door. Most people see the upright horseshoe over a doorway as benign protection; you can also put four thieves' vinegar or other protective potions in bottles you use for standard cleaning to keep what you do hidden.

Spell 11: It Followed You Home and You Don't Want to Keep it

Every so often, a person will go to a public gathering or be in a building with a dense population and one of the incorporeal beings also inhabiting that space will follow them home. This happens most in three places: college campuses, San Francisco, and bars. On college campuses, this spiritual activity is the byproduct of post-adolescent angst and near-constant stress. In San Francisco, rent prices even hurt ghosts: when people move in who can't sense them and won't give offerings or establish meaningful relationships to them or to the history of the city, it eventually forces those spirits to look for fresh energy sources in places that have awareness of them. Bars usually have the most malicious hangers-on—spirits that look for inebriated people, wide open and already toxic, to ride home and then exacerbate their addictions for amusement and food.

In most cases, the simplest act of protection is to just pay the spirits to leave you alone. Before leaving a crowd, especially one that memorializes a death, throw a coin behind you of any denomination and keep walking. Most of the time this is enough. While I prefer to stay out of bars, sometimes social obligations bring me to them. I rarely drink alcohol, wear warding jewelry, and when I get home, I throw a coin away from my front door. I then wash myself off with Florida water and salt.

Smudging Your Tracks

Another practice that helps is to pay close attention to your shoes. Depending on where you live, you may hear about "foot tricks" where people place nasty items in your path for you to step on. If you want to avoid engaging with this sort of thing or accidentally stepping in some nastiness, keep your shoes outside your home if you can. It's a good idea to have a spray to use on the bottom of your shoes to knock off negative energy. You can easily make one at home.

Spell 12: Evil Off Shoe Spray Recipe

You will need:

- Vodka/grain alcohol
- Alum crystal (you can get it from any grocery store spice aisle)
- 7 drops lemongrass essential oil
- 2 drops camphor essential oil
- One glass container with a screw cap
- A glass spray bottle
- A funnel
- Coffee filter or cheesecloth

In a glass bottle, combine the vodka, alum crystal, and essential oils. Allow to sit in a cool, dark place for a week, shaking once a day. At the end of the week, get out your spray bottle. Remove the cap and place the funnel in the neck of the bottle. Run the mixture through the coffee filter-lined funnel into the spray bottle until the bottle is full. Set aside any remaining mixture for future use. Keep this bottle by your front door and spray the bottom of your shoes before you take them off every day. This cancels out any trouble you might pick up while wandering the streets.

Integrating with City Energy

Cities stay in constant motion. The more populated the city, the more constant the motion. Most magick workings that are explicitly urban tap into that motion, or the way population density can form psychic clouds of moods—good or bad. The rest of these spells are about mood, motion, and integration, whether via a job or simply blending into the city grid.

Spell 13: Ambient Mood Change

The easiest way to shift the mood of a room is to scent it. There is risk with this option. Fragrance also backfires far too easily, because of asthma, allergies, and aversion. Please remember that a scent need not be strong to be potent.

While incense works best, as the burning stick has some clearing qualities, the following recipe is for a spray. This may not last as long as incense but also does not get the smell in the carpet in a way that won't come out. It also uses the (to most) innocuous scent of vanilla.

Since human drama is a daily occurrence in a city, making this light fragrance and keeping it on hand can come in handy, especially if you share a hallway with that couple that always has that epic fight on Saturday nights.

You will need:
- A place to heat water (a stove is ideal, but this can happen in a hot pot)
- A few drops of vanilla extract
- A small amount of vodka (to preserve)

Heat the water to a simmer and add a few drops of the vanilla extract. The smell should be faint, but present.

As it cools, speak this charm:

> *Shift like moon and tide*
> *shift like wind and wight*
> *Make this mood light,*
> *and calm as the reflected water,*
> *smooth like the flowing streets*

Store in a spray bottle. Lightly spritz the shared areas where arguments tend to happen.

Spell 14: Traffic to Move a Project Forward

This spell works best for people who work in skyscrapers and can get a view of the traffic in the city below. Those stuck in windowless offices or cubicles might need to use the geometry of the building they're in as a power container and get clever with an area traffic webcam. Even though it slightly dilutes the force of energy a window view offers, it still offers some energy to tap for your project.

In the movie *Trainspotting*, the first scene opens with the cast standing next to a barreling train, screaming into its oncoming energy. While much more dramatic in the movie (especially if you have screamed at trains), you do want to conjure this exact emotional state in yourself for this spell. Find your way to a place where you can observe traffic. If you don't work in a skyscraper, look for pedestrian bridges that cross highways. You can stand on the bridge and get the immediate effect of the traffic energy. Standing on the roof of a tall building—the sort that allow tourists—or even going to the roof of a parking garage might also work.

You will need:
- A bottle with a cap. Glass is ideal, but not if you're likely to drop it onto a passing car or train.

While timing is always nice but optional for a spell, in this case it's very important to do this after morning or evening rush hour has finished. Go to a place where you can feel the motion of passing traffic but are not obstructing traffic in any way. Open the bottle and imagine the vibration and force of the traffic going into the bottle. If you wish, place a paper with details of your project written on the bottle inside. When you feel you've grabbed enough of this energy, cap the bottle. When you get home, place it close to your work area and imagine it radiating force, moving you forward in your work.

Added challenge: If you live in a city with pedi-cabs, hire a ride and then hold the bottle to the side and imagine the energy scooping in off the motion of the people you pass.

Spell 15: City Spirit Job Finder

A well-cultivated relationship with a city spirit usually equals easily located places to live and work within the city. While political and economic manipulations from within a political system can seriously affect this, for the most part a healthy city spirit that likes you will make your city a healthy place to live. If a city spirit doesn't like you, you've got problems.

This spell works better after you've gotten out, walked in the city, found a few of its secret places, and praised the good while caring for the bad. Perform this spell at the place where the spirit of the city manifests with the most clarity. It may take a while for the city to reveal itself to you, so if that option is not quite available for you, go to the city hall or government center. If you are unable to find or access those easily, your nearest police or fire station will do.

You will need:

- A gold coin. Banks and post offices usually carry dollar coins.

- A talisman of your choice. It can be literally anything, whether it's a button you pin on a bag, a cufflink, or a credit card. I used a black onyx stone necklace.

At a time of day when you are least likely to be interrupted, go to the city spirit center. Hold up the coin and state, "City of _____, I come to this place to call to your spirit. I need to work here to live here. Please open the best pathways to steady work that pays what I need to continue to live here. I will do this for you while I live here: (name something you can do)." Leave the gold coin on the step. Touch your talisman to the coin, imagining the energy of acceptance flowing into it. Carry the talisman with you as you go about your job search or even as a form of enhanced luck as you walk through the city.

Spell 16: Home Finder

One of the trickiest parts of living in the city is, well, living there. Rents in cities with populations over 100,000 give the hardiest souls sticker shock, and mortgages can be hard to get when you already work three retail jobs just to barely make rent. If you need a place that also allows pets, you face even more of a challenge, especially with the popularity of pet rents. If you know the general neighborhood you want to live in, you can get a little help from the neighborhood spirit with this spell.

You will need:
- The map and pendulum (if still trying to find the right neighborhood)
- One penny for each person and pet that lives with you
- Some water in a portable bottle
- A blue glass jar candle
- A bowl of water
- A pinch of dirt from your desired neighborhood

If you are uncertain exactly where a good place is for you, plan a few questions to ask the pendulum, such as "Show me neighborhoods where people are friendly to outsiders," and "Show me neighborhoods that are good for my children and pets." You may worry that you can't afford some of these places; set that concern aside for now.

Visit the neighborhoods where you get the most positive feedback. When you find one that speaks to you most, find a tree or a bit of dirt (in some places you may need to dig between sidewalk cracks). In exchange, pour out a little bit of the bottled water and leave one penny for each person that will live in your home.

When you get home, light the blue candle and set it in a bowl of water for fire safety.[75] You may wish to write on the candle what features you need your home to have. Add all the details, including the rent you can afford and sustain, and at the end "or better." Add the pinches of dirt from the neighborhood. As you light the candle say, "(Name of neighborhood), we'd like to be part of you. Please find us a place we can live with all we need at a price we can afford or better."[76] Add a little offering to the water around the candle every day—sugar, honey, coconut flakes, or flowers make wonderful offerings to spirit.

---

75. Lady Rhea, *The Enchanted Candle* (New York: Citadel Press, 2004), 8–12.

76. Janina Renee, *Tarot Spells* (St. Paul, MN: Llewellyn Worldwide, 2000), 184.

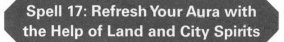

Spell 17: Refresh Your Aura with the Help of Land and City Spirits

The denser the population, the more important spiritual hygiene becomes. Every day you walk through the energies of others— and that means you pick up energy off the shoulders you rub, and your shoes grab gunk off the sidewalk. While mostly harmless, it can become as annoying as that gum that sticks to your shoe that ruins your gait. Along with purification practices you do at home, this outdoor method allows you to mediate between both land and city spirit, giving back the energy you picked up so that it can go back to where it belongs.

You will need:
- A bottle of water. A sipper or bottled water is fine.

Go to your favorite park. If you live in a coastal city, a beach is especially good because you can incorporate land and sea as well. Find a space you feel safe and lie on the ground. Speak to the ground, saying, "Ancestors of the land, take from my energy what is not mine that is yours." As you imagine the draining of the fertilizing gunk, expand your awareness to the sounds of the city around you—sounds outside the park and inside. Mentally connect to it as if it is all one being. Say, "Spirit of the city, give a home to what has gathered on me that is not mine." Relax, allowing the process to complete as best you can. As you leave, pour out a little water on the ground for the land and a little bit more for the city. As you work magick with the city spirit, that spirit will begin to take notice of you and make room for you. It is not a fast process. It may never want you for service—not every magickal person working with city spirits becomes a priest to it. In fact, such people are rare and uniquely imbued with community responsibility. But anyone can work *with* the city spirit, and the city, your neighbors, the land, and you can benefit from this cooperative work and expanded understanding of engaging secular structures for sacred purpose.

The first cities were meant to make life easier; today's cities have the potential to do that for real. You can take that city energy and make your own life a little easier. Most city-based magick spells address safety, transportation, and home. What makes them different is that the energy used does not always pull from sky and sun—it takes the energies of traffic and foot and combines them into new pathways. The above spells are to help you set up your foundations; what you do after those foundations have been set is up to you. There are no hard and fast rules for city magick beyond a call to find out exactly what works for you.

ELEVEN
SO NOW WHAT?

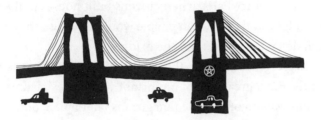

If there is one thing I hope readers take away from this book, it's that urban magick belongs to everyone. While city spirit work does have *a* priesthood, priests do not decide who may work it (although in some cases a city spirit might ask some of us to intervene when someone is leveraging the energy for reasons a little too selfish). We do not even have any sway over what people who practice urban magick believe—all that is between you and spirit. Yes, urban magick can be your practice (this book is a step toward making that more possible), but often it is a practice that comes in conjunction with practices you already developed.

The one person that urban magick is not for (aside from someone who falls ill in cities): someone who demands too much control. Letting go of outcomes after setting a standard by which to measure success is a fundamental magical skill. You especially must let go of how an outcome manifests with urban magick because very few people can imagine the chain of synchronicities necessary to make events fall in to place.

In terms of that non-organization of magickal urbanism, it is not the same as taking a disorganized approach. Humans, after dabbling in it for centuries, really only caught on to city planning and urban design as beneficial standard practices in the past 150 years. Until then, cities routinely had situations like the one in nineteenth-century Paris, when citizens built houses in the middle of bridges, and then when people wouldn't budge, the city had to burn down the houses and the bridges.

Yes, a great deal of out-in-the-city urban magick happens spontaneously. But a great deal of important work takes planning and execution. All too often, when magicians fail to plan, they end up burning down the houses they built on bridges, never realizing how much of an obstacle they created for themselves. Planning ahead also gives your city spirits an opportunity to communicate to you resources you can use in your work. Yes, in some cases, structuring a ritual format so it imitates a city layout will definitely help with what it is you are doing. Creating that structure will require you to do some research and experiment, finding what structures the city spirits work with most comfortably.

I have (sometimes without knowing) worked with spiritual energy for so long that sometimes I forget that things which are obvious to me are not so obvious to others. When studying anything magickal, it can be hard to create a cohesive whole of all the small subjects that make up a big one, especially in the case of magickal urbanism. In order to avoid anyone having a *"that* would have been good to know" moment, I will provide a few bits of closing advice below and do my best to make them easy to parse. A few things that do need to be answered before I go, such as what makes a priest different from a witch and whether one can be both, are a little hard to explain using language. I will do my best.

City Priest versus City Witch

Don't let the labels provided in the opening chapters limit you. The four paths named—Hearth and Home, Chaotic, Civil, and Priesthood—are not the only options available, just the ones I know of. There are certainly other ways, so if you don't see yourself here, don't sweat it—there is room for you. You do not have to be a city priest to work urban magick, and not all city spirits even want priests.

Some of you are asking yourselves whether you might be a city priest. Given the dogma and loaded history of the word *priest*, I can see why that possibility might cause some distress. Others may also struggle with the connection between priest/ess and Wicca, especially if Wicca does not fit your spiritual makeup.

For the purposes of urban magick working, the major difference between a priest and a witch is calling. While religious calling isn't discussed much in Pagan circles (we tend to use other names for it), priesthood always requires exactly this experience. When called, an energy puts forth messages to specific people who align with that energy. Everyone that energy taps can refuse—but often most feel uncomfortable refusing, because opening to that request fulfills something that the person called always sensed was missing.

Priesthood is a service. Witchcraft is either a choice, or a condition of being, depending on who you are. Witches can simultaneously be priests, but it's not a requirement. When someone feels called to practice witchcraft, a spirit can be behind it, but often it's a call from deep within.

The way you know you're a city priest depends on the city. Sometimes those priests have no idea they're even serving a spirit: one man I know who is a priest at the top of that spirit's hierarchy in the Midwest considers himself a staunch atheist. He might explode if he ever finds this out, so please, no one tell him. Even so, the actions he took when we went out almost always ended up serving some need of that spirit. As long as the work got done, he didn't need to believe. In my own case, the city spirit of San Francisco marched up to me as I stood at the top of Twin Peaks and offered me the job. By the end of that vacation, my then-partner had a job offer and we had a cross-country move to plan.

Other city spirits that want priests may communicate in other ways. Some call their priests from other places by sending dreams about their city. Others may use synchronicity, planting little messages around a priest to call him or her there. The most common experience is a sort of knowing, either that you need to do something for your city without necessarily knowing why, or a knowing that you need to get yourself to a certain city and stay there for a long time.

Priesthood is not required to work with a city spirit. Worship is not required to act as a priest to a city spirit. Some city spirits don't even want worship. As for the ones who do, they don't always need that worship … they just like it.

Best Practices in Urban Magick

Magickal people work their magick in different ways, and that is especially the case in big cities. While there is no one true way to work urban magick, there are a few habits and practices that can consistently improve results. Many are not, on the surface, magickal. Even though mundane in nature, they open up opportunities for spirits to communicate and knowledge to manifest. As you do this work, you may find your own practices to add to this list or find practices to replace the practices I recommend.

Pay Attention to New Populations Coming to Your City

Whenever a city receives a large human migration, its energy changes. These people bring their own folklore, witchcraft, and wishes with them. If you make an effort to know a little bit about these new people, you can get ahead of new spirit manifestations. For example, as more Muslim communities come to the United States, more spirits from those countries arrive too. In my own city work, I now have to account for encounters with djinn who originate from Middle Eastern countries and who also, for the most part, practice Islam.

Visit the Cemeteries and Say Hello

If you work with urban energies for any length of time, you will at some point encounter the dead. The most effective way to make sure this begins and ends as a peaceful encounter is to do almost exactly the same thing you might with your living neighbors. Go around and introduce yourself, and definitely bring a little treat to sweeten the relationship.

The following practice is strictly my own, although it has roots, in part, in practices learned from visiting ancestral graves as a child, listening to conjure people talk about cemetery work, and observing how friends of various cultures behaved when they visited their departed.

When you first visit a cemetery, bring water or rum to pour out at the entrance, and ask permission to enter. If the answer is yes, you'll either feel welcome or neutral. If the answer is no, you will likely feel as though you are not be able to get away from there fast enough. If the spirits allow you in, respectfully walk through the paved pathways. If you see a grave that needs cleaning off, do so, and sprinkle a little water on the grave when done. Introduce yourself and let the spirits know you just want to get to know your neighbors. Name your boundaries, i.e., that you prefer they not follow you home, how you prefer they communicate with you, and how you can help them. As you leave, place a dime and any cookies or other treats you brought with you at the inside entrance. Most of the time this alleviates many issues you might encounter when handling hauntings or spirits looking to inhabit your space.

Learn Your Resources

One of the main causes for struggling in a city is a lack of knowledge about its resources. This is not just for people new to a city: it's stunning, the number of lifelong residents that consult me that have no idea how many useful things are freely available to them. Also, while not on the list, make sure to visit local metaphysical shops—often the management knows all about various groups in the area and how to contact them.

The following list is just the bare surface of places you can look for things to do, useful information, and interesting opportunities. Often if you know where to look, you can find things that at the very least make life in the city affordable:

- Library event calendars
- University and college events and calendars

- City government websites
- Chambers of Commerce
- Museum and hospital newsletters
- Parks and Recreation Department websites
- Community education services
- Arts organizations newsletters and events

Check In with the City Spirit

It's helpful to have a regular check-in with the city spirit. While priests may sometimes need to do this daily, for those on other paths, setting up a regular one-on-one time to build a relationship may keep you apprised of energetic shifts that can affect you. If you do this, make sure the relationship has give-and-take. Constantly approaching a spirit with your needs can have diminishing returns. Make sure you ask the spirit what it might need, or what you can do. In some cases, the spirit might just need someone to listen. Spirits can get demanding too, so maintain polite but firm boundaries.

Stay Up-to-Date on Local History

Yes, it does sound paradoxical. Historians discover new additions to old stories all the time. Sometimes an urban archaeological dig reveals a building everyone forgot existed. Other times, new information reframes an entire set of assumptions around something that happened in the past. For cities that still have local newspapers, these new historical reveals are a common go-to for stories. Keep an eye on these; they can turn up old news about everything from forgotten trades to rediscovered serial killers. These discoveries often explain some aspect of a city or neighborhood spirit that seems odd. The better you understand the history of the city, and the way understanding of that history changes, the better you can understand the quirks of your city spirit.

Read the Local Rags

Many cities still have a hyperlocal press, and not just online. Before the day of blogs, the neighborhood newspaper covered goings-on of a single neighborhood, giving people a chance to find out about everything from church fish fries to local yard sales that the big city paper might skip printing. A lot of neighborhoods still print these papers and distribute them for free in coffee shops, bank lobbies, and occasionally to your door. These papers still cover things often skipped online.

While stories such as the writeup of a local bank manager's retirement may not make for the most exciting news, to a neighborhood spirit, such shifts matter. Someone that served its energy flow is leaving and now it has to get used to a whole new bank manager, and a whole new way of having a particular stream of energy flow in and out. These papers do help those spirits communicate.

Take Mass Transit at Least Once a Week

If your health allows it, try to take mass transit in the city at least once a week. This connects you to the city's rhythm and lets you check your energy against the city's movement: Are you in step this week? Do you need to be? This also gives the city spirit opportunities to show you something you need to see or hear, either with other people taking transit with you, or in the places that you visit.

Go Ahead and Miss Out

Do not try to keep track of everything in a city. We live in an age where the volumes of information and entertainment coming at us is too large to process in a lifetime. Even within a single city, it's neither reasonable nor possible to know every single thing that goes on. Cultivate trust: trust that the city spirit shows you what you can do something about, and trust that you can find out what you need to know when you need to know it.

No magickal practice can ever be perfect, nor should it be. It is in the imperfections in life that we learn, and this is just as true in magick as it is in every other discipline. I have given you the beginnings of guidelines and structures and based on who you are and where you are, some will work and some will not. Go out and fail with glee. Go out and succeed with joy. Please share what you find out—urban magick is a big world, waiting for discovery and rediscovery.

BIBLIOGRAPHY

ONLINE

American Civil Liberties Union. "Overview of Lesbian and Gay Parenting, Adoption and Foster Care." ACLU, https://www .aclu.org/fact-sheet/overview-lesbian-and-gay-parenting- adoption-and-foster-care.

BayArea.com. "Fairy Door Brings Magic to Golden Gate Park." February 22, 2016. https://www.bayarea.com/things-to-do /get-involved/look-for-the-fairy-door-in-golden-gate-park/.

BBC. "Primary History—Ancient Greeks—the Olympic Games." BBC.co.uk. http://www.bbc.co.uk/schools/primaryhistory /ancient_greeks/the_olympic_games/.

Biography.com. "Isaac Newton—Philosopher, Astronomer, Physicist, Scientist, Mathematician." https://www.biography.com/people/isaac-newton-9422656.

Boundless. "The Three Laws of Thermodynamics." *Boundless*, https://www.boundless.com/chemistry/textbooks/boundless-chemistry-textbook/thermodynamics-17/the-laws-of-thermodynamics-123/the-three-laws-of-thermodynamics-496-3601/.

Brown University. "Brownfields: How Can Abandoned Industrial and Commercial Properties Be Cleaned up and Returned to Productive Use?" http://www.brown.edu/Research/EnvStudies_Theses/summit/Briefing_Papers/Brownfields/Vacant_Lots.

Buckminster Fuller Institute. "Geodesic Domes." https://www.bfi.org/about-fuller/big-ideas/geodesic-domes.

California Department of Conservation. "Tsunami Inundation Map for Emergency Planning." Sacramento, CA: State of California, 2009. https://www.conservation.ca.gov/cgs/tsunami/maps.

Center for Climate Change and Energy Solutions. "Buildings Overview." https://www.c2es.org/technology/overview/buildings.

Center for New Media and Promotions. "US Census Bureau 2010 Census." US Census, https://www.census.gov/2010census/.

Center for Problem-Oriented Policing. "What Does Research Reveal About Street Access and Crime?" University of Albany, http://www.popcenter.org/responses/closing_streets/2.

Center for Urban Design and Mental Health. "Need and Opportunity." http://www.urbandesignmentalhealth.com/need-and-opportunity.html.

Chicago Architecture Foundation. "Great Lakes Symposium: Designing for Life Along the Water's Edge." https://www.architecture.org/experience-caf/programs-events/detail/great-lakes-symposium-designing-for-life-along-the-waters-edge/.

City of Chicago. "City of Chicago : Chicago History." https://www.cityofchicago.org/city/en/about/history.html.

City of Redwood. "Who Was Dona Arguello?" *Redwood City Voice*, 2015. http://www.redwoodcityhistory.org/blog/2017/1/30/who-was-dona-arguello.

CNN Library. "Flint Water Crisis Fast Facts." http://www.cnn.com/2016/03/04/us/flint-water-crisis-fast-facts/index.html.

Destination DC. "Monuments & Memorials." Destination DC, (no date). https://washington.org/topics/monuments-memorials.

Diffen. "Kinetic and Potential Energy—Difference and Comparison." http://www.diffen.com/difference/Kinetic_Energy_vs_Potential_Energy.

Digital Public Library of America. "Building the First Transcontinental Railroad." https://dp.la/exhibitions/exhibits/show/transcontinental-railroad/human-impact/native-americans.

The Earth Institute. "A Major Source of Air Pollution: Farms." 2016. https://www.earth.columbia.edu/articles/view/3281.

The Editors of Encyclopedia Britannica. "Heinrich Cornelius Agrippa Von Nettesheim." Encyclopedia Britannica, Inc., 2018.

EnergyShifter.com. "Camphor Burning to Clear Negative Energy." http://www.energy-shifter.com/camphor.html.

Environmental Protection Agency. "Sources Greenhouse Gas Emissions." https://www.epa.gov/ghgemissions/sources -greenhouse-gas-emissions.

Feast of the Lord. "Joseph's 7 Years Feast & Famine Prophecy." http://www.feastsofthelord.net/id140.html.

Federal Trade Commission. "Buying a Cemetery Site." Federal Trade Commission, July 2012. https://www.consumer.ftc.gov /articles/0304-buying-cemetery-site.

[no author.] "Field Sports of Assyria." *The Illustrated Magazine of Art* 4, no. 23 (1854): 276–277. https://archive.org/details /jstor-20538491/page/n1.

Food and Agriculture Organization of the United. Nations "Organic Agriculture." United Nations, http://www.fao.org /organicag/oa-faq/oa-faq5/en/.

Fox Business. "How the Mega-Rich Avoid Paying Taxes." Fox News, 2015. https://www.foxbusiness.com/features/how-the -mega-rich-avoid-paying-taxes.

Golden Gate Park. "History and Geography of Golden Gate Park." Golden Gate Park, https://goldengatepark.com /history-geography.html.

"Glamorous at Times, Dire at Others, South Shore History a Fascinating Ride." The Hammond Times, January 19, 2014. https: //www.nwitimes.com/business/local/glamorous-at-times -dire-at-others-south-shore-history-a/article_f70d0fe9-3443 -59c4-8e56-ec7205c32a8a.html.

Grantspace. "How Many Nonprofit Organizations Are There in the U.S.?" http://grantspace.org/tools/knowledge-base /Funding-Research/Statistics/number-of-nonprofits-in-the-u.s.

Graphiq. "Find the Data." https://country-facts.findthedata.com /compare/1-28/United-States-vs-United-Kingdom.

Grass Roots Recycling Network. "What Is Zero Waste?" Grass Roots Recycling Network, http://www.grrn.org/page/what -zero-waste.

Greek Gods Info. "Greek Stories About Poseidon-the Contest of Poseidon and Athena." http://www.greek-gods.info/greek -gods/poseidon/stories/poseidon-athena-contest/.

Hennepin County. "Hennepin County Government Center Tunnel and Revolving Door: Contract 4619a7." Minneapolis, MN: Hennepin County, 2017.

History of American Women (blog). "Marie Laveau." 2012. http:// www.womenhistoryblog.com/2012/07/marie-laveau.html.

Lake.access.org. "Lake Minnetonka History." http://www.lakeaccess .org/historical.html.

Literacy First Open Court. "Urban Roosts: Where Birds Nest in the City." https://sites.google.com/a/lfcsinc.org/opencourt /third-grade-1/urban-roosts-where-birds-nest-in-the-city.

"Merkaba, Platonic Solids & Sacred Geometry." Patinkas, http: //www.patinkas.co.uk/Merkaba_Feature_Article/merkaba_ feature_article.html.

Michigan Land Use Institute. "10 Principles of New Urbanism." http://www.mlui.org/mlui/news-views/articles-from -1995-to-2012.html?archive_id=678#.WSuQ0Ma1vIV.

Minnesota Playlist. "Local Playwrights Tackle Wikileaks." Minnesota Playlist, December 15, 2010. https://minnesotaplaylist .com/magazine/article/2010/local-playwrights-tackle- wikileaks.

MPR News. "The How and Where of Sex Trafficking in Minnesota." *MPRNews,* April 25. 2013. http://www.mprnews.org /story/2013/04/25/daily-circuit-sex-trafficking.

National Park Service. "Archaeology Program." https://www.nps .gov/archeology/visit/urbanarch.htm.

National Park Service. "Discover History (U.S. National Park Service)." National Park Service, https://www.nps.gov /history/index.htm.

———. "Green Roof Benefits." https://www.nps.gov/tps/sustainability /new-technology/green-roofs/benefits.htm.

———. "Washington, DC—Octagon House." National Park Service, https://www.nps.gov/nr/travel/wash/dc22.htm.

Nature: International Weekly Journal of Science 131, no. 834, 1993, "Exchange of Goods During Economic Depression." https:// www.nature.com/articles/131834b0.

Natural Resources and Environment Department. "Keeping the Land Alive: Soil Erosion Its Causes and Cures." Food and Agriculture Organization of the United Nations. http://www .fao.org/docrep/t0389e/t0389e02.htm.

Norse Gods Asatru. "The Landvaettir or Land-Wights of the Asatru/Heathen Religion." http://www.norsegodsasatru.net /land-wights.html.

Organisation for Economic Co-operation and Development. "Urban Population by City Size." OECD Data. https://data .oecd.org/popregion/urban-population-by-city-size.htm.

PlumbingSupply.com. "The History of Plumbing in America." https://www.plumbingsupply.com/pmamerica.html.

The Museum of Russian Art. "History." The Museum of Russian Art. http://tmora.org/about/history/.

themystica.com. "Crossroad." https://www.themystica.com
/mystica/articles/c/crossroad.html.

Office for Victims of Crime. "Sexual Assault: The Numbers |
Responding to Transgender Victims of Sexual Assault." Office
of Justice Programs, https://www.ovc.gov/pubs/forge/sexual
_numbers.html.

Oxford University. "The Electronic Text Corpus of Sumerian
Literature." http://etcsl.orinst.ox.ac.uk/cgi-bin/etcsl.cgi?text
=t.1.3.1&charenc=j#.

Partners for a Livable Community. "Public Art: More Than Just a
"Picture on the Wall"—A Vehicle for Crime Prevention." (no
date). http://livable.org/component/content/article/9-livability
-live/474-public-art-more-than-just-a-picture-on-the-wall-a
-vehicle-for-crime-prevention.

Physics for Idiots. "Thermodynamics." http://physicsforidiots.
com/physics/thermodynamics/.

Prairie Restorations, Inc. "Prairie Restoration Minnesota Native
Landscapes | Project Photo Gallerys Mn." http://www.prairieresto
.com/gallery_overview.shtml.

Principia Discordia. "The Five Commandments." http://principia
discordia.com/book/11.php.

RAINN. "Victims of Sexual Violence: Statistics." https://www
.rainn.org/statistics/victims-sexual-violence.

Revolvy.com. "Core Frame Model." https://www.revolvy.com
/main/index.php?s=Core+frame+model&item_type=topic.

Senseware (blog). "Building Efficiency is the Key Driver to
Reducing US Energy Consumption." https://blog.senseware
.co/2016/05/09/increase-building-efficiency.

Soul & Spirit Magazine. "Attract the Fairies with Our 3 Must-Have Crystals!" 2018. http://www.soulandspiritmagazine.com/attract-fairies-3-must-crystals/.

TeacherTECH. "Newton's Laws of Motion." http://teachertech.rice.edu/Participants/louviere/Newton/law3.html.

TinyLiving.com. "Tiny Houses, Less Stuff, More Freedom." https://tinyliving.com/.

University of Michigan. "Traditions of Magic: Babylonian Demon Bowls." https://www.lib.umich.edu/files/exhibits/pap/magic/def2.html.

The Ugly Indian. "The Ugly Indian." http://theuglyindian.com/.

Union of Concerned Scientists. "Is There a Connection between the Ozone Hole and Global Warming?" UCS, http://www.ucsusa.org/global_warming/science_and_impacts/science/ozone-hole-and-gw-faq.html#.WRIdXJ-qO70.

U. S. Department of Justice. "History of the Federal Use of Eminent Domain | Enrd | Department of Justice." US Department of Justice, https://www.justice.gov/enrd/history-federal-use-eminent-domain.

The Virtual Museum of the City of San Francisco. "Norton I, Emperor of the United States." http://www.sfmuseum.org/hist1/norton.html.

Western Neighborhoods Project. "San Francisco History." Western Neighborhoods Project, http://www.outsidelands.org/.

Wonderopolis. "How Do Water Towers Work?" https://www.wonderopolis.org/wonder/how-do-water-towers-work.

The World Bank Group. "Surface Area (Sq. Km)." http://data.worldbank.org/indicator/AG.SRF.TOTL.K2.

Abbey-Lambertz, Kate. "There's a Profoundly Simple Explanation for San Francisco's Housing Crisis." *Huffington Post*, 2016. https://www.huffpost.com/entry/san-francisco-housing-crisis_n_5750a95ee4b0eb20fa0d682e.

Akash, Singh. "Top 7 Indian Places Named After Gods." *Native Planet*, 2018. https://www.nativeplanet.com/travel-guide/top-7-indian-places-named-after-gods-004468.html.

Alexander, Bryan. "When the Mobile Revolution and the Digital Divide Combine." *Bryan Alexander: Futurist, Educator, Writer*, 2018. http://www.bryanalexander.com.

Alter, Lloyd. "Instead of Vertical Cities, Should We Be Thinking About Linear Cities?" *Treehugger*. Narrative Content Group, 2014. https://www.treehugger.com/urban-design/instead-vertical-cities-should-we-be-thinking-about-linear-cities.html.

Anderson, James A. M., Benjamin Franklin, and Paul Royster. *The Constitutions of the Free-Masons (1734): An Online Electronic Edition*. Lincoln, NE: University of Nebraska-Lincoln, 1734. https://digitalcommons.unl.edu/cgi/viewcontent.cgi?article=1028&context=libraryscience.

Andrews, Evan. "8 Legendary Ancient Libraries—History Lists." History.com. http://www.history.com/news/history-lists/8-impressive-ancient-libraries.

Anonymous. "Code of Ur-Nammu." http://www.polk.k12.ga.us/userfiles/644/Classes/177912/Code%20of%20Ur-Nammu.pdf.

Badger, Emily. "The Evolution of Urban Planning in 10 Diagrams." *The Atlantic* CityLab, 2012. https://www.citylab.com

/design/2012/11/evolution-urban-planning-10-diagrams
/3851/.

———. "'White Flight' Began a Lot Earlier Than We Think." *The Washington Post*. https://www.washingtonpost.com/news /wonk/wp/2016/03/17/white-flight-began-a-lot-earlier-than -we-think/.

Baez, John. "Platonic Solids in All Dimensions." University of California—Riverside. http://math.ucr.edu/home/baez /platonic.html.

Banks, Edgar James. "Cutha." *The Biblical World* 22, no. 1 (1903): 61–64. https://archive.org/details/jstor-3140532.

Baumann, John, and Vicki Baumann. "Sedona's Energy Vortexes." http://www.lovesedona.com/01.htm.

Bechtel, Robert B. *Environmental Psychology*. Wiley Online Library, 2002. https://www.wiley.com/en-us/Hand-book+of+Environmental+Psychology-p-9780471405948.

Bellis, Mary. "How Henry Bessemer Made Skyscrapers Possible." DotDash. https://www.thoughtco.com/henry-bessemer-the -steel-man-4075538.

Berg, Nate. "U.S. Urban Population Is Up … But What Does 'Urban' Really Mean?" *The Atlantic* CityLab 2012. https: //www.citylab.com/equity/2012/03/us-urban-population -what-does-urban-really-mean/1589/.

Bernstein, Jeffrey. "Political (De)Formation Ancient and Modern." *Society* 51, no. 6 (2014): 693–97.

Beyer, K. M. M., A. Kaltenbach, A. Szabo, S. Bogar, F. J. Nieto, and K. M. Malecki. "Exposure to Neighborhood Green Space and Mental Health: Evidence from the Survey of the Health of Wisconsin." [In English]. *International Journal of Environmental Research and Public Health* 11, no. 3 (2014): 3453–72.

Blanchette, Aimee. "Black Bear Is Shot, Killed in West St. Paul." *Star Tribune,* June 7, 2014. " http://www.startribune.com /black-bear-killed-in-west-st-paul-may-have-been-same -bear-seen-elsewhere/262238231/.

Blavatsky, Helena Petrovna. *Studies in Occultism.* BookRix, 2016. https://www.bookrix.com/_ebook-h-p-blavatsky-studies -in-occultism-a-series-of-reprints-from-the-writings-of-h-p -blavatsky-no-1/.

Bloom Sluggett, PC. "Urban Farming and the Michigan Right to Farm Act." http://www.bsmlawpc.com/_blog/Municipal _Law_Grand_Rapids_Michigan/post/Urban_Farming_and _the_Michigan_Right_to_Farm_Act/.

Blumberg, Naomi, and Ida Yalzadeh. "Urban Planning: City Beautiful Movement." *Encylopedia Britannica.* Encyclopedia Britannica Inc., 2019. https://www.britannica.com/topic /City-Beautiful-movement.

Bohannon, John. "There Are Only Four Types of Cities." *Science Magazine,* October 7, 2014. https://www.sciencemag.org /news/2014/10/there-are-only-four-types-cities.

Bond, John Michael. "2.1 million people still use dial-up internet from AOL, and other mind-boggling facts." *The Daily Dot*: TIME Inc., 2017. https://www.dailydot.com/debug/dvd-rental -windows-3-aol-2017/.

Boothman, Chris. "Why Is the Needles Highway Such an Amazing Experience?" *A Brit and a Southerner,* 2016. https: //abritandasoutherner.com/needles-highway/.

Bradford, Alina. "Pollution Facts & Types of Pollution." LiveScience, February 28, 2018. http://www.livescience.com/22728-pollution-facts.html.

Branch, John. "The Town of Colma, Where San Francisco's Dead Live." *The New York Times*, February 5, 2016. https://www.nytimes.com/2016/02/06/sports/football/the-town-of-colma-where-san-franciscos-dead-live.html.

Brasuell, James. "Renewing the Idea of a Linear City." *Planetizen*: Planetizen Inc., 2014. https://www.planetizen.com/node/72536.

Brisch, Nicole. "Marduk." Oracc Museum. http://oracc.museum.upenn.edu/amgg/listofdeities/marduk/.

Brown, Cynthia Stokes. "Uruk: The World's First Big City." *Khan Academy*, 2015. https://www.khanacademy.org/partner-content/big-history-project/agriculture-civilization/first-cities-states/a/uruk.

Butts, George, dir. *Hoarders* (TV Series 2009–). A&E Network, 2009. https://www.aetv.com/shows/hoarders.

Calter, Paul. "Geometry in Art & Architecture, Unit 6." Dartmouth College. https://www.dartmouth.edu/~matc/math5.geometry/unit6/unit6.html.

Cashmore, Catherine. "Population density, demand and house prices." *Macrobusiness*. Sydney, Australia, 2013. https://www.macrobusiness.com.au/2013/07/population-density-demand-and-house-prices/.

Castelow, Ellen. "The Origins and History of Fairies." http://www.historic-uk.com/CultureUK/The-Origins-of-Fairies/.

Cavazzi, F. "The Founding of Rome." http://www.roman-empire.net/founding/found-index.html.

Cesaretti, Rudolf, José Lobo, Luís M. A. Bettencourt, Scott G. Ortman, and Michael E. Smith. "Population-Area Relationship for Medieval European Cities." *PLOS ONE* 11, no. 10 (2016): 1–27.

Cheng, Rev Patrick S., PhD. "What Was the Real Sin of Sodom?" *Huffington Post*. Washington, DC: Huffington Post, 2011. https://www.huffpost.com/entry/what-was-the-real-sin -of_b_543996.

Christensen, Erik. "14 American Cities with Crazy Underground Tunnel Systems." *Thrillist*, 2015. https://www.thrillist.com /travel/nation/14-american-cities-with-crazy-underground -tunnel-systems-chicago-boston-new-york.

Clay, A. T. "Ellil, the God of Nippur." *The American Journal of Semitic Languages and Literatures* 23, no. 4 (1907): 269–279. https://www.jstor.org/stable/527959.

Coffey, Maureen. "Urban Legends: Cities Are Fundamentally at Odds with Environmental Quality and Safety, Right? Not So Fast." *Colgate Scene*, November 24, 2014. https://news.colgate .edu/scene/2014/11/urban-legends.html.

Compagni, Vittoria Perrone. "Heinrich Cornelius Agrippa Von Nettesheim." *The Stanford Encyclopedia of Philosophy*, edited by Edward N. Zalta. February 2017. https://plato.stanford .edu/entries/agrippa-nettesheim/.

Correnti, Madison. "Outsourcing Overseas and Its Effect on the US Economy." National Customs Brokers & Forwarders Association of America, Inc. http://www.ncbfaa.org/Scripts /4Disapi.dll/4DCGI/cms/review.html?Action=CMS _Document&DocID=14050&MenuKey=pubs.

Cory. "Blog Post 127—Summoning Devils." *New World Witchery* (blog). NewWorldWitchery.com, 2011. https://newworldwitchery.com/2011/05/09/blog-post-127-%E2%80%93-summoning-devils/.

———. "Blog Post 142—Coins." *New World Witchery* (blog). NewWorldWitchery.com, 2011. https://newworldwitchery.com/2011/11/09/blog-post-142-%E2%80%93-coins/.

Curtis, Edward Lewis. "Early Cities of Palestine." *The Biblical World* 7, no. 6 (1896): 411–424. https://archive.org/details/jstor-3140126.

Danielsdottir, Gudbjorg, Sigrun Sigurgeirsdottir, Helma Einarsdottir, and Erlendur Haraldsson. "Interrogative Suggestibility and Its Relationship with Personality, Perceptual Defensiveness and Extraordinary Beliefs." in *Personality and Individual Differences* 14, no. 3 (March 1993): 499–502. https://doi.org/10.1016/0191-8869(93)90323-U.

Dastrup, R. Adam. *Open Geography Education.* (no date). https://www.opengeography.org/.

David, Anthony E. "A Biographical Dictionary of Ancient Egypt." Taylor & Francis, 2002. https://www.taylorfrancis.com/books/9780203498514/chapters/10.4324/9780203498514-4.

Deaton, Jeremy. "The Sahara Desert Used to Be Green and Lush. Then Humans Showed Up." *Popular Science*, March 20, 2017. https://www.popsci.com/sahara-desert-drought-humans/.

De Sousa, Ana Naomi. "Death in the city: what happens when all our cemeteries are full?" *The Guardian UK*, January 21, 2015. https://www.theguardian.com/cities/2015/jan/21/death-in-the-city-what-happens-cemeteries-full-cost-dying.

Dell'Amore, Christine. "How Wild Animals Are Hacking Life in the City." *National Geographic*, April 18, 2016. https://www.nationalgeographic.com/news/2016/04/160418-animals-urban-cities-wildlife-science-coyotes/.

Dhwty. "The Ingenious Invention of the Tower of the Winds." *Ancient Origins*, 2014. https://www.ancient-origins.net/ancient-technology/ingenious-invention-tower-winds-001902.

Ditmore, Melissa. "Sex Work, Trafficking: Understanding the Difference." *Rewire*, 2008. https://rewire.news/article/2008/05/06/sex-work-trafficking-understanding-difference/.

Editors (various). "The Dark History of San Francisco's Cemeteries." *7x7*, October 24, 2013. https://www.7x7.com/dark-history-of-cemeteries-in-san-francisco-1786563925.html.

Eliades, Savvas Jack. "Plato's Theory of Forms." Fordham University, 1991. https://fordham.bepress.com/dissertations/AAI9118836/

Elliott, Sarah K. "How American Indian Reservations Came to Be." PBS.org. http://www.pbs.org/wgbh/roadshow/stories/articles/2015/5/25/how-american-indian-reservations-came-be/.

Ellwood, Taylor, and Lupa. "Polarity in Sex Magick." *Spiral Nature Magazine*, July 2, 2006. https://www.spiralnature.com/magick/polarity/.

Faust, Jack. "What the Fuck Is a Fluid Condenser?!" In *Agent of Chaos*, 2012. http://vonfaustus.blogspot.com/2012/10/what-fuck-is-fluid-condenser.html (no longer online, no cache.)

Fernandez, Lisa, and Elyce Kirchner. "Rogue 'Get Your S--- Together' Anti-Hate BART Campaign." NBC Bay Area.

December 2, 2016. https://www.nbcbayarea.com/news/local
/Get-Your-S----Together-BART-Campaign-Part-of-Rogue
-Unauthorized-Campaign-404315886.html.

Ferraro, Nick, and Josie Clarey. "I-35W Bridge Collapse: Five
Stories, Five Years Later." *Twin Cities Pioneer Press*, July 30,
2012. https://www.twincities.com/2012/07/30/i-35w-bridge
-collapse-five-stories-five-years-later/.

Floyd, Allison. "Farm Expenses Increase 43% in Five Years."
Growing Georgia, May 7, 2014. https://chattooga1180.com
/farm-expenses-increase-43-in-five-years/.

Franklin, Benjamin. "Benjamin Franklin Quote." http://www
.azquotes.com/quote/663602.

Frank, Tenney. "The Economic Life of an Ancient City." *Classical Philology* 13, no. 3 (1918): 225–240. https://www.jstor.org
/stable/263254.

Frazer, James George. *The Golden Bough*. https://link.springer
.com/book/10.1007/978-1-349-00400-3.

Frey, William H. "The Suburbs: Not Just for White People Any-
more." *The New Republic*, 2014. https://newrepublic.com/article
/120372/white-suburbs-are-more-and-more-thing-past.

Friedersdorf, Conor. "When the State Takes Kids Away from Parents: Three Perspectives." *The Atlantic*, July 24, 2014. https:
//www.theatlantic.com/national/archive/2014/07/when-the
-state-gets-between-kids-and-parents-3-radically-different
-perspectives/374954/.

Frost, Robert. "Mending Wall" Poetry Foundation, https:
//www.poetryfoundation.org/poems-and-poets/poems
/detail/44266.

Frothingham, A. L. "Babylonian Origin of Hermes the Snake-God, and of the Caduceus I." *American Journal of Archaeology* 20, no. 2 (1916): 175–211. doi:10.2307/497115.

Gallagher, Mari. "USDA Defines Food Deserts." *Nutrition Digest* 38, no. 2, October 12, 2011. http://americannutritionassociation.org/newsletter/usda-defines-food-deserts.

Garkavenko, Alex. "Revealed: The Underground Secrets of the Buildings We Thought We Knew." *Architizer*, December. 19, 2016. https://architizer.com/blog/inspiration/stories/architecture-flip-side/.

German, Dr. Senta. "White Temple and Ziggurat, Uruk." Khan Academy. https://www.khanacademy.org/humanities/ancient-art-civilizations/ancient-near-east1/sumerian/a/white-temple-and-ziggurat-uruk.

Geva, Anat. "Passive Energy Systems in Frank Lloyd Wright's Sacred Architecture." Paper presented at the PLEA International (Passive and Low Energy Architecture) Conference Proceedings: Design With the Environment, Toulouse, France, 2002. http://papers.cumincad.org/data/works/att/sigradi2009_697.content.pdf.

Goldenberg, Corrinne, Sarah Gunther, Anne Lieberman, Jesse Wrenn, and Gitta Zomorodi. "Sex Worker Rights: (Almost) Everything I Wanted to Know but Was Afraid to Ask." American Jewish World Service, July 2013. https://www.nswp.org/sites/nswp.org/files/sex_worker_rights.pdf.

Goldenberg, Suzanne. "Climate Change: The Poor Will Suffer the Most." *The Guardian*, March 31, 2014. https://www.theguardian.com/environment/2014/mar/31/climate-change-poor-suffer-most-un-report.

Goldstein, Jacob. "A Primer on the Goldman Sachs Scandal." *The Daily Beast*. New York: Gawker Media, 2010. https://www.thedailybeast.com/a-primer-on-the-goldman-sachs-scandal.

Gramlich, John. "Voters' Perceptions of Crime Continue to Conflict with Reality." Pew Research Center. http://www.pewresearch.org/fact-tank/2016/11/16/voters-perceptions-of-crime-continue-to-conflict-with-reality/.

Grammatikopoulou, Christina. "Ritual, Reality and Representation: From Ancient Theatre to Postmodern Performance" *Interartive: A Platform for Contemporary Art and Thought*. https://interartive.org/2013/01/theatre-and-performance.

Grammenos, Famis. "The Fused Grid: A Contemporary Urban Pattern." http://www.fusedgrid.ca/fusedgrid.php.

Gray, Alistair. "Regulators Find 'Pervasive Pattern' of Abuse at Wells Fargo." *The Financial Times*, March 28, 2017. https://www.ft.com/content/b5bc46a8-13de-11e7-b0c1-37e417ee6c76.

Gray, Louis H. "The Indian God Dhanvantari." *Journal of the American Oriental Society* 42 (1922): 323–337. https://www.jstor.org/stable/593645?seq=1#metadata_info_tab_contents.

Greene, H. B. "Hebrew Rock Altars." *The Biblical World* 9, no. 5 (1897): 329–340. https://www.jstor.org/stable/pdf/3140288.pdf.

Gross, Daniel. "Is U.S. Manufacturing Really in Decline?" *Strategy & Business*, July 26, 2016. https://www.strategy-business.com/blog/Is-US-Manufacturing-Really-in-Decline?gko=37098.

Haggi, Ty. "11 Worst States for Human Trafficking in America." *Insider Monkey*: InsiderMonkey, 2017. http://www.insidermonkey

.com/blog/11-worst states-for-human-trafficking-in-america -524251/.

Halbherr, Federico. "Cretan Expedition Xvii. Ruins of Unknown Cities at Haghios Ilias and Prinià." *American Journal of Archaeology* 5, no. 4 (1901): 393–403. https://www.jstor.org /stable/496582?seq=1#metadata_info_tab_contents.

Hanson, Steve. "Mind the Gap: Psychogeography as an Expanded Tradition." *Street Signs* (2007): 10–13. https://www.academia. edu/5674808/_2007_Mind_the_Gap_Psychogeography_as _an_expanded_tradition_from_Street_Signs_-_the _Goldsmiths_College_Centre_for_Urban_and_Community _Research_journal.

Harjani, Ansuya. "How Much Do the Ultra-Rich Give to Charity?" In *CNBC Philanthropy*. New York, 2014. https://www .cnbc.com/2014/10/05/how-much-do-the-ultra-rich-give-to -charity.html.

Heath, Wallace G. "Some Biophysical Bases for the Human Energy System." https://www.energeticfitness.com/Support%20Files/Some%20Biophysical%20Bases%20for %20the%20Human%20Energy%20System.pdf.

Hess, Amanda. "Race, Class, and the Stigma of Riding the Bus in America." In *CityLab*: The Atlantic Group, 2012. https://www .citylab.com/solutions/2012/07/race-class-and-stigma-riding -bus-america/2510/.

Hill, J. "Gods of Ancient Egypt: Osiris." www.ancientegyptonline .co.uk/osiris.html.

Hill, Steven. "Evictions and Conversions: The Dark Side of Airbnb." *American Propsect Longform*, October 19, 2015.

https://prospect.org/economy/evictions-conversions-dark -side-airbnb/.

Hirsch, Makaso. "Detecting Stolen Metal Takes Vigilance at Scrapyard." *Star Tribune*. June 9, 2012. http://www.startribune .com/detecting-stolen-metal-requires-vigilance-at-scrap -yard/158320835/.

Hodge, Scott A. "The Distribution of Tax and Spending Policies in the United States." Tax Foundation, https://taxfoundation .org/distribution-tax-and-spending-policies-united-states/.

Holmes, Frank. "What Does It Take to Be in the Top 1 Percent? Not as Much as You Think - U.S. Global Investors." US Global Investors, 2014. http://www.usfunds.com/investor-library /frank-talk/what-does-it-take-to-be-in-the-top-1-percent -not-as-much-as-you-think/#.XeWsDuhKg2w.

Holmes, William Henry. "Archeological Studies among the Ancient Cities of Mexico: Part II, Monuments of Chiapas, Oaxaca and the Valley of Mexico." *Publications of the Field Columbian Museum. Anthropological Series* 1, no. 1 (1897): 143–338. https://archive.org/details/archaeologicalst01holm /page/n4.

Horry, Ruth. "Enki/Ea." Oracc Museum, http://oracc.museum .upenn.edu/amgg/listofdeities/enki/index.html.

Ikeda, Sandy. "Urban Mass Transit Out of Suburban Sprawl." In *Market Urbanism*: Market Urbanism, 2016. https://marketurbanism .com/2016/12/13/urban-mass-transit-out-of-suburban -sprawl/.

Ingersoll, Alex M. "Divining the Network with the Forked Twig: An Archaeological Approach to Locative Media." January 20, 2012. https://networkarchaeology.wordpress

.com/2012/01/20/divining-the-network-with-the-forked
-twig-an-archaeological-approach-to-locative-media/.

Islahuddin, Islah. "1. Linear, Radial and Grid Iron Layout Patterns."
2016. www.scribd.com/presentation/241478529/Roman
-Townplanning.

Janz, Wes. "This Is Flint, Michigan, in All Its Pain and All Its
Glory." *Grist*, February 17, 2011. https://grist.org/urbanism
/2011-02-15-this-is-flint-michigan/.

Jastrow, Morris. "The God Ašur." *Journal of the American Oriental Society* volume 24 (1903): 282–311. https://www.jstor.org
/stable/592800?seq=1#metadata_info_tab_contents.

———. "Sumerian and Akkadian Myths of Beginnings." *Journal
of the American Oriental Society* vol. 36, (1916): 274–299.
https://www.jstor.org/stable/pdf/592686.pdf.

Jiquanda, Johnson. "Flint, Detroit among Nation's Poorest Cities,
New Census Data Show." http://www.mlive.com/news/flint
/index.ssf/2015/09/flint_detroit_among_nations_po.html.

Johnson, Maisha Z. "4 Lies You've Fallen for If You Think the
US Is A 'Melting Pot.'" *Everyday Feminism*, August 29, 2016.
https://everydayfeminism.com/2016/08/melting-pot-lies/.

Jones, Lindsay, Catherine Bell (editor). "Eventfulness of Architecture: Teaching About Sacred Architecture Is Teaching
About Ritual." in *Teaching Ritual* 2007: 251–272. 10.1093/acp
rof:oso/9780195176452.003.0020.

Keeling, Brock. "San Francisco Votes to Confiscate Homeless
Tents, Fails to Pass Funding to House Them." In *Curbed
San Francisco*. San Francisco: CurbedSF, 2016. https:
//sf.curbed.com/2016/11/10/13576508/san-francisco-home-
less-tents-election.

Keen, Jeffrey S., Bsc Hons, Arcs Minstp, and Cphys Ceng. "2-Body Interaction with Space-Time and the Effects on the Mind's Perception." (2011). https://www.semanticscholar.org /paper/2-Body-Interaction-with-Space-Time-and-the -Effects-Keen/1df8542ff8c8cb2c562444a8c56a3f8c0d37c5b2.

Kivari, Kristel. "Dowsing as a Link between Natural and Supernatural. Folkloristic Reflections on Water Veins, Earth Radiation and Dowsing Practice." 2016. https://www.semanticscholar.org /paper/Dowsing-as-a-link-between-natural-and-supernatural .-Kivari/c7385c4755cac98043c9e9f7499b0dde1c556c14.

Kloc, Joe. "Tech Boom Forces a Ruthless Gentrification in San Francisco" in *Newsweek*, April 25, 2014. https://www.newsweek .com/2014/04/25/tech-boom-forces-ruthless-gentrification-san -francisco-248135.html.

Klontz, Brad. "Do You Have a Money Disorder?" *Psychology Today*, January 30, 2010. https://www.psychologytoday.com /us/blog/mind-over-money/201001/do-you-have-money -disorder.

Kotler, Steven. "Flow States and Creativity" in *Psychology Today*, Feb 25, 2014. https://www.psychologytoday.com/us/blog/the -playing-field/201402/flow-states-and-creativity.

Kristof, Nicholas. "Opinion | Meet a 21st-Century Slave." *The New York Times*, October 25, 2015. https://www.nytimes .com/2015/10/25/opinion/sunday/meet-a-21st-century -slave.html.

Kroh, Kiley. "Here's Why Suburban Sprawl Cancels out the Benefits of City Living." *ThinkProgress*, January 7, 2014. https:// thinkprogress.org/heres-why-suburban-sprawl-cancels-out -the-climate-benefits-of-city-living-970dd4173bfa/.

Langdon, S. "Babylonian Proverbs." *The American Journal of Semitic Languages and Literatures* 28, no. 4 (1912): 217–243. https://www.journals.uchicago.edu/doi/pdfplus/10.1086/369693.

Lawler, Andrew. "City of the Dead" *Archaeology Archive* vol. 59, no. 3, May/June 2006. http://archive.archaeology.org/0605/abstracts/saqqara.html.

Leonard, Andrew. "Save the Artists, Inc." *San Francisco Magazine*, April 27, 2016. https://sanfran.com/save-the-artists-inc.

Le Coz, Emily. "Fry Fuel: Mcdonald's Franchisee Runs Cars on It." National Broadcast Corporation, http://www.nbcnews.com/id/11809771/ns/us_news-environment/t/fry-fuel-mcdonalds-franchisee-runs-cars-it/.

Levitin, Michael. "The Triumph of Occupy Wall Street." in *The Atlantic*, June 10, 2015. https://www.theatlantic.com/politics/archive/2015/06/the-triumph-of-occupy-wall-street/395408/.

Livius. "Rome's Cloaca Maxima Sewer Needs Love." *The History Blog*, 2012. http://www.thehistoryblog.com/archives/21511.

Long, Heather. "U.S. Has Lost 5 Million Manufacturing Jobs since 2000." *CNN Money*, March 29, 2016. https://money.cnn.com/2016/03/29/news/economy/us-manufacturing-jobs/index.html.

Loomans, Taz. "7 Reasons Why High-Rises Kill Livability." Blooming Rock, September 25, 2014. http://bloomingrock.com/2014/09/25/7-reasons-why-high-rises-kill-livability/.

Marks, Tracy. "Elemental: The Four Elements from Ancient Greek Science and Philosophy to Poetry." http://www.webwinds.com/thalassa/elemental.htm.

Marlene. "The Historic 1856 Octagon House." http://www.marle-nesheirlooms.com/octagon.html.

Masani, R.P. M.A. *Folklore of Wells Being a Study of Water Worship in East and West.* D.B. Taraporevala & Sons Co., 1918. archive.org/details/FolkloreOfWellsBeingAStudyOfWater-WorshipInEastAndWest.

McArdle, Megan. "Density and Crime." in *The Atlantic*, May 16, 2011. https://www.theatlantic.com/national/archive/2011/05/density-and-crime/238944/.

McCollum, Brian. "Sixto Rodriguez Making Another Bid for Detroit Mayor?" *Detroit FreePress*, April 4, 2017. https://www.freep.com/story/entertainment/music/2017/04/04/sixto-rodriguez-making-another-bid-detroit-mayor/100043458/.

McConnell, Anna. "US Down 18,000 Farms in 2015 USDA Says." *Successful Farming*, February 8, 2016. https://www.agriculture.com/news/business/us-down-18000-farms-in-2015-usda-says_5-ar52340.

McCraw, Jim. "Ghosts of Detroit's Past in Ford's Old Buildings." *New York Times*, October 15, 1999. https://www.nytimes.com/1999/10/15/automobiles/ghosts-of-detroit-s-past-in-ford-s-old-buildings.html.

McDermid, Riley. "Here Are the Bay Area Counties with the Most People Earning More Than $1 Million a Year, Including San Francisco, San Mateo and Marin Counties." *San Francisco Business Times*, 2017. https://www.bizjournals.com/sanfrancisco/news/2017/02/14/bay-area-san-francisco-millionaires-per-mile.html.

McEllistrem, Steve. "The Myth of Equal Opportunity." http://www.mcellistrem.com/2015/03/03/the-myth-of-equal-opportunity/.

McKean, Cameron Allan. "How Blue Lights on Train Platforms Combat Tokyo's Suicide Epidemic."Next City, March 20, 2014. https://nextcity.org/daily/entry/how-blue-lights-on-train-platforms-combat-tokyos-suicide-epidemic.

McLaren, Kevin Todd. "Pharaonic Occultism: The Relationship of Esotericism and Egyptology, 1875–1930."San Luis Obispo, CA: California Polytechnic State University, 2016. digitalcommons.calpoly.edu/theses/1658/.

McNerthney, Casey. "Police Alerted to 'Superheroes' Patrolling Seattle." In Seattle PI. November 18, 2010. https://www.seattlepi.com/local/article/Police-alerted-to-superheroes-patrolling-Seattle-821425.php.

Mears, Bill. "Michigan's Ban on Affirmative Action Upheld by Supreme Court" CNN, April 22, 2014. https://www.cnn.com/2014/04/22/justice/scotus-michigan-affirmative-action/index.html.

Mehta, Barjor, and Arish Dastur. "Approaches to Urban Slums." http://documents.worldbank.org/curated/en/547701468346439819/Approaches-to-urban-slums-a-multimedia-sourcebook-on-adaptive-and-proactive-strategies. Washington, DC: International Bank for Reconstruction, 2008.

Melosi, Martin V. "The Automobile in American Life and Society." University of Michigan, http://www.autolife.umd.umich.edu/Environment/E_Overview/E_Overview4.htm.

Mendoza, Rubén. "Sacrament of the Sun: Eschatological Architecture and Solar Geometry in a California Mission" Boletín:

The Journal of the California Mission Studies Association, vol. 22, no. 1: 87–110. https://digitalcommons.csumb.edu/sbgs _fac/14/.

Meyer, B. H. "Fraternal Beneficiary Societies in the United States," *American Journal of Sociology* vol. 6 (March 1901): 646–651. http://historymatters.gmu.edu/d/5048/.

Millet, Joyce. "Understanding American Culture—from Melting Pot to Salad Bowl." www.culturalsavvy.com/understanding _american_culture.htm.

Montgomery, David. "Mass Transit Is More Than Light Rail— and Still Costly." *Twin Cities Pioneer Press*, March 30, 2015. https://www.twincities.com/2015/03/30/mass-transit-is -more-than-light-rail-and-still-costly/.

Morrow, Ashley. "Hubble Finds Universe Expanding Faster Than Expected." NASA, June 2, 2016. https://www.nasa.gov/feature /goddard/2016/nasa-s-hubble-finds-universe-is-expanding -faster-than-expected.

Moyer, Liz. "For Richer or Poorer? Rich Families Face a Marriage Problem." in *The Wall Street Journal*, May 16, 2014. www.wsj .com/articles/for-richer-or-poorer-rich-families-face-a -marriage-problem-1400280084.

Muss-Arnolt, W. "The Babylonian Account of Creation." *The Biblical World* 3, no. 1 (1894): 17–27. https://archive.org/details /jstor-3135405.

Neff, Otten Johnson Robinson, and P. C. Ragonetti. "Installation of Ten Commandments on City Hall Lawn Is Government Speech, Violates First Amendment." Lexology, November 21, 2016. https://www.lexology.com/library/detail .aspx?g=104fc69e-ce15-422b-84f9-c247678e04ef.

Newitz, Annalee. "Why Do We Build Walls around Our Cities?" *io9*. September 3, 2014. https://io9.gizmodo.com/why-do-we -build-walls-around-our-cities-1630142347.

Nicholson, B. A. R. "Notes on the Ancient City of Balabhipura." *The Journal of the Royal Asiatic Society of Great Britain and Ireland* 13 (1852): 146–163. https://www.jstor.org/stable /25228640.

Niddle, Nadra Kareem. "Myths and Misconceptions About Multiracial People in the U.S." *ThoughtCo*, September 22, 2019. https://www.thoughtco.com/myths-about-multiracial-people -2834944.

O, Janet, and Katie Marzullo. "2 Children Bitten by Rattlesnakes within Week in Northern Ca." *ABC7*. Oakland, CA, June 10, 2015. https://abc7news.com/775850/.

Paton, Lewis B. "The Civilization of Canaan in the Fifteenth Century B. C." *The Biblical World* 20, no. 2 (1902): 113–122. https://www.journals.uchicago.edu/doi/10.1086/473017.

Pereira, Alyssa. "Have You Seen These Hidden Fairy Doors around Sf and Berkeley?" 997now, http://997now.cbslocal .com/2014/05/16/have-you-seen-these-hidden-fairy-doors -around-sf-and-berkeley/.

Plake, Sarah. "More Murals & Public Art Decrease Crime, Increase Pride." 13WIBW, http://www.wibw.com/home /headlines/More-Murals—Public-Art-Decrease-Crime -Increase-Pride-262129391.html.

Plaza, Beatriz. "Valuing Museums as Economic Engines: Willingness to Pay or Discounting of Cash-Flows?" *Journal of Cultural Heritage* 11, no. 2 (4// 2010): 155–162. https://doi .org/10.1016/j.culher.2009.06.001.

Polat, R. T., and A. Tunali. "Characterisation of the Ancient City of Teos Western Necropolis Sherd Samples." *Acta Physica Polonica Series a,* iss. 129, April 2016. 521-523. 10.12693/APhysPolA.129.521.

Popow, W Bro Victor G. "A Report on Psychology & Architecture." *Grand Lodge of Manitoba* (2000). kimstevewri101.wordpress.com/annotated-bibliographies/popow-v-g-2000-a-report-on-psychology-architecture-vol-1/.

Preston, Julia. "Immigrants Aren't Taking Americans' Jobs, New Study Finds." *The New York Times,* September 21, 2016. https://www.nytimes.com/2016/09/22/us/immigrants-arent-taking-americans-jobs-new-study-finds.html.

Price, Ira Maurice. "Notes on the Pantheon of the Gudean Cylinders." *The American Journal of Semitic Languages and Literatures* 17, no. 1 (1900): 47–53. https://www.journals.uchicago.edu/doi/abs/10.1086/369386?mobileUi=0.

———. "Some Observations on the Financial Importance of the Temple in the First Dynasty of Babylon." *The American Journal of Semitic Languages and Literatures* 32, no. 4 (1916): 250–260. https://www.jstor.org/stable/528194?seq=1#metadata_info_tab_contents.

Prone, Simon. "Sacred Geometry: A Beginner's Guide." AscensionNow. http://www.ascensionnow.co.uk/sacred-geometry-beginners-guide.html.

Quednau, Rachel. "Skyways: Helping or Hurting Downtown?" in *Strong Towns,* 2016. https://www.strongtowns.org/journal/2016/6/27/skyways.

Radford, Benjamin. "The Lore and Lure of Ley Lines." *Live Science*, 11/19/2013 2013. https://www.livescience.com/41349 -ley-lines.html.

Raguso, Emilie. "Authorities Clear out Gilman Homeless Camp in Berkeley." *Berkeleyside*, June 16, 2016. www.berkeleyside .com/2016/06/16/authorities-clear-out-gilman-homeless -camp.

Richiele3@aol.com. "Rootsweb: Folklore-L [Folklore] Insects, Bugs, Spiders." Ancestry.com, http://archiver.rootsweb.ancestry .com/th/read/FOLKLORE/2000-04/0954963854.

Rinkesh. "10 Current Environmental Issues." In *Conserve Energy Future*, 2013. www.conserve-energy-future.com/current -environmental-issues.php.

Romero, Maureen. "The Cotton Gin." SCORE, http://score.rims .k12.ca.us/score_lessons/cotton_gin/pages/reading.html.

Rose, Christopher. "Ancient Cairo 3000 Bce-200 Ce." www.laits .utexas.edu/cairo/history/ancient/ancient.html.

Rosemeyer, Joe. "Bobcats Move Back into Southwest Ohio, Including Butler County." *Journal News*, February 24, 2017. https://www.journal-news.com/news/bobcats-move-back- into-southwest-ohio-including-butler-county/LjTxmaqqYg- JoXEkC8BMz8M/.

Rosin, Paul L. "On Serlio's Constructions of Ovals." *The Mathematical Intelligencer* 23, no. 1 (2001): 58–69. https://link. springer.com/article/10.1007/BF03024523.

Ruth, Michael. "Urban Revolution." In *Salem Press Encyclopedia*, 2017. [EBSCO only.]

Sahadi, Jeanne. "The Richest 10% Hold 76% of Wealth." In *CNN Money*. Washington, DC: Time Warner Inc., August 18, 2016.

https://money.cnn.com/2016/08/18/pf/wealth-inequality /index.html.

Sala, Nicoletta. "Fractal Models in Architecture: A Case of Study." Paper presented at the Proceedings International Conference on Mathematics for Living, 2000. www .semanticscholar.org/paper/Fractal-Models-in-Architecture %3A-A-Case-of-Study-Sala/77686c72a9564b3bea32fe93f-f5e8f590dbb6dab.

Sampson, Robert J. "Structural Density and Criminal Victimization." *Criminology* 21, no. 2 (May 1983): 276–293. https://doi .org/10.1111/j.1745-9125.1983.tb00262.x.

Sandiopoulis, John. "What Is the Source of Poltergeist Activity?" In *Pentecostal Resources*, 2011. www.johnsanidopoulos .com/2011/05/what-is-source-of-poltergeist-activity.html.

Sayce, A. H. "The Babylonian and Biblical Accounts of the Creation." *The American Journal of Theology* 9, no. 1 (1905): 1–9. www.jstor.org/stable/3154114.

Schwarz, Hunter. "State Capitol Buildings That Don't Look Anything Like State Capitol Buildings, Ranked." *The Washington Post*, November 20, 2014. https://www.washingtonpost.com /blogs/govbeat/wp/2014/11/20/state-capitol-buildings-that -dont-look-anything-like-state-capitol-buildings-ranked/.

Semuels, Alana. "Suburbs and the New American Poverty." in *The Atlantic*, January 7, 2015. https://www.theatlantic.com /business/archive/2015/01/suburbs-and-the-new-american -poverty/384259/.

Sergi, G. "Primitive Rome." *The Monist* 14, no. 2 (1904): 161–176. https://philpapers.org/go.pl?id=SERPR&proxyId=&u

=http%3A%2F%2Fdx.doi.org%2F10.5840%2Fmonist
19041426.

Short, Steven. "John McLaren: The Man Who Planted Two Million Trees." KALW Local Public Radio, September 25, 2012.
https://www.kalw.org/post/john-mclaren-man-who-planted-
two-million-trees#stream/0.

Silver, Nate. "Most Police Don't Live in the Cities They Serve."
Fivethirtyeight.com. August 20. 2014. https://fivethirtyeight.
com/datalab/most-police-dont-live-in-the-cities-they-serve/.

Singh, Rana P. B. *Sacred Geometry of India's Holy City, Vara-
nasi: Kashi as Cosmogram.* National Geogr. Soc. India,
1994. https://www.academia.edu/12915203/_103-94_
._Singh_Rana_P.B._1994._Sacred_Geometry_of_India_s
_Holy_City_Varanasi_Kashi_as_Cosmogram._National
_Geographical_Journal_of_India_N.G.S.I._Varanasi.
_ISSN_0027_9374_0944_vol._40_pp._189_216_.

Sisson, Patrick. "Detroit's Creative Enterprises Engage with Miles
of Vacant Land." Curbed.com, November 20, 2015. www
.curbed.com/2015/11/20/9898180/detroit-abandoned-lots
-vacant-artists-urban-farming-business.

Skipwith, Grey Hubert. "Ashtoreth, the Goddess of the Zido-
nians." *The Jewish Quarterly Review* 18, no. 4 (1906): 715–738.
https://www.scribd.com/document/427056539/Ashtoreth
-the-Goddess-of-Zidonians-Grey-Hubert-Skipwith-pdf.

Sohma, Marina. "The White Temple and the Great Ziggurat in
the Mesopotamian City of Uruk." In *Ancient Origins: Recon-
structing the Story of Humanity's Past*, 2016. www.ancient
-origins.net/ancient-places-asia/white-temple-and-great
-ziggurat-mesopotamian-city-uruk-006835.

Stellen, Debra. "Get the Look: Southern-Style Architecture." In *Traditional Home*. http://www.traditionalhome.com/design /get-look-southern-style-architecture.

Stoll, Nate. "The City Functional Movement." https://ds.lclark .edu/nstoll/2013/04/03/the-city-functional-movement/.

StormPhoenix. "Danu." Sisters in the Goddess Tree. thegoddesstree.com/GoddessGallery/Danu.html.

Struck, Peter T. "University of Pennsylvania Classics." University of Pennsylvania. http://www.classics.upenn.edu/myth /php/tools/dictionary.php?regexp=VENUS+LIBITINA .&method=standard.

Svenja, Lohner. "Drinking Water Cleanup." *Scientific American*, July 21, 2016. https://www.scientificamerican.com/article /drinking-water-cleanup/.

Sze, Kristen. "Data Shows SF Has 2nd Highest Homeless Population in US." *ABC7* June 29, 2016. http://abc7news .com/1407123/.

Taille, Anthony. "The Truth About New York's Legendary 'Mole People.'" *Narratively*, October 29, 2015. https://narratively .com/the-truth-about-new-yorks-legendary-mole-people/.

Taylor, Timothy. "Analogies for America: Beyond the Melting Pot." *StarTribune*, June 29, 2013. http://www.startribune.com /analogies-for-america-beyond-the-melting-pot/213593491/.

Thomas, June. "The Gay Bar: Is It Dying?" *Slate Magazine*, June 27, 2011. http://www.slate.com/articles/life/the_gay _bar/2011/06/the_gay_bar_6.html.

Thorpe, J. R. "Why Don't We Like Talking to Strangers?" *Bustle*, September 29, 2016. https://www.bustle.com/articles/186760 -why-dont-we-like-talking-to-strangers.

Tierney, John. "Do You Suffer from Decision Fatigue?" *The New York Times*, August 17, 2011. www.nytimes.com/2011/08/21 /magazine/do-you-suffer-from-decision-fatigue.html.

Treuhaft, Sarah, and Allison Karpyn. "The Grocery Gap: Who Has Access to Food and Why It Matters." PolicyLink and the Food Trust. March 2010. https://community-wealth.org/content/grocery-gap-who-has-access-healthy-food-and-why-it-matters.

Trope, Jack F. "Existing Federal Law and the Protection of Sacred Sites: Possibilities and Limitations." in *Cultural Survival Quarterly Magazine*, 1995. https://www.culturalsurvival.org/publications/cultural-survival-quarterly/existing-federal-law-and-protection-sacred-sites.

Trout, Daniel. "How Many Feet Are in an Anchor?" Daniel Trout & Associates. http://www.troutdaniel.com/how-many-square-feet-are-in-an-acre/.

Ungerman, Katya. "Life on the MUNI, as Told by San Franciscans." In *Roomi Blog–Resources for Coliving*. San Francisco, CA: Roomi Blog, 2015. https://roomiapp.com/blog/life-on-the-muni-as-told-by-san-franciscans/.

Van Leusen, Martin. "Dowsing and Archaeology." *Archaeological Prospection* 5, no. 3 (1998): 123–138. July 9, 2016. https://ahotcupofjoe.net/2016/07/dowsing-in-archaeology/.

Vercillo, Kathryn. "Lombard Street Is San Francisco's Crookedest Street." SFToDo, www.sftodo.com/lomabardcrookedstreet.html.

Vogel, Jennifer. "Old-Fashioned Cutting-Edge Radio." *The Rake*, June 22, 2005. http://rakemag.com/2005/06/old-fashioned-cutting-edge-radio/.

Waldstein, Charles. "The Panathenaic Festival and the Central Slab of the Parthenon Frieze." *The American Journal of Archaeology and of the History of the Fine Arts* 1, no. 1 (1885): 10–17. https://www.jstor.org/stable/495977?seq=1#metadata _info_tab_contents.

Walker, Jarrett. "Why We Should Stop Talking About 'Bus Stigma.'" In *CityLab*: The Atlantic Group, July 2012. www .citylab.com/transportation/2012/07/why-we-should-stop -talking-about-bus-stigma/2601/.

Wallis, Robert J, and Jenny Blain. "Sites, Sacredness, and Stories: Interactions of Archaeology and Contemporary Paganism." *Folklore* 114, no. 3 (2003): 307–321. https://www.tandfonline .com/doi/abs/10.1080/0015587032000145351.

Waxman, Elaine. "How Food Insecurity Is Adding to Our Health-care Costs." In *Urban Wire*: Urban Institute, August 25, 2015. https://www.urban.org/urban-wire/how-food-insecurity -adding-our-health-care-costs.

Weathers, Cliff. "Why Is Michigan Trying to Derail Detroit's Urban Farming Movement?" *Occupy.com*, May 20, 2014. http://www.occupy.com/article/why-michigan-trying -derail-detroits-urban-farming-movement#sthash.y9IBgutk .Ll6wO8L8.dpbs.

Webster, Nancy Coltun. "South Shore a Commuter Rail Survivor." *Chicago Post Tribune*, June 17, 2016. www.chicagotribune .com/suburbs/post-tribune/ct-ptb-bicentennial-south-shore -st-0619-20160617-story.html.

Weissberg, Robert. "The Gay Solution to Urban Blight." *Taki's Magazine*, February 13, 2013. https://www.takimag.com

/article/the_gay_solution_to_urban_blight_robert_weissberg
/#axzz4iF1tT4qE.

Welter, Ben. "Dec. 26, 1862: 38 Dakota Men Executed in Mankato." *Star Tribune*, December 26, 1862. www.startribune .com/dec-26-1862-38-dakota-men-executed-in-mankato /138273909/.

Wheeler, Heather. "History on the Net." Regnery Publishing. https://www.historyonthenet.com/ancient-egypt-timeline-2.

White, Martha C. "So Long, Middle Class: Middle Income Jobs Are Disappearing the Fastest." *NBC News*, August 5, 2016. https://www.nbcnews.com/business/economy/so-long -middle-class-middle-income-jobs-are-disappearing-fastest -n623886.

Wilczek, Frank. "Beautiful Losers: Plato's Geometry of Elements." PBS, December 29, 2011. www.pbs.org/wgbh/nova/blogs /physics/2011/12/beautiful-losers-platos-geometry-of -elements/.

Williams, Colter. "The Goddess Named Athena." Google, www .google.com/culturalinstitute/beta/usergallery/6wIyU2uq _W6TKw.

Wingergarner, Beth. "How Journalists Can Stop the Spread of Misinformation When Reporting on the Occult." *Poynter*, April 12, 2012. https://www.poynter.org/reporting-editing /2012/how-journalists-can-stop-the-spread-of-misinformation -stereotypes-when-reporting-on-occult-crimes/.

Wong, Byron. "The Default Human Being." *bigWOWO: Asian American literature, ideas and common sense*, 2010. [no URL.]

Dr. Y. "Why the Name: Cairo?" In *African Heritage*, September 8, 2014. https://afrolegends.com/2014/09/08/why-the-name -cairo/

Yang, Jeff. "A Quick History of Why Asians Wear Surgical Masks in Public." *Quartz* Media, November 19, 2014. qz .com/299003/a-quick-history-of-why-asians-wear-surgical -masks-in-public/.

Yeung, Chris. "The American Studies Project." http://xroads .virginia.edu/~ug02/yeung/baberuth/home.html.

Yronwode, Catherine. "Peace Water Spiritual Supplies." Lucky Mojo Inc., http://www.luckymojo.com/peacewater.html.

PRINT

Al Sayyad, Nezar. *Cairo: Histories of a City*. London: Harvard University Press, 2011.

Alberto, Angela. *A Day in the Life of Ancient Rome*. New York: Europa, 2009.

Ascher, Kate. *The Heights: Anatomy of a Skyscraper*. New York: Penguin Press, 2011.

Badea, Lucian. "The Ancient City of Callatis and the Neotectonic Movements." *Vechiul oraş Callatis şi mişcările neotectonice*. 9 (2010): 5–8.

Barrie, Thomas. *The Sacred In-Between: The Mediating Roles of Architecture*. New York: Routledge, 2013.

Beguin, Gilles, and Dominique Morel. *The Forbidden City: Center of Imperial China*. New York: Harry N. Abrams Publishers, 1997.

Berger, Judity. *Herbal Rituals: Recipes for Everyday Living*. New York: St. Martin's Press, 1999.

Berlyn, Patricia. "The Biblical View of Tyre." *Jewish Bible Quarterly* 34, no. 2 (2006): 71–82.

Bonewits, Isaac. *Real Magic*. San Francisco: Weiser Books, 1989.

Branfoot, Crispin, George Michell (editor, 2001). "Encyclopaedia of Indian Temple Architecture: South India, Drāviḍadeśa, Later Phase AD 1289–1798." *Bulletin of the School of Oriental and African Studies* 66, no. 1 (2003): 105–107.

Caffrey, Cait. "Neolithic Revolution." *Salem Press Encyclopedia*, 2019.

Carr-Gomm, Philip, and Richard Heygate. *The Book of English Magic*. New York: Overlook Press, 2010.

Croome, Derek J. "The Effect of Geopathic Stress on Building Occupants." *Renewable Energy* 5, no. 5 (1994): 993–996.

Curtiss, Samuel Ives. "The Local Divinities of the Modern Semites." *The Biblical World* 19, no. 3 (1902): 168–177.

Devereux, Paul. "Acculturated Topographical Effects of Shamanic Trance Consciousness in Archaic and Medieval Sacred Landscapes." *Journal of Scientific Exploration* 7, no. 1 (1993): 23–37.

Dyson, Stephen L. *Rome: A Living Portrait of an Ancient City.* Baltimore, MD: Johns Hopkins University Press, 2010.

Ely, Richard T. PhD. *Urban Land Economics.* Ann Arbor, MI: Edwards Brothers Publishers, 1922.

[no author.] "Egypt Culture and Religion." *Encyclopedia of World History: The Ancient World Prehistoric Eras to 600 C.E.* New York: Houghton Mifflin, 2012.

Fairs, Marcus. *21st Century Design: New Design Icons from Mass-Market to Avant Garde.* London: Carlton Books Limited, 2006.

Farrar, Janet and Stewart Farrar. *The Witches' God: Lord of the Dance.* Blaine, WA: Phoenix Publishing, 1989.

———. *The Witches' Goddess.* Blaine, WA: Phoenix Publishing, 1987.

Ferguson, William Scott. "Legalized Absolutism En Route from Greece to Rome." *The American Historical Review* 18, no. 1 (1912): 29–47.

Filan, Kenaz. *Vodou Money Magic: The Way to Prosperity through the Blessings of the Lwa.* Rochester, VT: Inner Traditions, 2010.

Froese, Tom, Carlos Gershenson, and Linda R. Manzanilla. "Can Government Be Self-Organized? A Mathematical Model of the Collective Social Organization of Ancient Teotihuacan, Central Mexico." *PLOS ONE* 9, no. 10 (2014): 1–14.

Galal, Tarek M., and Hanaa S. Shehata. "Bioaccumulation and Translocation of Heavy Metals by Plantago Major L. Grown in Contaminated Soils under the Effect of Traffic Pollution." *Ecological Indicators* 48, 244–251.

Galvin, Terrance Gerard. *The Architecture of Joseph Michael Gandy (1771–1843) and Sir John Soane (1753–1837): An Exploration into the Masonic and Occult Imagination of the Late Enlightenment.* Philadelphia, PA: University of Pennsylvania, 2003.

Gifford, Robert. "The Consequences of Living in High-Rise Buildings." *Architectural Science Review* 50, no. 1, March 2007.

Gin, Jerry. "The Science of Biogeometry." *Cosmos and History: The Journal of Natural and Social Philosophy* 11, no. 2 (2015): 290–309.

Gladwell, Malcolm. *Outliers: The Story of Success.* London: Hachette UK, 2008.

Glaesen, Edward. *Triumph of the City.* New York: Penguin Press, 2011.

Goldberger, Paul. *Why Architecture Matters.* New Haven and London: Yale University Press, 2009.

Gophna, Ram, Itamar Taxel, and Amir Feldstein. "A New Identification of Ancient Ono." *Bulletin of the Anglo-Israel Archaeological Society* 23 (2005): 167–176.

Grantz, Roberta Brandes. "The Genius of Jane Jacobs." *The Nation* 303, nos. 1–2 (2016): 16-17.

———. *We're Still Here Ya Bastards: How the People of New Orleans Rebuilt Their City.* New York: Nation Books, 2015.

Graves, Tom. *Needles of Stone*. London: Turnstone Books London, 1978.

Graves, Tom, and Liz Poraj-Wilczynska. *The Disciplines of Dowsing*. Colchester, UK: Tetradian Books, 2008.

Greer, John Michael. *The Celtic Golden Dawn: An Original & Complete Curriculum of Druidical Study*. Woodbury, MN: Llewellyn Worldwide, 2013.

Gross, Craig. "Salvation on the Strip." *Christianity Today*, Spring 2009.

Halsted, George Bruce. "The Message of Non-Euclidean Geometry." *Science* 19, no. 480 (1904): 401–413.

———. "Non-Euclidean Geometry: Historical and Expository." *The American Mathematical Monthly* 1, no. 5 (1894): 149–152.

Hardaker, Chris. "The Hexagon, the Solstice and the Kiva." *Symmetry: Culture and Science* 12, nos. 1–2 (2001): 167-83.

Hare, Timothy, Marilyn Masson, and Bradley Russell. "High-Density Lidar Mapping of the Ancient City of Mayapán." *Remote Sensing* 6, no. 9 (2014): 9064–9085.

Harmanşah, Ömür. "Beyond Aššur: New Cities and the Assyrian Politics of Landscape." *Bulletin of the American Schools of Oriental Research*, no. 365 (2012): 53–77.

Hart, Aidan. "The Sacred in Art and Architecture: Timeless Principles and Contemporary Challenges." Paper presented at the Beauty Will Save the World: Art, Music, and Athonite Monasticism Conference, 2005.

Hellmund, Cawood Paul and Smith, Daniel Somers. *Designing Greenways: Sustainable Landscapes for Nature and People*. Washington: Island Press, 2006.

Hermary, Antoine. "Building Power: Palaces and the Built Environment in Cyprus in the Archaic and Classical Periods." *Bulletin of the American Schools of Oriental Research*, no. 370 (2013): 83–101.

Hollis, Leo. *Cities Are Good for You: The Genius of the Metropolis.* Bloomsbury Publishing USA, 2013.

Hughes, Jeff. "Occultism and the Atom: The Curious Story of Isotopes." *Physics World* 16, no. 9 (2003): 31.

İezci, Yusuf, Serdar Kaya, Onur Erdem, Cemal Akay, Cahit Kural, Buğra Soykut, Okşan Başoğlu, et al. "Paleodietary Analysis of Human Remains from a Hellenistic-Roman Cemetery at Camihöyük, Turkey." *Journal of Anthropology* (2013): 1–7.

Iwaniszewski, Stanisław. "Vii. Archaeology, Folklore and the Recovery of Past Astronomies." *Archaeologia Baltica*, no. 10 (2008).

Johnson, Marc T.J., Thompson Ken A., and Saini,Hargurdeep S. "Plant Evolution in the Urban Jungle." *American Journal of Botany* 102, no. 12 (2015): 1951–1953.

Joost-Gaugier, Christiane L. *Pythagoras and Renaissance Europe: Finding Heaven.* Cambridge, UK: Cambridge University Press, 2009.

Kak, Subhash. "The Axis and the Perimeter of the Temple." *arXiv preprint arXiv:0902.4850* (2009).

Kaldera, Raven, and Tannin Schwartzstein. *The Urban Primitive: Paganism in the Concrete Jungle.* Saint Paul, MN: Llewellyn Worldwide, 2002.

Kaldera, Raven, and Tannin Schwartzstein. *The Urban Primitive: Paganism in the Concrete Jungle.* Saint Paul, MN: Llewellyn Worldwide, 2002.

Kalra, Gurvinder, and Dinesh Bhugra. "Sexual Violence against Women: Understanding Cross-Cultural Intersections." *Indian Journal of Psychiatry* 55, no. 3 (Jul-Sep 2013): 244–249.

Kappraff, Jay. "A Secret of Ancient Geometry." *MAA NOTES* (2000): 26–38.

Katz, Bruce and Bradley, Jennifer. *The Metropolitan Revolution: How Cities and Metros Are Fixing Our Broken Politics and Fragile Economy*. Washington, DC: Brookings Institution Press, 2013.

Keplinger, John G. "Who Were the Mound Builders?". *Journal of the Illinois State Historical Society (1908-1984)* 12, no. 1 (1919): 45–52.

Kondolf, G. Mathias, David R. Montgomery, Hervé Piégay, and Laurent Schmitt. "Geomorphic Classification of Rivers and Streams." In *Tools in Fluvial Geomorphology*, 171–204: John Wiley & Sons, Ltd, 2005.

Kriwaczek, Paul. *Babylon: Mesopotamia and the Birth of Civilization*. New York,: St. Martin's Press, 2010.

Lady Rhea. *The Enchanted Candle*. CreateSpace Independent Publishing Platform, 2016.

Larsen, Mogens Trolle. *Ancient Kanesh: A Merchant Colony in the Bronze Age Anatolia*. New York: Cambridge University Press, 2015.

Levine, Neal. *The Urbanism of Frank Lloyd Wright*. Trenton, NJ: Princeton University Press, 2015.

Lima, Kevin (director). *Enchanted*. Buena Vista, CA: Walt Disney Productions, 2007.

Loria, G. "Sketch of the Origin and Development of Geometry Prior to 1850." *The Monist* 13, no. 1 (1902): 80–102.

Lydon, Mike; Bartman, Dan; Woudtra, Ronald; Khawarzad, Aurash. "Tactical Urbanism Beta: Shoft Term Action Long Term Change" pamphlet, edited by The Street Plans Collaborative, 2015, 1–11.

Marcinoski, Christopher. *The City That Never Was*. New Jersey: Princeton Architectural Press, 2016.

Mark, Joshua J. "Athens." In *Ancient History Encyclopedia*, 2011.

———. "Tyre." In *Ancient History Encyclopedia*. UK: Ancient History Limited, 2009.

———. "Uruk." In *Ancient History Encyclopedia*. UK: Ancient History Limited, 2011.

Matz, David. *Daily Life of the Ancient Romans*. Westport, CT: Greenwood Press, 2002.

Meredith, Leda. *The Forager's Feast: How to Identify, Gather and Prepare Wild Edibles*. San Francisco: Countryman Press, 2016.

Miles, Richard. *Carthage Must Be Destroyed: The Rise and Fall of an Ancient Civilization*. New York: Viking, 2011.

Mohamed, N, Aisha Al Tohamy, and Ehab Y Ali. "Shiite Connotations on Islamic Architecture in Cairo in the Fatimid Era (358-567 Ah/969-1171 Ad)." *Journal of Faculty of Tourism and Hotels, Fayoum University* 10, no. 1/2 (2016).

Moss, Robert. *Sidewalk Oracles: Playing with Signs, Symbols, and Synchronicity in Everyday Life*. New York: New World Library, 2015.

Nicholson, Ben, Jay Kappraff, and Saori Hisano. "A Taxonomy of Ancient Geometry Based on the Hidden Pavements of Michelangelo's Laurentian Library." *Nexus* 98 (1998).

Oates, Joan, Augusta McMahon, Philip Karsgaard, Salam Al Quntar, and Jason Ur. "Early Mesopotamian Urbanism: A New View from the North." *Antiquity* 81, no. 313 (2007): 585–600.

Orvell, Miles, Klaus Benesh, and Dolores Hayden (eds.). *Rethinking the American City: An International Dialogue* (Anthology). Philadelphia: University of Pennsylvania Press, 2014.

Ostrow-Koloski, Ann. *The Archaeology of Sanitation in Roman Italy: Toilets, Sewers and Water Systems.* Chapel Hill, NC: University of North Carolina, 2015.

Palanichamy, Malliya Gounder, Bikash Mitra, Monojit Debnath, Suraksha Agrawal, Tapas Kumar Chaudhuri, and Ya-Ping Zhang. "Tamil Merchant in Ancient Mesopotamia." *PLoS ONE* 9, no. 10 (2014): 1–6.

Penczak, Christopher. *City Magick: Spells, Rituals, and Symbols for the Urban Witch.* Newburyport, MA: Red Wheel Weiser, 2012.

Plummer, William, and Meg Grant. "Shoeless Joe: His Legend Survives the Man and the Scandal" *People* magazine vol. 32 no. 6, August 7, 1989.

Popescu, Oana, and Jianca ŞTefan-Gorîn. "The First Cities of the World in a Bird's-Eye View." *Urbanism. Architecture. Constructions / Urbanism. Arhitectura. Constructii* 7, no. 3 (2016): 171–184.

Rajchel, Diana. *Mabon: Rituals, Recipes & Lore for the Autumn Equinox.* Woodbury, MN: Llewellyn Worldwide, 2015.

Randsborg, Klavs. "KEPHALLÉNIA: Archaeology & History: The Ancient Greek Cities." *Acta Archaeologica* 73, no. 2 (2002): 292–307.

Renee, Janina. *Tarot Spells*. Saint Paul, MN: Llewellyn Publications, 2000.

Rose, Jeffrey I. "New Light on Human Prehistory in the Arabo-Persian Gulf Oasis." *Current Anthropology* 51, no. 6 (2010): 849–883.

Saggs, Henry W. F. "Babylon." In *Encyclopedia Britannica*, 2017.

Sapir-Hen, Lidar, Yuval Gadot, and Israel Finkelstein. "Animal Economy in a Temple City and Its Countryside: Iron Age Jerusalem as a Case Study." *Bulletin of the American Schools of Oriental Research*, no. 375 (2016): 103–118.

Segal, Arthur, and Michael Eisenberg. "Sussita-Hippos of the Decapolis: Town Planning and Architecture of a Roman-Byzantine City." *Near Eastern Archaeology* 70, no. 2 (2007): 86–107.

Serageldin, Ismail. "Ancient Alexandria and the Dawn of Medical Science." *Global Cardiology Science & Practice* 2013, no. 4 (2013): 1–18.

Smith, P. D. *City: A Guidebook for the Urban Age*. New York: Bloomsbury, 2012.

Taylor, Claire. "Women's Social Networks and Female Friendship in the Ancient Greek City." *Gender & History* 23, no. 3 (2011): 703–720.

The Count, J. de Bertou. "Extract from a Notice on the Site of Ancient Tyre." *The Journal of the Royal Geographical Society of London* 9 (1839): 286–294.

Townsend, Amy. *Smart Cities: Big Data, Civic Hackers and the Quest for a New Utopia*. New York/London: WW Norton and Company, 2013.

Townsend, Anthony. *Smart Cities: Data, Civic Hackers, and the Quest for a New Utopia*. New York/London: W. W. Norton and Company, 2013.

Tutt, Patricia Adrienne. "Defining the Island City: Ancient Right Versus Modern Metropolis, as Considered at Peel, Isle of Man." *Island Studies Journal* 9, no. 2 (2014): 191–204.

Veenhof, Klaas R. "Ancient Assur: The City, Its Traders, and Its Commercial Network." *Journal of the Economic & Social History of the Orient* 53, no. 1/2 (2010): 39–82.

Walters, Jennifer. "Magical Revival: Occultism and the Culture of Regeneration in Britain, C. 1880-1929." (2007).

Weschcke, Carl Llewellyn, John C. Sulak, Oberon Zell, and Morning Glory Zell. *The Wizard and the Witch: Seven Decades of Counterculture, Magick & Paganism*. Woodbury, MN: Llewellyn Worldwide, 2014.

INDEX

To Write to the Author

If you wish to contact the author or would like more information about this book, please write to the author in care of Llewellyn Worldwide Ltd. and we will forward your request. Both the author and publisher appreciate hearing from you and learning of your enjoyment of this book and how it has helped you. Llewellyn Worldwide Ltd. cannot guarantee that every letter written to the author can be answered, but all will be forwarded. Please write to:

Diana Rajchel
℅ Llewellyn Worldwide
2143 Wooddale Drive
Woodbury, MN 55125-2989

Please enclose a self-addressed stamped envelope for reply,
or $1.00 to cover costs. If outside the U.S.A., enclose
an international postal reply coupon.

Many of Llewellyn's authors have websites with additional information and resources. For more information, please visit our website at http://www.llewellyn.com

GET MORE AT LLEWELLYN.COM

Visit us online to browse hundreds of our books and decks, plus sign up to receive our e-newsletters and exclusive online offers.

- **Free tarot readings • Spell-a-Day • Moon phases**
- **Recipes, spells, and tips • Blogs • Encyclopedia**
- **Author interviews, articles, and upcoming events**

GET SOCIAL WITH LLEWELLYN

Find us on   🐦 @LlewellynBooks

www.Facebook.com/LlewellynBooks

GET BOOKS AT LLEWELLYN

LLEWELLYN ORDERING INFORMATION

Order online: Visit our website at www.llewellyn.com to select your books and place an order on our secure server.

Order by phone:
- Call toll free within the US at 1-877-NEW-WRLD (1-877-639-9753)
- We accept VISA, MasterCard, American Express, and Discover.

Order by mail:
Send the full price of your order (MN residents add 6.875% sales tax) in US funds plus postage and handling to: Llewellyn Worldwide, 2143 Wooddale Drive, Woodbury, MN 55125-2989

POSTAGE AND HANDLING

STANDARD (US): (Please allow 12 business days)
$30.00 and under, add $6.00.
$30.01 and over, FREE SHIPPING.

CANADA:
We cannot ship to Canada. Please shop your local bookstore or Amazon Canada.

INTERNATIONAL:
Customers pay the actual shipping cost to the final destination, which includes tracking information.

Visit us online for more shipping options. Prices subject to change.

FREE CATALOG!

To order, call
1-877-NEW-WRLD
ext. 8236
or visit our
website

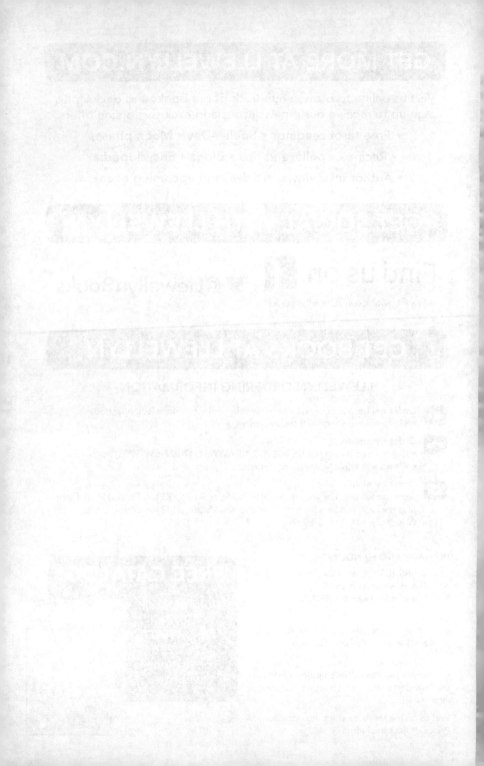

21982319472951